ADVICE FOR ALL MY GOOD READERS, SO-AND-SO READERS AND BAD READERS

Be sure to write your name *on the inside of the cover*. If only my printer allowed it, I would have marked a space for your *ex-libris* large enough to fit phone numbers, snail-mail and e-mail addresses, not to mention the reward to be paid to any stranger who happens to buy or find the book, should it stray. At first, I thought the circulating library was a *juggler* in this 19c punning illustration by Thomas Hood. Then, noting the position of his hands and worried brow, I came to think, instead, that he, like me, cannot find books he lent once upon a time to whomever he no longer recalls. *So*, before *you* lend *this* book to a friend, be sure to prepare your *ex-libris,* and *also* write down his or her name and this book inside *another* book you will never lend. Or, if you have a good eye and hand and are blessed to own a home, you may prefer to draw your friend riding a dolphin through the woods or straddling a surfing boar right there on the wall. Do not forget that friends can move, lend borrowed books to other friends, lose their memories or their books under accretions of printed matter where they will only be found if said friend passes on before you and a thoughtful person cleans up, or a saint with time to spare buys your book at the used book-store and looks you up. I do not know about *you*, but the books *I* have lost would fill a library! A fine one, too, for we usually lend the books we like, not the bad

A CIRCULATING LIBRARY.

ones that should be sent to Heckamondike (Did I get that right? My books of light-verse by Chesterton are in a box in a basement in Japan waiting for their owner to make good). So, guard this book as if it were worth something, which it may well be one day if your author dies before he is discovered by a reviewer who did not know he was alive when he was, and his dingy-sized readership *finally* grows into a junk (a big one like The Eunuch sent around Africa). *On second thought, I should not write such things.* It is better to *burn* books than collect them as an investment. Burning them, though misguided, is at least altruistic. Collecting them is selfish. As Aldous Huxley put it, "the bibliophile's point of view is, to me at least, unsympathetic and his standard of values unsound" (*Bibliophily* in *On the Margin* 1923/9). So, if you do not like this book, give it away. If you do like it, please be sure to mark it up *profusely* or make your personal index as you read so you will not lose what you find. After all, the real value of a book is not what it can be sold for but the time you put into it and the time you will save later finding things *if* you mark it up right. Then, *buy a lending copy* for your friends!

IN SEEKING TO DO CONJURING
FEATS OF VARIATION ON A SINGLE THEME,
△△△△△△△△△△△△△△△△△△△△△△△△
THERE IS DANGER OF EXHIBITING A DOLPHIN IN THE WOODS,
IN THE FLOODS A WILD BOAR
▽▽▽▽▽▽▽▽▽▽
HORACE (65 – 8BC)
▽▽▽▽▽▽▽
Dean of Lincoln
Oxford, 1900
transl.
▽▽

骨折りし一題を無限に枝分けてみるに危あり

★ ∘ ∘ ∘ Quote ∘ ∘ ∘ found ∘ ∘ ∘ in ∘ ∘ ∘ Loci ∘ ∘ ∘ Critici ∘ ∘ ∘ by ∘ ∘ ∘ George ∘ ∘ ∘ Saintsbury ∘ ∘ ∘ ★

何ぞ森に海豚、海に豚が

About the Cover Picture & Title of the Book

Thomas Hood made a practice of punning with pictures. *A SOW WESTER OFF THE CAPE: – PIGS IN THE TROUGH OF THE SEA* is at least a double pun but probably triple – I would not be surprised to find there was a corrupt politician named Wester. Punning images are extremely common in Japan, and I would love to offer you a book full of them; but playing with pictures takes access through affiliation or an abundance of what *time* is said to be. Your author is not fortunate enough to enjoy either. Hood's pictures are an exception. I *have* ten volumes of Hood to do what I would with (got them all for a few pounds in the basement of a big church in Edinburgh). So I can share them with you – as I would share so much more if I only had it! – for they are truly pictures for the lover of words. As to whether Hood thought of Horace's words *"delphinum sylvis appingit, fluctibus aprum,"* who knows! *Aprum* is no "sow," nor, for that matter, is it the "pig" I made it in Japanese because 1) a dolphin is written with the Chinese characters for "sea 海" and "pig 豚," *i.e.,* 海豚 (★our *porpoise,* too, *porcus marinus,* the *porc-peis,* pork-fish in Latin) 2) boar are identified with *whales,* as mountain whale (*yama-kujira*) is a euphemism for their meat – not because eating it was considered bad but because eating all four-legged mammals (whales were considered *fish*) was thought to be particular- ly sinful by Japan- ese Buddhists – that the larger semantics of the original, *i.e.,* putting things where they don't belong, might be lost. Anyway, if I *did* take that *boar,* I would also make the *forest mountain* (equated with wilderness in Japan), make the *dolphin* a *whale* and remove the rest of Horace's framing to create an allusive aphorism suitable for the Sinosphere: *mountain-picture-whale, ocean-picture-boar:*

山画鯨、海画猪

I appreciate the way the Dean of Lincoln came up with that *"floods/woods"* rhyme, for to my mind, the additional wit gained more than offset the slight loss in the perfect semantic symmetry of Horace's topographic reversal. Some might take issue with his "exhibit." The more usual translation of *appingo* is "paint;" but, note that it was chosen to link with "conjuring feats" (itself a very creative reading), bring out the *paint-in, fasten to* connotation of this rare verb and connect with readers in an age (c1900) where odd-juxtapositions were all too common, as demonstrated by the wildly popular international exhibitions. I might have translated the lead-in (*Qui variare cupit rem prodigialiter unam*) more succintly and, loving alliteration and rhyme, ditched the "dolphin in the woods" altogether

to put a whale in the willows and in the billows a boar.

◆ and speaking of sea swine ◆

While dolphin are known to jump up on sandy beaches chasing schools of fish, they have not, so far, been found in the woods. Aquatic swine and sheep actually exist.

> Today, a glimpse of a possible transitional process from land to sea may be found on the Tokelau Islands of the South Pacific, where pigs have developed the habit of wandering widely over coral reefs during low tide in search of food. According to the Bangkok Post (May 5, 1983), about three hundred pigs living on the island of Fakaofo forage along the shallow coral reefs for small molluscs, sea slugs, and fish. Apparently the pigs are excellent swimmers; they spend much of their time wading with heads submerged as they search for food. (Marianne Riedman. 1990. *Pinnipeds: Seals, Sea Lions, and Walruses*. University Of California Press: Berkeley, pp 50-83.)

Since swine are known to forage with their noses, I find this extraordinary. We may imagine that the pigs first got a taste for sea cucumber on the beach or in puddles on the reef at low tide, later stuck their head in the water to get them and eventually came to look for them, eyes open under water. If the swine have not by now all been eaten by humans, one would like to see an underwater video of this!

> On the other side of the world along the coasts of Scotland are domestic sheep that survive by grazing on algae in the intertidal zone. Described by Thomson (1954) as "scraggly creatures(s), long in the leg and neck, goatlike and wild, but with fine wool like the Shetland," these "marine sheep" have foraged on kelp and seaweeds for hundreds of years. They seem at home in the sea and often venture far out on surf-pounded promontories and swim in shallow waters to reach a new patch of seaweed. According to a native Orkney Islander, "If ye study the sheep, ye'll see how they follow the way o'the sea. They'll shift round to the lee side o' the island afore a storm, and they'll ken the run o' the tides afore ye'll ken it yersel'." The sheep actually share the beaches with grey seals; the seals tend to ignore the sheep, who in turn seem to go out of their way to avoid the seals. (Ibid)

Coincidentally, the Chinese character for the ocean is 洋 and it fuses a radical for literal liquidity 氵 and that for sheep 羊, allegedly because the white tops on waves in the ocean resembled the manes of the sheep. Whoever came up with many of these characters was a character himself, or herself, for making the associations.

A RADICAL DEMON-STRATION.

Were *Demonstrators* depicted as (to borrow a benighted term) "the axis of evil"? Not knowing Thomas Hood's politics, I'll not guess his intent, but the triple-punning gestalt-rebus is a faithful commentary on the times (See Desmond & Moore's 800-page biography of Charles Darwin to get a good grasp of mid-19c upper-class fear of radicalism). Punning a name on such a cartoon would make for a fine magazine contest, would it not?

PARAVER*SING*PARAVER*SING*PARAVER*SING*PARAVER*SING*PARAVERSE

"delphinum sylvis appingit, fluctibus aprum"

A DOLPHIN IN THE WOODS,
Composite Translation, Paraversing & Distilling Prose
IN THE FLOODS *A* WILD BOAR

一題もって神業の如き変種を求めば

森に海豚
〜 オブジェーなす多面翻訳を考えて 〜
大海に猪

robin d. gill
敬愚
paraverse press

A sensitive Lafcadio Hearn once wrote, *"Words will eventually have their rights recognized by the people."* — Our radically creative nonfiction sets them free to play and grow in a garden of fanciful thought far from the well-crafted, beautiful, but utterly boring journalism & plodding personal 'reality' narratives taught to a generation of **U**sanian writers, but close to the playful Aubrey, Borges, Chesterton, Darwin (Erasmus), Gennai, Li Yû, Lucretius, Montaigne, Newcastle (Duchess of ~), Ô Sukkwôn, Ôta Nanpô, Plutarch, Rabelais, Sei Shônagon, Sterne, Twain, Wilde, Yayû, *etc.* Or so your author-designer-editor-publisher likes to think. Critics, am I full of it?

**2009
paraverse press
all rights reserved**

But, please quote freely, so long as you cite this book, and take care to check the latest *Errata* at **http://www.paraverse.org**

Again, we invite the LC to help us catalog, meanwhile please enjoy our Publisher's Cataloging-in-Publication:

A Dolphin in the Woods, In the Floods a Wild Boar –
Composite Translation, Paraversing & Distilling Prose

by robin d. gill (also known as Gill, Robin 1951~)

ISBN # 0-9840923-1-5 (pbk)
13-digit: 978-0-9840923-1-4

1. Poetry – rhyme, paraversing, composite translation as a game.
2. Translation of poetry – multiple readings. 3. Japanese poetry in translation.
4. Chinese poetry in translation. 5. Metaphysical poetry – take-offs and retorts.
6. Found poetry – distilling prose. 7. Y. Hoffmann, D. Hofstadter, J. Mostow,
H. Sato, E. Weinberger. 8. Puzzles creating a product – contesting poetry.

1st edition: harvest moon 2009
(*please call it a reading copy, too*)

Printed by Lightning Source
in the United States and United Kingdom.
Distributed by Ingram, Baker & Taylor, etc..
Available from Amazon, Barnes & Noble & elsewhere.

Please visit our web site, *www.paraverse.org., for more information* or just for the hell of it. Further questions? Try uncoolwabin at hotmail dot com, or other e-mail addresses at the website, or catch me if you can at a social net-working site. *Forget snail-mail. At present,* your poor author-publisher *is* a snail.

ORDINAL TABLE OF CONTENTS

01 *The Way of Ways,* or count the ways to translate the first 6 characters of the *Tao-Te-Ching.* 21
02 *Rise, Ye Sea Slugs!* or the miraculous birth of elegant composite translation clusters. 35
03 *"Still to be neat," "The Essay on Man"* and other challenges for metaphysical paraverse 51
04 *God without turns demon within,* or how *aphorisms* may be multiplied to no end. 63

05 *100 Frogs,* or why a perfect translation of the world's most famous haiku is impossible! 69
06 *Fly-ku!* – the more you swat, the more they come . . . or composite-translation normalized. . . 77
07 *A Prayer to Silence the Howl-monster,* or how to translate an untranslatable Chinese lullaby 87
08 *Haikuing Thoreau's Flies & making Dillard's Mockingbird a pelican.* Distilling good stuff 95

09 *Nineteen Ways* to kill a poem in translation and a few more of my own! 101
10 *Cherry Blossom Epiphany* – a petal blizzard of composite-translation . . . 111
11 *Rabid ghost crabs, & gallant man-o-war – distilling* a contemporary amateur's poems 125
12 *Any Moonshiners out there?* An appeal to my readers for examples of prose distillation: 131

13 *A Hundred Poets,* making one by Michitsuna's mother interesting, anyway! 133
14 *The 5th Season* – the re-creation of the world & Japanese in English. More composite, yet. 139
15 *Sunflower Heads & Naked Trees* – amateur haiku, or *paraversing* as improvement 147
16 *Riding a Spruce Through a Storm* – *distilling* 19c nature-writing's purple prose 151

17 *Le Ton Beau de Marot's* A une Damoyselle malade: reading the plump variations. 165
18 *Octopussy & The Woman Without a Hole,* or composite translation for *senryû,* too. 179
19 *Wedged between her Symplegades,* or let's stand up for wonderful translations from Latin! 185
20 *Piss not on the moon* – double-take: did I paraverse *that* soon? 193

21 *Issa's* Fart-bug, or going out with a blast: my boldest paraversing. 201

22 *Ten Thousand Leaves* blowing in the wind: earliest paraverses, found last. 209
23 *Mad In Translation,* a neglected genre of poetry just asking for it! 221
24 *Crossword to Paraverse:* Why just pleasure yourself? 235

CATEGORICAL TABLE OF CONTENTS

I *Multiple Translations*: Watts/Tao-Te-Ching; Sato/Bashô's Frog; Mostow/100-poets, Hofstadter/Le Ton Beau de Marot, Weinberger/Nineteen Ways ch. 1, 5, 9, 13, 17. & my own 20, 21, 22.
II *Composite Translation* exampled by my work: *Rise, Ye Sea Slugs, Fly-ku!, Cherry Blossom Epiphany, The 5th Season, Octopussy, Dry Kidney & Blue Spots (aka The Woman Without a Hole),* and *Mad In Translation.* respectively, ch. 2, 6, 10, 14, 18, 23. & unpublished:
III *Playing w/ Poems. Paraversing great poems, Distilling & paraversing* poor poems , *Paraversing* translated nursery rhyme, *Multiplying* poems to improve them, ch 3, 7, 11, 15, 19, 24
IV *Prose-to-Prose & Prose-to-Poem paraversing. Multiplying Aphorisms, Distilling and paraversing a long prose piece,* 4, 8, 12, 16, 20
V *Finale, The argument for paraversing yet,* and the reason why *paraversing* should be as common as doing *crossword puzzles* 24

I like to think my work (as bad as it is) is for the greater good.

A MAGNUM BONUM.

apologiarspoeticapologia

For the less we are helped by our language, the better fight we must make in originality of matter. – Quintilian AD 35-96

from Saintsbury: *Loci Critici*

As all the well-read know, an *apologia* is not, strictly speaking, an apology at all, but rationalizations as to *why* one must do what one does. When I read Quintilian's words I identify with him and his fellow Roman writers and readers. If Latin was disadvantaged, or fancied itself to be so *vis-à-vis* Greek, my command of English, compared to that of better writers I know, is, to use two Japanese expressions, *as different as mud to a cloud* or, *as different as the full moon and a marsh turtle* (except that Japanese, following the Chinese, need not make "as different as" explicit). For me to write a book for word-lovers is audacious. As someone who writes better than I do in Japanese once wrote when I checked her translation for accuracy, *please pardon me for dirtying your (honorable) eyes.* She was only being polite. *Her* writing did no such thing. Mine, I am afraid, is a different matter. As to whether or not I have overcome my handicap by making "the better fight" – that judgment, my friend, is *yours*.

The title of this book, from Horace's *Ars Poetica,* is a warning to the author and his readers, some of whom may be writers, who would let their imagination leap like a dolphin or run hog-wild. But, it is also *a confession*, as I not only suspect but *know* my excesses are, in part, compensation for my weakness, which I do not exaggerate. Not that I *mind* overdoing it sometimes. Unlike the writers and readers Horace wrote for, I do not fear the unnatural, especially that we might now call *surreal*. If my variations on a poem (translated or not) occasionally leave a dolphin in the woods or a boar at sea, I should clap my hands with glee. That would be quite a feat, would it not? Of course, it must be done in a way that makes it *seem* right. Reason does not need nonsense but nonsense needs reason lest it be mistaken for nothing, which is another thing altogether. That reason, or proof can be obvious as *rhyme,* or a more subtle sort of *rightness* we might call *metaphysical fitness.* Dolphin grazing like cows would not convince, while dolphin dancing through the tree-tops, snatching balls or birds on the fly, competing with hunters (the equine breed) jumping obstacles in a horse show, or chasing hares through the landed equivalent of a coral forest would be in their proper element though it were completely out of water.

Quintilian's *Comparison of Greek and Latin Style* is a delight to read, even in English. Eg. *"The genius of the Greeks, even in its minor examples, has ports open to it alone; let us spread, whenever we can, an ampler canvas, and bid a mightier wind fill our sails."*

"SEE ME, SKATE!"

If I compiled a book of Thomas Hood's work, I might call it *Doggerel Drawings*. I do not mean that in a critical way. As Ernest Tubbs of *"Walking the Floor"* and *"Nails in My Coffin"* fame once noted, his lack of finesse (helped by a bass voice which covers all sins) inspired more would-be C&W singers than fancy vocal artists, who psyched them out. Hood at his worst (much worst than the above!) is inspirational. Though hilarious humor may be better to cheer us up and improve our immune system, it does no good for nausea. When we feel really bad, only *groaning aloud* makes one feel better, perhaps because it oxygenates the brain. Moreover, there is something about bad art that draws us together, makes all men kin in a way mother nature cannot. Shakespeare, who could be slick as a sea slug when he wanted to be, knew that nothing draws sympathy like a pathetic pun (Is it not because the unguarded mouth shows a good heart?). And, finally, just as there are far more varieties of human ugliness than of beauty, and of potential creatures than of actually selected ones, poor quality humor, by not censoring the fruit of the imagination, allows for more creative possibilities than the good. By this, I do not mean to imply that all the wit in this book will be vulgar, just that if some is, you should know that it may, indirectly, benefit you more than the elegant variety.

> *One must be an inventor to read well. As the proverb says, "He that would bring home the wealth of the Indies, must carry out the wealth of the Indies." There is then creative reading as well as creative writing. When the mind is braced by labour and invention the page of whatever book we read becomes luminous with manifold allusion. Every sentence is doubly significant, and the sense of our author is as broad as the world."*
>
> Ralph Waldo Emerson: *The American Scholar*

Emerson is not here to beg the indulgence of the reader who will be called to read beyond the call of duty, though that, too, may be true, but to make a claim. From nursery school, I took to print like a fish in water and read a book a day for a decade before becoming a book-scout for a Japanese publisher in 1980 and reading *more*, if I may combine books partially read. Yet, only correcting the translations of scores of books we published took my reading skill to a more exacting, if not higher level. Then, playing with multiple translation in the 1980's and improving those skills in the 1990's translated *me* to yet another world. It is the one described by Emerson, above. Such a state was probably far from rare among *his* highly literate readers, because they all read languages, dead or alive, and many if not most, could translate, themselves. Likewise, for Japanese up to the end of the twentieth century, for even if many of the top thinkers and writers never mastered a foreign tongue, the Chinese style writing (*kanbun*) and the ancient Japanese all of them studied and translated into modern Japanese ensured their minds were "braced by labour and invention." What I do not know and hope to find out through the publication of this book – not immediately, but *after* and *if* it inspires those who have read it to try for themselves – is whether or not monolinguals, *i.e.*, people who cannot read books in even one foreign language without constant resort to a dictionary (most moderns are probably in that boat) can, by practicing the arts demonstrated within these covers, experience the same growth, that does not come naturally to, say, those who confine their word play to crosswords and other barren puzzles.

Much is lost in translation. *That is true from the point of view of the reader; it is false for the translator, to whom every such loss to the world is his or her gain, as it illuminates a part of our language not only obscure but otherwise invisible because it does not even exist. Such discoveries, compounded, nurture a bitter-sweet nostalgia for an ideal language capable of expressing all this beauty found only when it is lost.* (From *Loving Two Tongues,* a book-to-be in my mom's closet)

More Gain in Loss. "*Poetry, indeed, cannot be translated; and therefore it is the poets that preserve languages; for we would not be at trouble to learn a language if we could have all that is written in it just as well in translation. But as the beauties of poetry cannot be preserved in any language except that in which it was originally written, we learn the language.*" (Samuel Johnson in Boswell's *Life of* ~ AD 1776). But how many people learn tongues for aesthetic pleasure today?

THE STAMP DUTY ON SCOTCH LINEN.

All pictures are puzzles. Rather than explain why Hood's pun specifically fits the Scotts, here is one of his poems found elsewhere in his writings. Note: if you cannot solve a picture, explanation does *not* hurt the humor, it revives it.

In walking one morning I came to the green,
Where the manner of washing in Scotland is seen;
And I thought it perhaps would amuse, should I write,
A description of what seemed a singular sight.
Here great bare-legged women were striding around,
And watering cloths that were laid on the ground.
While, on t'other hand, you the lasses might spy
In tubs, with their petticoats up to the thigh,
And, instead of their hands, washing thus with their feet,
Which they often will do in the midst of the street,
Which appears quite indelicate, – shocking, indeed,
To those ladies who come from the south of the Tweed! (10-9)

♪ *Prefatory Notes* ♪

The Way is not *a* way.

"Poetry is what cannot be translated" – Robert Frost [1]

Mark Twain, lamenting the fortunes of his "Jumping Frog of Calvares County" in France might have remonstrated *"Bob, what about prose?"* He would have a point, for the extent to which translation is or isn't possible varies less between *genres* of literature than between *cognate* and *discognate*, or familiar and exotic languages. With the former, much can be carried intact across the river of difference; with the latter, a translator must pretty much start from scratch, re-creating the work on the other bank. How could it be otherwise when the syntax (order of the major parts of speech) is almost completely contrary, the vocabulary utterly different and the cultural assumptions and knowledge allowing us to read between the lines without even being aware we do it, is absent?

I hope this sampling of ways to 1) *re-create* poems in order to do justice to foreign language originals, 2) *invent* alternate poems, or *paraverses,* by expanding upon or diversifying originals, 3) *turn* prose or ideas found in prose into poetry, or even 4) *multiply* a maxim to no end, will inspire readers to try the same – and editors to give them that chance – for it is a waste of good brainpower to kill time doing crossword puzzles and other such games that create nothing but scrap-paper, when we can gain the same pleasurable stimulation and thrill of completion while creating *literature* we can keep and share with others. If experienced translators find the appeal of multiple translations or *paraverses*, presented in clusters as singular composite-translations, too irresistible not to emulate, good! But whether or not such comes to pass, all readers will gain something from the insights translation brings to poetry and vice versa.

The preface title comes from one of *scores* of translations I did of the 6-character first line of the *Tao Te Ching* after Alan Watts, who noted the skeletal nature of Chinese not only permits but *asks for* multiple readings. Because most of his examples were notably bad, I tried *my* hand, which, I found to my astonishment, easily beat his (ch.1). I was tempted to turn *Way* into *Wei*, for Eliot Weinberger's annotated selection of nineteen translations of Wang Wei's six-line poem, *Deer Park* is perhaps *the* best-known essay of multiple translation. Like Watt's work, it only strengthened my resolve to do my own book, because, despite the author's elegant preface and Octavio Paz's cultured postscript, the examples were, excluding the Nobel laureate's bold re-creation in Spanish, uniformly boring. In other words, we must thank Watts and Weinberger for their vision and marvel at their strong stomach for digesting poor translation.

Three other books featuring multiple translation bear mentioning. The best known is Hiroaki Sato's *One Hundred Frogs* (1983), though the collection of over a hundred translations of Bashô's famous frog *ku* only fills one of ten or so chapters.² Jonathon Mostow's *Pictures of the Heart*: *The Hyakunin Isshu* (University of Hawaii Press: 1996), which I know only through a book review by Sato, has ten translations each of famous *waka* (32-syllabet poems) by a hundred poets. These books, like *Nineteen Ways*, give us *previously published or collected translations* by many translators, but the commentary is minimal and the translations lack the brilliance of those from Classic (Greek or Roman) poetry I have seen compared.³ The third book, *Le Ton Beau de Marot* (1997), is far more impressive, for Douglas R. Hofstadter realized that making diverse translations from a single original could be enjoyed *as a social game* and got dozens of brilliant people to cooperate. I also started doing diverse translation of single poems in the early 1980's, but did not solicit translations until the mid-90's, when I found myself doing dozens of translations for scores of individual haiku by Issa. With few friends to ask, however, *Pangur Ban* – the white cat who hunted for mice in nooks with his sharp claws and clear eye while the Irish monk sought wisdom in books with his duller senses – was graced with only two good readings, one by Jack Stamm, one by me. More recently, Liz Henry's website for *composite translation* (a term she may have been the first to coin) did the same in magazine form with more success than me, but less than DRH.)

Then, in 2003, as I worked on my first book of translated haiku for publication (900+ *ku* about sea cucumber), I realized it was not *just* a game. For many *ku*, more than one translation was *needed* to cover ambiguity, express manifold meaning, or supply enough cultural background for it to be fully understood without the wit destroyed by explanation and extra beats. At the same time, I came to feel that multiple translations, conceptually justified or not, *looked* bad. Presented in serial, strung-out down a page, or even spanning pages, a multiple-translation fails to convince; *many* poems are not *a* poem. Moreover, as haiku lines are very short, the waste of space/paper/trees represented by the broad margins was troubling. So, I started to experiment with mixes of single, double and even triple columns. It was not easy, for Microsoft Word columns have many quirks which are exaggerated when one mixes Japanese and English. But the torture was worth it, for the effect was stunning. Presented in side-by-side pairs or more complex clusters such as 1-2-1, 2-1-2, 2-3-2, 1-2-3-2-1, the multiple readings are experienced as a singular translation, a composite, *i.e.,* one multi-faceted *crystalline(?)* objéct of word art, a poem! Unless someone else has done this before, I would seem to have come up with a *major literary invention,* albeit one with limited use, for clusters only work with tiny poems, such as Japanese *haiku, senryû* or short Chinese rhymes that can be written in squares as small as 4 x 4 characters.

1. Robert Frost's Epigram. The poet was probably familiar with the following passage from Percival Shelley's *Defense of Poetry* (via Saintsbury):

Sounds as well as thoughts have relation both between each other and towards that which they represent, and a perception of the order of those relations has always been found connected with a perception of the order of the relations of thoughts. [misprint?] . . . Hence the vanity of translation; it were as wise to cast a violet into a crucible that you might discover the formal principle of its colour and odour, as seek to transfuse from one language into another the creations of a poet. The plant must spring again from its seed, or it will bear no flower – and this is the burthen of the curse of Babel.

I doubt Frost cooked Shelley, though anyone with good taste would agree that the latter *is* better boiled down. Chances are Frost instead took Dante's short but dull pronouncement *Convito* i.7.

"Let it be known to all, that nothing harmonized by the laws of music (i.e., metrical harmony = Saintsbury) *can be translated from its own tongue into another without breaking all its sweetness and harmony."* (also, from Saintsbury)

– and shrank it to generalize the idea into his witty definition of poetry that indirectly explains why translators who do the impossible deserve the same respect (& payment) accorded the author of the original. If we think of "poetry" in its broad sense as *all that is magical, rather than humdrum,* Frost's six words may be distilled yet further:

Translation kills.

The prefatory notes ended here. Then, I read Hofstadter's entire book for the first time (Previously, I only found time for his treatment of haiku, opinions on Chinese, and translations of the central poem.) and found this *re.* Frost: *"Although I have not managed to find it in his writings, I have seen it quoted in print in the following manner: 'Poetry is what disappears in translation.' In a sense, this whole book is a riposte to Frost's thrust."* Hofstadter expressed those feelings in a 32-line poem titled *Star Frost Bite Dust*, which starts *"From Robert Frost, this sound bite I found: / "Poetry's that that's lost in translation."* and ends *"Thou unsound Frost bite, just bite the dust! / For poetry's found, not lost in translation."* Hofstadter's intent (increasing appreciation for the translator as artist/creator) is good, but I wonder if Frost and Hofstadter are really at odds. Frost's comments about the impossibility of translation *might* be interpreted as *support* for Hofstadter's (and my) understanding of *translation as re-creation.* What cannot be carried over (*trans-lated*), must be made, not necessarily from scratch, but not merely reassembled either, for, depending on the text to be translated and the languages, not only the whole, but many, if not most, of the parts are lost. *To be found something must first be lost.* Could it not truly be said that *a poem must die to be reborn?*

2. *Impossibility of (Faithful) Translation.* Hofstadter also brings up 1) the old French riddle posed by Mann, the answer to which he rhymfully Englishes as *When they are beautiful they're never dutiful; and when they are dutiful they're never beautiful*, calling it "cute, but stupid and insulting to both referents at the same time," and 2) G.K. Chesterton's remark about FitzGerald's *Omar Khayyam* as *"too good a poem to be faithful to the original,"* which he calls "clever . . but nonetheless quite silly." Again, Hofstadter could not be more right *or* wrong! If keeping the word order and/or flow of the original is considered being faithful and not doing so being unfaithful, then faithful is indeed ugly, while beauty must play. That is what an experienced translator means when speaking of the impossibility of perfect translation. Yet, twenty years of work correcting translations also taught me that Hofstadter is, *practically speaking*, correct in so far that translations following the original closely in the mechanical manner some consider faithful are not only ugly but far more likely to mistranslate the sense of the original, while exceptionally beautiful translations that do not follow the original "word for word" tend to have the fewest major misreadings. This is not so much intrinsic to the style of translation as to the type of translator who does it. Those who cling tightly to the original tend to do so either because they do not have a full enough understanding of it to dare let go, or because they are so fixated upon the mechanics of translation either because it is in their character, for they lack imagination, or because they hold prejudicial views about the foreign language they want reflected in the translation that they fail to catch the author's intent.

2. *A Poem must Die to be Reborn?* Though I read Spanish, some Portuguese and Russian, most of my experience is with the mutually exotic English & Japanese. When translating between cognate tongues, far less is lost in translation. I beg the reader who, nonetheless feels my claims excessive to see more detailed explanation of the limits of translation in *Orientalism & Occidentalism* (2004).

~~~~~~~~~

3. What is a *ku*? An individual *haiku* or *senryu*. What are they? Both are 17-syllabet Japanese poems, the difference of which will be addressed in the text. Why *syllabet*? Because the Japanese "syllable" is short and may be expressed with a single letter of their syllabic alphabet. To count out 17 *syllables* in English is *not* following form, for the resulting *ku* are *very irregular* in duration and tend to be far longer than Japanese *ku*. Content aside, the "formal constraint" of a haiku is, first and foremost, *to sound right*. Count out 7 or 8 beats if you would approximate the Japanese form.

~~~~~~~~~

4. *Classic (& Russian) Translation.* I had examples, but seeing some from Ronald Storr's *Ad Pyrrham* (OUP 1959) and Pushkin's verse-novel, *Eugene Onegin,* in Hofstadter's *Le Ton Beau de Marot*, I will stop before I start and keep them to myself. Storr gives 63, 20, 15, 13, 12 & 21 versions of Horace's poem, in English, French, Spanish, German, Italian and sundry tongues, respectively!

~~~~~~~~~

★ **Frost's sentence on translation** is *itself* a good example of inadvertent prose paraversing, for it is found in many slightly different versions. (Compare, say, *"Robert Frost once remarked, disparagingly, that what gets lost in translation is the poetry itself"* to my version and Hofstadter's.) There seems to be no source; the credit for this "well-known witticism" or, simply, *"it"* is just *"according to Frost,"* who "famously/ notoriously" "once said/remarked /put" the same. So things stood until MMcM dug up enough information to fill a book. Let me try to squeeze it into the remaining column on this page. The first source (or *one* first-hand context) of the Frost maxim is Untermeyer's *Robert Frost: a Backward Look*. Untermeyer explains that " 'Stopping by Woods on a Snowy Evening,' . . . a poem that says much in little . . . has been subjected to many interpretations and even more misinterpretations" turning "the homegoing man into a symbol of all men lost in the world," the woods into "a universal desire to withdraw from life with possible thoughts of suicide" and so forth, which irritated Frost who told him that criticism of that ilk *"analyses itself—and the poem—to death."* If Untermeyer recorded his words correctly, Frost's summation was

"You've often heard me say—perhaps too often—that poetry is what is lost in translation. It is also what is lost in interpretation. That little poem means just what it says and it says what it means, nothing less but nothing more."

Frost's final claim is the sort of thing a monolingual with no experience translating, or at least none with exotic tongues where one *must* interpret because even the parts of speech are apples and oranges, might make. I recall laughing at ridiculous stipulations about exact translation in publisher-to-publisher contracts made by benighted monolingual Usanian lawyers who think that language can be as precise as Frost claimed his "little poem" was.

~~~~~~~~~

★ *G.K. Chesterton on Fitzgerald*. MMcM notes that Hofstadter paraphrased Chesterton, who, discussing "the great Victorian poets" in the Victorian Age in Literature (1913) wrote, "But it is quite clear that Fitzgerald's work is much too good to be a good translation." In the original, Chesterton's point is not "silly," but *witty* because it plays upon two different connotations of "good." The second does indeed mean "faithful," but it is not the same as saying so.

~~~~~~~~~

A New Twist. MMcM, apologetic for giving me too much information, wrote that "while checking out fellow LibraryThing member MoonPublisher's poetry small press [moonpie press] in Maine, [he discovered that] one of her poets, Ted Bookey, wrote: *"what gets lost in any good translation is translation."* I read it in context ("Language as a Second Language" 2004), but remain unsure what it means. If it means *a good translation is not a translation*, I agree. If it means *a good translation never reveals it is a translation,* I disagree.

~~~~~~~~~

A Fine Way to Think About "Composite." Liz Henry offered a fine complement of definitions of "composite" at her Composite Translation dot com:

1) The composite sketch made from interviews with various near-sighted witnesses with imperfect memories. Together these descriptions and sketches may help to catch the wanted criminal. 2) A complex material in which two or more distinct, structurally complementary substances combine to produce some structural or functional properties not present in any individual component. 3) A weed, an aster, wormwood, a dandelion, a thistle (said to be the favorite food of donkeys).

i
Paraversing the Tao Te Ching
道　可　道　非　常　道
way-can-way-not-usual-way

In his autobiography *Cloud-hidden, Whereabouts Unknown*, Alan Watts claims there are at least eighty translations for the first six characters of the *Tao Te Ching*. In *Tao: The Watercourse Way* (1975), he wrote it was "usually translated *'The Tao which can be spoken of is not the eternal Tao,'* "but many translations were possible because the original was vague: "Tao can be Tao not eternal [or regular] Tao." In other words, the first/third/sixth character =道 means *way/ road/path /course*, the second =可 *can/able/possible,* the fourth = 非 *not/un-/ir-* and the fifth = 常 *normal/regular/ ordinary,* except against the transient world of appearance, when such constancy becomes "eternal" (The Christian *Rock of Ages* is characterized as a "usual-rock" 常磐). With Chinese so skeletal, translation resembles forensic anthropology; the imagination has a job on its, hopefully skilled, hands. Watts evidently found the freedom to flesh out those bare bones exhilarating, for many of his reincarnations were so wild that a Chinese reader who knew English would have little chance of identifying the original from them. The six best (which is not to say they are good) and one bad:

> 1) *The Way that can be described is not the eternal Way.*
> 2) *The Course [course:1975] that can be discoursed is not the eternal Course.*
> 3) *The Go that can be gone is an emergency Go.*
> 4) *The Way that can be weighed is not the regular Way.*
> 5) *The Flow that can be followed is not the real [eternal:1975] Flow.*
> 6) *Energy which is energetic is not true energy.*
> 7) *Force forced isn't force.[The Force that is forced isn't true Force: 1975]*

Translation 1) is direct and boring. 2), is based on the hypothesis that the "road" character rendered as *Tao* also meant "be spoken of" is clever, but "discourse" seems too highbrow for the original. 3) is the bad one. Watts jokes is out of place and time: the last three characters, in *modern* Chinese and Japanese mean "emergency exit." The pun in 4), "weighed," *is* good English but little help for the meaningless "regular Way." The "flow" in 5) is a valid reading of "way," but *following* does not follow. 6) is true, but the polysyllabic "energy/etic" *sounds* wrong and light-years removed from the original. 7), likewise, is such a stretch that one less liberal than I might call it a *mistranslation*. "Force" does, however, *sound* better [x]. One can say, as a movie script later did, *"May the force be with you!"* because *force* works with *poetic* language such as "May the ~." Big words like "energy" are only poetry in the hands of an Ogden Nash. "May the energy be with you?" *Never!* Well, maybe there is a way: "May the Energy be *in* you!" might work, perhaps because of the alliteration (*En* and *in*).

21

道 可 道 非 常 道
way-can-way-not-usual-way

Setting aside the meaning of *way-can-way-not-usual-way* for a moment, I would like to point out that, despite the puns and clever vocabulary, *none* of the readings offered by Watts can shake a stick at the original because they fail to take full advantage of *our* way, the *Way of English*, which has rhetorical tricks Chinese (and, for that matter, Japanese) cannot match, as we cannot match theirs. These are expressed by our choice of *a/the* or *nil*, for which they have no close equivalent, and writing devices their languages lack, such as italics for marked cases (emphasis), capitalization, explanation and interrogative marks. Compare –

    8) The discoursable course is not *the* course.

– with translation 2). Doesn't *"the,"* alone, honor the Course (even uncapitalized) more than "the eternal," where "eternal" oddly cancels *"the one and only"* meaning of the marked case (*i.e.,* emphatic) "the"? *That* is the magic of rhetoric. It is not *what* you say, but how you say it.

    9) To choose a way is to lose the way.

One reason we cannot match the original is that Chinese is just too compact for English, for us. Note what is *not* in the word-for-character gloss. Articles are not the only thing missing. There is no "is." Either the negative character "no/not-/ir/un" 非 itself functions as a verb meaning "is not" or Chinese needs no verb to indicate a state of being. If brevity is the soul of wit, we are left, comparatively speaking, witless. But parity is possible if we use the natural rhymes and rhythms of our tongueand, most important, taking advantage of idioms and devices Chinese lacks. This is why Pound's translation of the Shi-ching (Book of Songs) is worth a hundred translations purporting to be more accurate. With 9), "choose" as a sense-translation of "way-can-way" was hard to come up. I myself forget where it came from. Perhaps I lucked upon it while fishing for a rhyme for "lose," itself a creative way to English that "not." The *a* vs. *the* contrast came more easily and the delightful ambiguity of "the" as part of standard idiom for being lost and indicating *The Way* was fortuitous.

    10) The Way of Ways is never a way.

This is the favorite of my *paraverses*, a term I use because translation between exotic tongues is largely a matter of invention, *i.e.,* creating "alternative readings" rather than the *conversion* people familiar with translation between cognitive tongues might imagine. Note how 10) takes advantage of our precise articles "the" and "a," while the pun "a way = away" comes alive with that "never," a fine word with no Chinese (or Japanese) equivalent. Created by Young English (dictionaries call it *Old* English) by fusing "not" and "ever," this word does not grace our classical tongues either. If the Way is *never away*, it is, by implication, regular/constant/eternal, and the untranslateable modifier is moot.

道　可　道　非　常　道

way-can-way-not-usual-way

~~~~~~

11) *The* Way of Ways is not *a* way.

With "not," rather than "never," and italics, the "a way/away" pun, which, in 10), implies the Way is always near at hand, vanishes, leaving us with a didactic paradox: How can something *called* a "way" not be a member of the *category* "way?" I think such a paradox is more interesting than a straight contradiction, such as 12) *No way is the Way of Ways*, but what about the following?

13) *The Way* is not *this* way or *that*.

I do not know about Chinese, but, Japanese not only lacks a match for "the," but cannot follow the equivalent of "this way" with a mere "that." Japanese boasts more ellipsis than does English, but this is not such an instance. 13) works stylistically, but seems too simple.

14) The Way of Ways is not *this* way or *that*.

Is 14), with its colorful English *Way of Ways,* better than 13)? This Indo-European rhetoric you might have noticed in 10), 11) and 12) is good for being light. If we were to back-translate into Japanese or Chinese, the closest match "Way-among-way/s" (道の中の道 (the の are Japanese)) would be too heavy, so, by Frost's definition it must be poetry, *for us*. The strongest question about this reading, and some others, is whether the constant/eternal 常 idea is implicit in the grandeur we feel in rhetoric such as the marked *the* or the "Way of Ways."

15) The Way of all ways is not *this* way or *that*.
16) The *Always* is not this way or that.
17) *Always* is not this way or that.

A pun such as that in 15) is *always* intended. And, that takes care of the constant/eternal problem. 16) goes further and makes the constant/eternal modifier the very word for the Tao, for if the Way is Eternal, isn't it *always*? 17) brings out the thingatude of *always* by *not* articling it. And, speaking of "out,"

18) The Way of Ways is out of the way.
18b The Way of Ways lies out of the way.

The *regular/eternal* is lost again, but the *way-can-way* is well covered by the contrary "out of the way. If the Way is not one that is a way to speak of, or a road not generally taken, that is where it would be. Not a few idioms are, themselves, worthy of contemplation and this is one. But the reading is still too plain in comparison with the original, which seems poetic and enigmatic to Chinese, themselves. The colloquial "lies" (18b) helps, but makes the Tao seem too static.

道　可　道　非　常　道
way-can-way-not-usual-way

---

    19) Out of the way is the way of ways.

English need only put the predicate last to create what looks like poetry: Unfortunately, that does not always help the content. Here, it showed it was too thin, until decapitalization put just enough ambiguity in the line to give us something to chew on.

    20) Out of the way of ways is The Way.

It would be fun to feed this, 10) and 11) into an AI (artificial intelligence) translating program (English⇒Chinese ⇒English) to see if the readings contradict each other. Obviously, for HI (human intelligence), they should not, because the "way of ways" here has nothing to do with the "Way of Ways," though the ever-so-slight echo of that idiom tricks us just long enough to keep the words hopping.

    21) Out of the way of ways is a way.

Away, indeed. But, pun aside, what differentiates this with 20) is how "a" makes the 6-character line a low-key or humble start for the Tao narrative. The mood is that of a fable, while *The* Way has a religious if not evangelical overtone. Still, perhaps because our language has incorporated the rhetoric of an absolutist faith, the latter seems more natural to us, whether we believe in it or not.

    22) The Way that may truely be regarded as the Way is other than a permanent way
    23) The Tao which is truely Tao is not a fixed Tao
    24) The Waycanway is nowhere bound

22), by Duyvendak (*Tao Te Ching: The Book of the Way and Its Virtue* 1954), is another translation introduced by Watts in *The Watercourse Way*; and 23) is how Watts would translate the same idea. Duyvendak could win a prize for bad writing, but his idea is fresh, for he sees the *way-can-way* half of the line as the authentic Tao and the *usual* or, to use Watts' good words, "fixed and definable" way/s usually held to be the sought for real thing as "not the true Tao at all." While I confess to having wondered the same, for Chinese has changed over the centuries and who is to say whether, once upon a time, the *Waycanway* 道可道 may not have meant *The Tao=Way* 道 and being "normal/fixed/conventional" 常 etc., or to use 70's language, *hung up,* was precisely what it was *not*, rather than what it was. My first try to improve this reading was *The Waycanway is not fixed,* but I decided to go with the more meaningful ambiguity of "bound." I do not want to give readers an exaggerated idea of translator's license. Grammatically speaking, Duyvendak's reading is definitely *possible,* but all the dictionaries are clear about the "usual way" being the true Tao, and none even admit "way-can-way" as a word. So, these readings should be taken with a grain of salt.

道　可　道　非　常　道

way-can-way-not-usual-way

21) The Tao that can be *tao*-ed is not the invariable Tao

Watts credits this translation to "Fung Yu-lan [Bodde]." Since Bodde translated Fung's books (several are given in Watts' bibliography), one might assume all the credit should go to Bodde, but it is always possible that he translated from a gloss of the *Tao Te Ching* by Fung rather than the thing itself, so I leave the credit as is. Be that as it may, Fung/Bodde make/s us think about the possible meaning of "road." Watts explains, after Wieger (who has a 1927 book on Chinese characters) that 道, or road, originally 衜, includes " 'a going and pausing movement,' where going (彳) is *yang* and pausing (亍) is *yin*." That sounds good to me, but I would be remiss to readers not to mention that Shirakawa Shizuka, probably the top world expert on the etymology of Chinese characters, takes the head 首 in the road character seriously. It was, he writes, held by its hair and waved above the road, or crossroad, to hallow it . . . [1] Be that as it may, there is appeal in the idea of verbing the Tao/Way. If only a road could be rode rather than ridden, I would do it, too. Maybe there is *another* line somewhere in the *Tao te Ching* I could render: *The ridden can not ride the Road* – but that is little help for our *way-can-way-not-constant-way*. I can, however, offer one idea *for the road*. Chinese have long taken the written spells we hide from the public eye in the West (I do not just mean incantations by witches and magicians, but an attitude of secrecy with respect to charms, including the very name of YWH found in the Old Testament) and publically posted them on walls by the roadside, at crossroads, or even scratched right into clay road surfaces. One nursery rhyme (mistranslated) in I.T. Headland's *Chinese Mother Goose* (c.1900) asks a morally upstanding stranger to repeat an incantation three times when he comes across it to save the family from . . . guess what! . . . their *cry-monster*, which is to say little baby, who was keeping them up all night. If such practices were around at the time the Tao Te Ching was composed, the *road-can-road* may well have referred to this sort of crass public practice (matched today by Christian churches who pray for strangers in the USA) as opposed to the more subtle Tao, which neither depended on nor expected miracles.

22) Get out of the way, if you would find It!

Here, I am admittedly pushing it, for my reading has but one way of the three and even if the capitalized *It*, which may or may not be the same "it" about which Watts asked his famous question (What is this *it* that rains?), is clearly the Tao, advice to get out of the way, by which I mean to lose your self, though found elsewhere in Taoist writings is a bit of a stretch for *road-can-road-not*.

23) Give way to all ways: that's The Way!

Likewise, here. Even if we interpret the *road-can-road-not* as advice not to take takeable-roads, that is not quite the same as *jujitsu* (the art of going with the flow to win).

道 可 道 非 常 道
way-can-way-not-usual-way

~~~~~~~~~~~~~~~~~~~~~~~~~~~~~~~~~~~~~~~

24 All ways lie in the way of the Way!

25) No ways lie in the way of the Way!

Oddly, the assertion that all ways get in the way and the opposite assertion that none do are not at odds. I am a bit tired of typing after that last page and must go out to feed the cows, so I leave this *koan* for the reader to figure out.

26) The Way is all ways and none.

If we have an infinite number of ways to go, then there is no way to start. But this "all" is no fiction, for we know it means all extant ways, *i.e.*, the variously established religious ruts, which, being within The Way can not *be* it, itself. But logic can not make a boring translation fun. This next is better:

27) No way is a way to the way.

The sense here is right. If a way is a way to something it is a way-can-way and the only major divergence from the original is the "no" at the start rather than two-third's of the way through the line. "The Way" would be proper in English, but I find the read is sweeter if we are made to make it out for ourselves, so I decapped it.

28) To take a way is to lose It.

For some reason, "To choose a way is to lose *the way*" (9)) required *the way*, while this version with "take" does better with *It*. Either way, the idea would be that 31) *All ways lead away from The Way*, which I tried to improve:

29) All ways stray from the Way that stays.

It is good "that stays" means the same as "regular/eternal," for even if Chinese poetry is more consistently and thoroughly rhymed than English poetry ever was, the line from the Tao te Ching is not so much rhymed as repetitive, so my wordplay must rest on reason. The "always" version (see 16 & 17) would be: 30) *All ways stray from Always.*

31) All ways lost! Always found!

This is more along the lines of an association than a translation. I came up with it after feeling fed up with the following versions of the "all ways/always" idea: 32) *All ways lead not to Always;* 33) *Forget all ways to find Always;* 34) *No way is always the Way;* 35) *No way is Always;* 36) *The Way is always – all ways are not;* 37) *The Way of always, all ways is not;* 38) *No way but The Way is all ways.*

道　可　道　非　常　道

way-can-way-not-usual-way

---

39) All ways are not the Way of Ways.

This is the plural version of the didactic paradox 11). The next will be our last translation with "Way of Ways."

40) The Way of Ways is weigh enough!

Way enough is a nautical term for "put up your oars," the implication being that the Way found, there is no need to keep rowing. Or, that one could not row there to begin with.

41) The Way is every which way but.

42) Every which way but is the Way.

Lucretius, the agnostic poet-scientist, said about all that can be said about religion and knowing what can not be known. If I am drawn to my own hard-to-grasp reading, 41), is it because I do not care to know what is what? Is it because I prefer to leave religion, or bonding with the supernatural, entirely to my unconscious to do *if it so wishes?* 42) is not a different version of 41). It is a taste of grammar common until the 20c. Thoreau overused it, perhaps because *"but"* allowed him to sound offputting while actually welcoming the world (I joke, the word is similar to "quite" in that is simultaneously functions as an emphatic and a modest qualification. With the right language one can have one's cake and eat it too). For readers who have not paid close attention to pre-20c style, 42) is the Taoist version of God in all things. But, instead of a *thing* (spirit or concrete, light or matter, God is a *thing*), while the Way is *moving,* itself.

43) Only the Way is not in the way.

No explanation for 43) is needed. The idiom is one all English-speakers know. The next and final reading will take us back to Watts' undescribeable and undiscourseable Tao 1) and 2), saving the idea with a down-to-earth verb and impersonal yet familiar second-person. The Tao may flow, but never forget that Chinese snaps. Our translations should likewise be snappy.

44) The way you say is not the Way!

It has been about ten years since I did this exercise in what might be called exhaustive paraversing; and I can still remember the pleasure it gave me. I am not one to deliberately sit and meditate – unless composing haiku poetry is such – but I feel like that first line of the Tao pulled me into a meditative state. I came away refreshed, having learned how important it is to stick with the Way of our native tongue in order to get more from another one.

初心

I explained "paraversing" on the second page of this chapter and used the word in the penultimate sentence, on the last page, while I used "translation" many times. In retrospect, I probably shouldn't have because 1) I am not fluent in Chinese, much less ancient Chinese; but I was following Watts and it could be said that *most* "translation" of famous work is not translation in so far that it attracts "translators" who can only read it because others have translated it before; and 2) newly unearthed (since 1970's) older versions of the first line of the *Tao Te Ching* or *Daodejing* if you prefer the *au courant* spelling, favor some of the translations more than others enough that the others become unintended, or *post-facto paraverses*. Such updating could have been worked into what I wrote, but I am of the school that values 初心, literally "first heart/mind." Those two characters by themselves could support a chapter-full of translations, but in this case, I mean that I find something in my naive initial efforts worth preserving as is. And, in retrospect, the chapter is clearly about paraversing rather than multiple-translation, though the line between the two may only be drawn in pencil, erasable at will. I will explain *why* multiple translation is sometimes the only good translation in the next chapter, but let us jump the gun a bit here inorder to put this chapter into context before moving on. Correspondent MMcM notes that "it seems like there are a number of motivations for multiple translations, with some overlap –

> Exploring the nature of translation by contrasting different approaches to troublesome passages.
>
> Brainstorming toward a single correct translation. Gather up all the ideas with hopes of distilling after you have enough to work with.
>
> A truly multi-faceted translation because a single one just won't do. Just as you say, this has typographical challenges.
>
> Improvisations on the original theme. Here I'm again reminded of Pound, even though he tried to work out a single product. While as translations from Chinese (or Provençal or Old English), the results are sometimes just plain wrong, they are almost uniformly good English poetry. One can honestly come to believe that as well as making mistakes, when confronted with problems with the meaning, he deliberately ignored it. (e-mail: 2007)

What I have done with the Tao Te Ching is clearly the last of the above, though I doubt mine are "uniformly good." Improvisation is exactly what I mean by paraversing, and MMcM, the reader to beat all readers, picked up on it: "On the matter of translation, Watts says two things particularly relevant to your paraversing enterprise. First, of the eighty, *'All differ, and most are to some extent correct.'* And then later, *'But in my own feeling this kind of laconic and aphoristic Chinese is best translated by giving, in parallel, many of the different ways in which it may be understood: for it means all of them.'* Indeed, the first statement is as much as admitting they are mostly paraverses and not translations (Had Watts known the words *paraverse* and *paraversing*, can you doubt he would have used them?). The second statement implies the third option posited by MMcM, the multiple or composite translation (if you are not familiar with my work, the next chapter will clarify what is meant by "typographical challenges). However, Watts was a bit off. Paraversing and translation may overlap, but they are not identical. To some readers, the Chinese original doubtless can mean "all of them," but Lao Tsu, or whoever it was who first spoke or wrote the original words would surely have disagreed with such a claim. For the dreamers among us, who would preserve possibility in a world the doers would *fix* in every meaning of that word, hyper-polysemy is a blessing, but we need to be careful of spreading false hope born of ignorance, possibilities that do not exist.

☆ **Watts and the *Tao Te Ching***: Watt's autobiography is not on hand, but checking his earlier *Watercourse Way*, where the "real" in 5) is "eternal" and 7) is "The Force that is forced isn't true Force," it is clear that either his style improved=shortened over the years, or I touched up his translations just a little and forgot I did so. In the latter book, he also gave *awfully* prosaic translations by Lin Yutang: *"The Tao that can be told of is not the Absolute Tao;"* A. Waley: *"The Way that can be told of is not an Unvarying Way;"* W.G. Old: *"The Tao that is the subject of discussion is not the true Tao;"* and two others I mentioned in the main text. (I may be wrong about the autobiography being my first source, too, but does it really matter?)

Pronunciation of Chinese. Here are two renditions of the first 6 characters of the classic *Tao Te Ching* by Lao-tsu in the Wade-Giles Romanization or, *Daodejing* by Laozi in the pinyin, respectively:

tao k'o tao, fei ch'ang tao.
dao ke dao, fei chang dao.

As one can see from *Peking*, *Beijin*, the once popular WG romanization was crisp/cool/clean/sharp-edged, while the recent favorite is blunt/warm/dirty/soft-edged. The effect of the psychological mimesis of these sounds can be argued either way. Some Edo era (1603-1857) Japanese (noteably Norinaga) considered the latter type of consonant (d,g,z,b) *dirty* and more animal than the former (t,k,h,s), associated with a pristine spirit and godly language. But one could find the sharp edges on those pristine consonants too sharp, even aggressive in a cutting way, while the dull-edges ones can be seen as friendly for having the corners worn off. Or, conversely, blunt-edged consonants can be felt as heavy and clublike, rather than warm. Be that as it may, the correct Romanization and the correct pronunciation are different matters. Like all languages, Chinese itself changed over time.

My feel for Chinese is not good enough to settle the many quibbles concerning the meaning of the characters in this context. And there are complications. New, older versions of the *Tao Te Ching* found in the 70's (Mawangdui 馬王堆帛書 老子: 道可道也 非恆道也) and the 90's (Guodian 郭店 竹簡 老子) support "unvarying" *vs*. "eternal" as 恆 is used instead of 常, but I am not certain it makes much difference, for what does not change is eternal and vice-versa. Waley's translation (above), based on the long accepted Wang Bi redaction could be a translation of the new older varients. *The only way is always the way that won't stay put.* And neither now does the history of the words, which in one version come in the middle rather than start of the book. If my attitude seems awfully lacksidasical, it is because I agree with MMcM that even though it is fun to find out more about the roots of the words,

" . . . if these texts were lost to the Chinese themselves before the establishment of classical Taoism, then it is what it is already. The older perspective isn't invalidated. The history of ideas is as important as the truth. Translation can be seen as a dialog between China and the West and this is just a continuation of that. Even the Christians who saw their Trinity in the Tao are legitimate paraversers. (correspondence).

Japanese tend to quote the characters as they are and pretend they just mean what they mean in the same way Frost insisted his poem did; but, when those characters are translated or interpreted, the difficulty of reading them remains. Take this translation (the one at Wiki) by Fukunaga Mitsuji (福永光司?): 道の道とす可きは常の道に非ず which might be Englished as *"what makes the way the way is not [found?] in the constant way."* What does *that* mean? That the way is only found in flux? We are as confused as ever. I did find *one* exception, someone who dared go so far out on a limb that he pulled it right down to the ground (one of my favorite childhood games):

> In direct translation, it becomes *"What was previously a road/way is not necessarily a road/way now."* This idea would seem to link to the idea that though *"theorems are not constant"* one cannot make a theorem that *"theorems are not constant."* That is hard to grasp without explanation. In the end, it means *"You might follow the road another took to success but then it would no longer be the way to success."* . . . The situation is constantly changing and the world of music no exception. What I think is that to be successful is to constantly blaze a new way/path/trail." 直訳すると、「前まで道だったものが今でも道であるとは限らない。」となる。「定理は常でない。」にもかかわらず、「定理は常でない。」は定理にできない。という訳し方にも繋がるらしいどういう意味であるか、解説なしではわかりにくい。これは結局のところ、「人が成功した道をたどろうとしても、それはもう成功の道ではない。」という意味に捉えることが出来る。。。状況は常に変化し、音楽業界もまた例外ではない。。。私はこう思う。「成功するものは、常に新しい道を切り開こうとする。」
> redboot.noblog.net/blog/c/10299576.html

Forgive my unconstant translations of 道 : I could not settle on one of the choices (*road/way/trail/path*) and be idiomatic, which in translation means natural. What interests me here is how the musican took the old line and – whether or not you buy his translation – made it his own. Chinese who find Japanese timidity perplexing would applaud. Doubtless, there are more Japanese interpretations to be found, but we shall leave them to another edition.

Chinese Readings, as Least a Word on Way/Road.

While Chinese would not have any reason to translate, they have surely interpreted this line in many ways. I would love to add a couple pages of the best of these to another edition *if* a specialist could gather and translate them (For a model, see Makoto Ueda's compilation of interpretations of Bashô's *ku*). For now, let me summarize an extraordinary essay by a Chinese social scientist in a language *I* can read, Japanese: 中国の「道」と日本の「技」中国社会科学院　李兆忠 or *"China's 'Way' and Japan's 'Craft' "* by Li Shiu Chung.

First, Li notes that what in China was simply how to write, arrange flowers or brew tea, etc. became the formal "Way of Writing," "Way of Flowers," "Way of Tea," etc. in Japan, and that this, while an impres-sive development, seems a bit silly to Chinese who are amazed one can be so damn serious (*majime-kusaru*) about the arts, but that this is partly a misunderstanding due to Chinese not understanding that Japanese use 道 "way" differently than they do. To Chinese, "way" as a concept is diametrically opposed to "craft" 技 or "technique." It belongs to the metaphysical 形而上 (that which is above form), whereas craft belongs to the physical, or material world 形而下 (that which is below form), and, as such, (the six characters mean) *"The Way, generally speaking cannot be explained"* (道は一般的には、はっきりと説明することができない). Reading this, I am tempted to write: *The metaphysical road is on no map,* or, better yet, *The way that can be worked out is not the One none doubt.*

Because Chinese revere the Way, they feel that being hung up on technique is a shackle that prevents one from scaling the metaphysical heights and, indeed, in comparing the arts, Chinese are more playful than Japanese in their approach and despise work lacking the mark of special talent as "stinking of craftsmen"(職人臭). Indeed, they find the idea of a Way of this or that bound by strict rules a ludicrous contradiction of terms and cannot help being amused by the evident stiffness of Japanese artists who work according to the rules of their constantly splintering factions. And this is not only true for the arts but for traditional sports such as the Way of the Bow, where Chinese who follow the spirit and revere originality are amazed by the same factionalism based on fine points Chinese archers do not bother with (If Roger Aschaam's *Toxiphilia* has been translated into Chinese, the part advising us to shoot at lanterns at night so we learn to shoot from the heart should agree). This is not necessarily a bad thing, Japanese craftsmen in Edo were so proud of their skill and place in society that they boasted of keeping no money overnight, as they knew they could do good work and get paid for it the next day and a society does better with many fine craftsmen and few artists than the vice versa. (If you read Japanese, the full text may still be here: peopleschina.com/maindoc/html/fangtan/200108.htm)

~~~~~~~~~~~~~~~~~~~~~~~~~~~~~

140 Way of Ways! A website w/ a marvelous name, BUREAU OF PUBLIC SECRETS has 140 translations in chronological order. Each one is the entire first stanza (the first line and nine more). I am tempted to give *all* of them and may in a future edition if the authors are amenable. Let us see a dozen or so first lines: *The tau (reason) which can be tau-ed (reasoned) is not the Eternal Tau (Reason).* (John Chalmers tr. 1868). *The TAO, or Principle of Nature, may be discussed* [by all]; *it is not the popular or common Tao.* (Frederick Henry Balfour tr.1884); *This is what may be called a God (the great everlasting infinite First Cause from whom all things in heaven and earth proceed) can neither be defined nor named.* (G.G. Alexander tr. 1895); *The Reason that can be reasoned is not the eternal Reason.* (D.T. Suzuki and Paul Carus tr. 1913). Suzuki, the man who brought Zen to the West, follows Chalmers with his "reason," reminding us of Aristotle's *ratio* which links to the *logos* of the *Genesis.* This concept originated in the late-16c Jesuit policy of Accomodation worked out to facilitate the introduction of Christianity to the Far East. *The Tao that can be expressed is not the Everlasting Tao.* (Isabella Mears 1916) I cite this one because it is nice to see a woman in the game so early and because it gives me an excuse to introduce another of mine: *The way that can be expressed is not the Express Way. I know.* I am pushing it with "expressway." *There are ways but the Way is uncharted; / There are names but not nature in words: / Nameless indeed is the source of creation / But things have a mother and she has a name.* (R.B. Blakney tr. 1955). I had to keep going to the last line, an extraordinary paraverse. *The way that can be defined to death is not the Way to Life.* (Benjamin Hoff tr. 1981); *TAO called Tao is not TAO.* (Stephen Addiss and Stanley Lombardo tr. 1993). This is the first all-cap Tao, but why not? It makes you think. That first line is followed by *Names can name no lasting name,* good for taking advantage of the English name-as-verb. *The Way that can be experienced is not true* (Peter Merel tr. 1995). "Experience" is a good word, but reading Merel's entire stanza, all that perfect Latin vocabulary (*constructed, manifests, represents, exists, intention,* etc.) depressed me, for I long for more good short words than English has. *The way you can go / isn't the real way* (Ursula K. Le Guin tr. 1998). I like the terse quality of this. *A path is just a path, a name is just a name / What is, is, without sense or differentiation / And only divides itself into things when we give names* (Ted Wrigley tr. 2000). I had to give more than the first line, for Wrigley translates more than one line at a time, a practice acceptable to me – if done well, it may be the best way to translate because languages differ in their paragraphs as they do in theor sentences – but rare, for most translators and critics think it beyond the pale (as is Wrigley's use of the long Latin "differentiation"). *Who would follow the Way / must go beyond words.* (Douglas Allchin 2002) Allchin's bold "go beyond" is a good example of a paraverse. *The Way cannot be told. / The Name cannot be named* (A.S. Kline tr. 2003). Kline keeps it phonetically as short as the original but had to short-change the information to do so. *This book can tell you nothing; / the Tao leaves you where you began.* (Crispin Sartwell tr. 2004) After this enchanting paraverse, Sartwell tried to tell *everything* (the 9 lines became 13, and 2 horribly long). Let's see just a few entire translations. The first is by Charles H. Mackintosh (1926),

The way to which mankind may hold
   Is not the eternal way.
Eternal truths cannot be told
   In what men write or say.

The name that may be named by man
   Is not the eternal name
That was before the world began
   Or human language came.

In that the namable took root,
   The tree of fire and force,
Which, having blossomed and borne fruit,
   Returns then to its source.

Who warms his body at that fire,
   Sees nothing but its smoke;
But he who puts aside desire,
   The flame's self will invoke.

These two things are the same in source
   But different in name;
Who solves this mystery has recourse
To that from whence he came.

Compare Mackintosh's rhyming paraverse to Lionel Gile's straightforward prosaic rendition (1904):

The Tao which can be expressed in words is not the eternal Tao; the name which can be uttered is not the eternal name. Without a name it is the Beginning of Heaven and Earth; with a name it is the Mother of all things. Only one who is ever free from desire can apprehend its spiritual essence; he who is ever a slave to desire can see no more than its outer fringe. These two things, the spiritual and the material, though we call them by different names, in their origin are one and the same. This sameness is a mystery — the mystery of mysteries. It is the gate of all wonders.

While the original is more poetic than Giles, it is a prose poem, with only two rhyming lines right in the middle. James Legge (1891) captured them thus:

Always without desire we must be found,
If its deep mystery we would sound;
But if desire always within us be,
Its outer fringe is all that we shall see.

D.T. Suzuki and Paul Carus (1913) prefaced it with "Therefor it is said" and adjusted the last two lines:

"He who desireless is found
The spiritual of the world will sound.
But he who by desire is bound
Sees the mere shell of things around."

Most translations are all rhyme or none, like the next by Ron Hogan (1994) which is, to my mind, an extraordinarily good vernacular translation because Hogan takes the ideas in the original, makes them his own and presents them with snap.

If you can talk about it, it ain't Tao.
If it has a name, it's just another thing.

Tao doesn't have a name.
Names are for ordinary things.

Stop wanting stuff. It keeps you from seeing what's real.
When you want stuff, all you see are things.

These two statements have the same meaning.
Figure them out, and you've got it made.

Like most of my favorites, Hogan's does away with the "mother" found in the Chinese. There is some irony in the unmothering, to me, anyway, for I recall reading a book by one Sam Gill (no relation) about how European's brought their Classical idea of an Earth Mother to the Americas and impressed it on the natives. The other expression missing from all my full stanza examples, including Gile's who has said Mother, is the "ten-thousand things," which just means *all sorts of things,* what Christians call *creation,* anyway.

More, Yet! While the Bureau of Public Secrets had well over 100 translations/paraverses, there are more out there. MMcM notes that Pauthier put it into French and Latin in 1838 — *La voie droite qui peut être suivie dans les actions de la vie n'est pas le Principe éternel, immuable, de la Raison suprême.* / *Via (quæ) potest frequentari, non æterna-et-immutabilis rationalis Via.* — and Julien into French in 1842 — *La voie qui peut être exprimée par la parole n'est pas la Voie éternelle.* Both predate Chalmers and are found in *The Idea of God and the Moral Sense in the Light of Language: Being a Philological Enquiry Into . . .* by Herbert Baynes, who, himself offers: *"Reason which can be embodied in speech is not the Eternal Reason!"* MMcM also observes the first German translation, two years after Chalmers, also solved? the problem of translating 道 by Romanizing the Chinese: *Tao, kann es ausgesprochen werden,/ Ist nicht das ewige Tao.* (Victor von Strauss 1870). After considering the impossibility of translating Tao *in* a word, Watts came to the same conclusion: *"It has thus more or less come to the point where we have simply adopted the word tao into English ..."* I am not sure that was quite the case when he wrote, but the *Tao of Pooh* would eventually come and more recently, with Nelson's didactic but delightful *Dao of Willie*, it would indeed seem to have naturalized. And, I note, in what seems an encyclopedic introduction to *World Scriptures: An Introduction to Comparative Religions*, that though the translation is my "Way," the word is Anglicized so well you might mistake it for something on Wall Street or an international corporation producing more than the basic elements, *i.e,* the Dow). All in all, the Tao's first stanza has given birth to a hell of a batch of paraverses. The Tao's message would seem to inspire freedom . . . at least, with words.

This Book is Under-Construction

This book, like the *Tao* now called *Dao* will change with each edition so long as the author keeps changing, which is to say, living. Hopefully, this silly page will be replaced in the next edition with an illustration. Of the Dao? No. We already know that cannot be done. It will be a phenomenal illustration of the literal analog of *The Way* as *Road*, as described in the plural by Rabelais in *Gargantua and Pantagruel*. In case, the reader only knows Rabelais as an adjective, let me introduce a quote from the chapter about an Island with rascal roads that just would not stay put.

> After we had sailed for two days, the Isle of Odes hove into sight, and there we saw a strange thing. For the roads there are animals, if Aristotle is right when he says that one irrefragable sign of an animal is that it moves of its own accord. For the roads there move like animals, and some are roads errant, like the palanets, others roads passing, roads crossing, roads traversing. I noticed that travellers frequently asked some inhabitant of the island: 'Where does this road go?' The answer would be: 'From Noon to Fevrolles, to the church, to the town, to the river . . . The road you see there was born of water and will return to it. A couple months ago boats were passing down it but now it carries carts. (John Michael Cohen trans. 1955)

And, if you think Rabelais was drinking when he wrote that chapter, look up Chesterton's poem on the origin of the famously winding roads of England.

★*Amateur and professional scholars!* I would be *obligado* if you could dig up some early translations. Legge mentions a 1788 translation that introduced two connotations of the T/Dao: *ratio et via,* or *reason and road*, doing to a single word what I would do with composite translation. It would be interesting to have the Latin for the whole line, but even more interesting to find a comparison of the "tao" translation problem and the "logos" (from "our" *Tao te Ching, The Genesis*) translation problem. Speaking of which, when I tried to give the description of my last book to the Isbn agency and to my printer, I found nothing regarding "translation" among the allowable subjects *except Christian matters* (the Bible) about which there were *dozens of choices* including a handful *specifically about "multiple translation!"* I recall how Peter Farb relied upon Bible translation to make interesting points in his classic book on language, *Word Play* (Destroyed in Japanese, the basis for my *Goyaku-tengoku*=Mistranslation Paradise. Hakusuisha: 1989); but the Bible is hardly the only thing going! That a publisher is presented with such a choice is absurd. Only in pre-modern *Usania*. Let me add that I expect to find 16 or 17c translations by Ricci or Rodriguez.

ii
Rise, Ye Sea Slugs!
◎ Up to 26 Readings for One Haiku ◎

This, my first book in English, is the first I know to use deliberately created multiple-readings of individual poems *as a method of translation*. First, a couple pages from the Foreword demonstrating an aesthetic use of multiple-translation.

Each chapter of *RISE, YE SEA SLUGS!* focuses on a different type of sea cucumber, not a different biological species, but a different semiological species. In biology, the line between species is not always solid. Even with DNA called in to arbitrate, arbitrary lines, i.e. definitions, must be *made*. The same thing is true with respect to organizing a poetic typology.

直線を知らぬ存ぜぬ海鼠かな　マツク・ヒデ
chokusen o shiranu zonzenu namako kana – matsuku hide 20c
(straight-line/s[obj], know/ing-not, existing-not, seaslug/s[subj] !/?/ø)

allogical animal

straight lines
are beyond the ken
of a sea slug

Moreover, I had to do this work completely de novo, with no Linnaean system, indeed no prior system at all, to assist me. My *modus operandi* was simple. I collected every old haiku and senryu on the sea cucumber I could, and tried to divide them thematically. I wavered back and forth as I made new finds. It was something like playing cards, where a new draw might make you decide to go for a full-house rather than a straight. In the end, I had a good hand. As the *Table of Content* shows, I managed to invent no less than twenty-one semiological species – metaphorical groupings, if you prefer – and [abbrev.] many more sub-species, scores of which have been compiled into a large extra chapter of *Sundry Slugs*.

oh, sea slug!
not knowing not living
straight lines

If the range of individual difference for a given trait in a species can be listed in serial or drawn as a simple distribution curve, even a complex graph of overlapping curves – or for that matter, a tree cannot show the convoluted relationship of many species, sub-species and their various traits. That is to say, my chapters and the haiku within them not only overlap each other, but do so in ways that defy proper narrative. The overall relationship can only be grasped at a glance by three-dimensional modeling, or the next best thing, overlapping Venn diagrams, a sample of which, I plan to offer (below) in the best tradition of

Laurence Sterne. Arranging such material in a serial narrative was, to borrow holothurian expert and curator Philip Lambert's fine pun, truly a taxing problem! I hope that even if the ride is occasionally bumpy, good readers from every ilk of life will still find themselves transported by my sea slug serenade.

tristam sandy

straight lines
are beyond sea slug's
wildest dreams

> I Am now beginning to get fairly into my work; and by the help of a vegitable diet, with a few of the cold seeds, I make no doubt but I shall be able to go on with my uncle Toby's story, and my own, in a tolerable straight line. Now,
>
> These were the four lines I moved in through my first, second, third, and fourth volumes.——In the fifth volume I have been very good,——the precise line I have described in it being this:

I put a diagram from Laurence Sterne's *Tristam Shandy* above, in case my reader has missed out on the first modern novel written in English, but the point indirectly made with the above translations, was that even an unknown *ku,* with a little imagination, could be resurrected as a number of entertaining haiku in English. As the presentation was in serial and the detail strayed far from the original, the result was less a composite translation than what I call *paraversing*.

海底に一存在の海鼠哉　松本正氣
unazoko ni hito sonzai no namako kana – matsumoto seiki 1942
(sea-bottom/floor-on one/singular-existence's/- seaslug/s!/?/ό/'tis)

its world

a sea slug
on the floor of the sea
truly exists

place

a *namako*
on the seabed has
a presence

on the seabed
a *ding an sich* called
sea cucumber

beneath it all

on the bottom
a singular being
the sea slug

it goes deep

there's reality
on the floor of the sea
eg., namako

Now, it may be that the poet has recognized how a sea slug in its element has a far more impressive presence than one in a fish-shop or the chafing dish. But it is more likely that he finds its thingness – being nondescript, *namako* makes a far better thing than something with particulars messing with its generality – a fine excuse to pull philosophy down to solid ground, no, lower, to the very bottom of the sea. The Japanese, after their allies, the Germans, were big on existentialism at the time this *ku* was written. While I used the word "being" in one translation, the sea slug need not be alive to serve as proxy for existential reality. Like Bashô's sea slugs, frozen in a lump, Namako's life remains a question, as, ultimately, does ours.

on the seabed
a singular presence
holothurians

I added the above, for *namako* may be thought of collectively. But wouldn't you agree the cluster of five-readings on the previous page make composite translation *convincing* in a way a chain of readings would not? Without words, it *shows* translations may be *a* translation. Needless to say, it helps that haiku are short and I center-balance them. Part of a note from the page gives another reason why multi-translation is particularly useful for haiku:

A haiku, theoretically speaking, is itself supposed to be singular, but a few words, no matter how skillfully chosen, cannot rule out enough possibilities . . . to tell whether it stands for something other than what it purports to be. Knowing nothing about this poet's circumstances, I cannot say for sure that we do not have here a nod to a friend thrown in jail for being less than patriotic or to another in a submarine, or a sort of victimization mentality, where the oppressed individual (or nation) remonstrates *even us sea slugs have a life!*

For all my readings, the possibilities were not covered. Perhaps I needed more yet!

~~~~~~

<center>
海鼠あり庖厨は妻の天下かな　碧梧桐
namako ari hôchû-wa tsuma-no tenka kana – hekigoto (1872-1937)
(seaslug/s is/are kitchen-as-for wife's heaven-below[domain] 'tis!/?/ø)
</center>

a sea slug	a sea slug
my wife is now god	makes my wife shôgun
in the galley	of the kitchen

<center>女神</center>

with sea slugs	one sea slug
in the kitchen, my wife	turns the kitchen into
thinks she's god	the wife's realm

Paraphrasing my book – Either the difficulty of cutting up the featureless creature or the wife's knowledge that Hekigoto loved to eat sea slug elevates her; but it is hard to say if *tenka* (heaven-below=domain) simply means the kitchen is the wife's shôgunate or is meant to remind us that it was a goddess who first poked a sea slug when it did not pledge allegiance to the gods like others in the sea and its mouth was macerated by her dagger (a just-so for the ugly opening). In the traditional kitchen, man was usually the one with the knife . . . .

古 湯 婆 形 海 鼠 に 似 申 す よ　子 規
furu tanpo katachi namako ni ni môsu yo – shiki (1867-1902)
(old hot-water bottle: shape, sea slug-to resemble say-would/emph.)

appearances deceive   *sick-bed taxonomy*

a resemblance   i give a class
to the sea slug: my old   to my old foot-warmer:
    foot-warmer   *holothurian*

Shiki, who spent much of his adult life as a bedridden invalid, had a close acquaintance with hot water-bottles. His haiku gives a familiar form to the formlessness. . . . . Japanese readers of Shiki's time would also remember the reputation of the sea slug as a *cold* creature and chuckle at the false likeness. To wit:

my old hot-water bottle

another likeness:
abandoned, it is cool as
a sea cucumber

I thought Shiki's *ku* meant that rubber or leather hot water "bottles" were already in use over a hundred years ago – one nineteenth century term for holothurian was *scytodermata*, or "leather/hide-skin" – but OM writes "Until the 1970's, Japanese hot water bottles were not made of rubber or leather. They were flat oval-shaped tin (like a flattened football) with wave-like indentations which truly resembled *namako*." (corresp) [♪Let me add that the inert Shiki was himself the sea slug.]

徹 頭 徹 尾 せ ぬ を 身 上 海 鼠 か な 成 瀬 桜 桃 子
tettôtetsubi senu o shinjô namako kana – naruse ôtôshi 1993
(thorough-head-thor.-tail do/have-not merit/asset seaslug!/?/ó/'tis/am)

to a certain someone   *moderation*

not having it   sea slug sea slug
all together is what saves   you and me! we never
   you sea slug   go whole hog

the sea slug
bless you for never
going all out!

luke warm/cold   *the uncut gem*

sea slug nation   the saving grace
our only saving grace   for the sea slug is that
  is moderation   it is unfinished

I suspect an allusion (to the poet, prime-minister? national mentality?) here because it would be wrong to say the only good thing about the animal sea slug is *its* lack of thoroughgoingness. The last reading is highly unlikely, for the poet could have written the same more clearly, if he wished to, but, whomever is signified, the signifier is the literary sea slug, the invention of generations of poets. Keigu [my *haigo,* or haiku pen name, taken shortly before writing *Rise*] speaking for all who dislike exhaustive clarity, cannot help himself –

if black & white is not your bag

oh, happy day!
the sea slug is grey
in every way!

The only problem is that an overly thorough celebration of the un-thorough leads quickly to contradiction. Be that as it may, Keigu cannot help continuing [Here, he/I added 5 more paraverses, in both Japanese and English. If you would celebrate *the indeterminate*, by all means, read the rest of *Rise, Ye . . !*].

~~~~~~

尾 も 鰭 も な く ? 退 屈 な り 海 鼠　　小谷ゆきを
o mo hire mo naku[te?] taikutsu nari namako　kotani yukio 20c
(tail-even fin-even not, boring/monotonous becomes/is seaslug)

no tail or fins:
the monotonous life
of a sea slug!

boredom is
a sea slug, *sans* fin
sans tail

no fin no tail
no wonder sea slugs
look bored

no appendages
it's plain sea slug *is*
monotony

Life as a Torso. This haiku puts a new tooth on the old saw of have-not sea slugs while it plays with the idiom "put tail and fin on" (*obire-o tsukeru*), meaning to enliven a story with details. The double *sans* in my last translation was suggested by the line describing the "second childishness and mere oblivion" of old age in *"As You Like It,"* to wit: "Sans teeth, sans eye, sans taste, sans everything." I do not know if the *ku* is about the life of a sea slug or that of the poet. Either way, it reflects a modern attitude which, contrary to the traditional appreciation of doing nothing, assumes excitement is desirable. The poetry improves immensely when you reflect upon life without any protrusions to play with or look at. Imagine the disembodied brain of science fiction, minus the brain. Consider whether or not a brain could have evolved without appendages to stimulate their owner. Read Loren Eiseley's essay on why the handless dolphin would not build a civilization even if it were as bright as us. The *ku* can be read as hopelessly anthropocentric or laudably trans-specific and sympathetic. [♪ I just changed "no fin *or* tail" in the third reading to "no fin *no* tail" to better play on my "no wonder,", and added the last reading, as an afterthought. May future editors of my work do the same!]

39

尾も鰭も持たぬ海鼠の潔し 無名
o mo hire mo motanu namako no isagiyoshi – anon 20c
(tail-even fin-even have-not seaslug's gallantry/manliness)

> no fin or tail
> i'd call the sea slug
> very clean-cut

> no frilly stuff
> *viz* tail, or fin, to mar
> the manly slug

> no fin, no tail,
> no frills at all, sea slug
> man of men

> - for H.G. Welles -
> *Spartan Samurai*

> *ah, sea slugs,*
> *a truly gallant race*
> *doing without*
> *tail, fins and lace*

A meta-contradiction. The blatantly philosophical bent of the *ku* is far from the accepted haiku style, but the argument itself – that lack of frills is manly=good – is typical 20c Japanese thought originating in the late-nineteenth century's international boast to be more *manlier-than-thou*. What is now called Orientalism taught us to despise the supposedly effeminate East, exemplified by the ornate Byzantine civilization; Japanese, who had not a few stern and stark memes to boast of in their own culture, joined the race toward black, grey and khaki, tossing out colorful gallantry and putting down intricate century-old poetry as feminine (or contrived or Chinese) while praising the simpler millenium-old "manly" *Manyôshû*. To this day, neither Japan nor the West have overcome their prejudice. I appreciate what the poet does for the sea slug with his totally new take on its featurelessness; but, unless he is being facetious, cannot abide his (our) worldview. [♪ I revised the last from "Sea slugs are / a true gallant race"]

~~~~~~

海底にまなこ忘れてきしなまこ 鳥居真理子
unazoko ni manako wasurete kishi namako – torii mariko 2002
(sea-bottom-on/at eyes forgot/forgetting comes/came sea slug/s)

> the sea slug
> its eyes left behind
> on the seabed

> hi, sea slug!
> did you forget to bring
> your eyeballs?

> forgetful sea slug
> leaves his eyes behind
> on the sea floor

> are your eyes
> still on the sea floor
> mr namako?

What a sweet poem! I wonder if the poet, like me, if only for a second, misread Taigi's *ku* [♪ this famous *ku,* where the poet looks for but cannot find the *namako's* eyes, fills two page of *Rise*] and thought of a sea slug blindly groping for its own. [♪I wonder if she read the *senryû* I found recently with a ghost leaving her vagina in hell!] It also ought to be considered a *Just-so Sea Slug* [♪ the name of a chapter] *ku*. None of my readings matches the *manako/namako* rhyme in the original. . . . [♪Just added the last reading. The original is a Japanese style poem-as-chain-of-modification: *seabed-on eyes-forgetting-came-seaslug*.]

~~~~~~

天地を我が産み顔の海鼠かな　子規
ametsuchi o waga umigao no namako kana – shiki 1867-1902
(heaven-earth [accus.], myself-bore-faced seaslug!/?/ǿ/'tis/the)

apparent parent

the sea slug
a face that says "i bore
heaven & earth"

the sea slug   *original face?*

a face that says   the sea slug
the whole wide world   a countenance parent
was my doing!   to all creation

This, by the prophet of modern haiku, echoes the language and thought of earlier *ku* but, I think, is much better for its warm humor (This, not the oft-mentioned objective realism, is what makes *me* a Shiki fan). The Japanese use of "face" as "expression" fails in English. The boastful idiomatic nuance of "my face" in Japanese is "I did it!" Maybe, the sea slug really *did*. Chaos is as much a prerequisite for life as order. [♪ some changes in *ku* and text].

A boring title, "cosmic parenthood," was changed to "apparent parent," not just witty but good for drawing our attention to the holothurian's appearance. Let me add that the Japanese *namako* is more blobular, if I may coin a new word, and warty than our land cucumber-like image. One could spend a lifetime doing nothing but giving titles to haiku and have a fun time.

~~~~~~

ひと噛に千歳の思ひ海鼠哉　敬愚
hitokami ni chitose no omohi namako kana – keigu
(one-bite/chew-with, 1000-years' thoughts-even, seaslug!/ǿ/the/'tis)

time on the table   *the perennial food*

eating sea slug   in every chew
we gain/lose a century   a 1000 years of thought
with each bite!   eating sea slug

a thousand years
go by with each bite
of a sea slug

41

There is a Taoist connection I overlooked, the only one mentioned in Tsurumi Yoshiyuki's magnum opus, *Namako no Manako* (the sea cucumber's eye: 1993/ 2001), namely, that trepang is popular in the Sinosphere largely because of its association (as the ginseng of the sea) with *longevity*, the pursuit of which enthralled Taoists as the pursuit of *gold* did Occidental alchemists. But, I do not feel bad about the lacuna, for my focus has been on what makes namako *itself* Taoist rather than how it serves Taoist aspirations. [Some changes made.]

~~~~~~

鬼もいや菩薩もいやとなまこ哉　一茶
oni mo iya bosatsu mo iya to namako kana – issa 1814
(devil too, yuck! bodhisattva, too, yuck! [says/and] sea slug!/?/ø/the/behold)

no black, no white, just grey

phooey to saints
as well as to devils,
huh, sea slug?

Even with the literary *kana* pegged on, this is one of Issa's most colloquial haiku, and Issa was known for colloquialism. Simple words, but this *iya~iya*, or Double *Yuck!* (as in "no way!") *ku* is hard to crack, and my readings – or, rather, *guesses* – fill most of the next two chapters! If new information is found that makes a definitive reading possible, they will still serve to illustrate what is ambiguous about Japanese haiku and how easy it is for a translator to go wrong in fact, though arguably right!

With *twenty-six* translations, many if not most completely different interpretations of what Issa meant, this *ku* is the best demonstration of what purpose multiple translation serves that I know (number alone proves little, as most "translators" work off other translations and not the original). I am tempted to introduce them here, but too much of the significance of the exercise would be lost without the full text. Likewise for Issa's *uke namako,* the title *ku* for *Rise*.

~~~~~~

面目坊海中に入てなまこかな　大江丸
menbokubô watanaka ni irite namako kana – ôemaru? 1801
(appearance[-valuing] monk/man: ocean-in entered seaslug!/?/ø/the/'tis)

where is he?　　　　　　　　　　　　*occidental version*

that monk so　　　　　　　　　　narcissus, he
concerned about his looks　　　fell in the sea and turned
a sea slug now　　　　　　　　　into a sea slug

Ugliness is another way the sea slug relates to Buddhism that has nothing to do with its inactivity, meekness or circumstantial relationship to punishment for sin. According to the *Kokin-chôbunshû*, even attachment to the *appearance* of being religious was deeply sinful. So what should be done about a preacher whose vanity extended even to his own good looks? As a *senryû* put it, "not looking / in the mirror is decorous / for a monk (*kagami-o minai koto-wa so-no tashinami* [from my memory, imperfect]), whereas samurai were supposed to use the mirror.

One wonders what the snooty diva Sei Shonagon (c.965-) would have thought about Oemaru's poetic punishment – she who wrote that a preacher "ought to be good looking" to hold our attention, while an ugly preacher who could not, "may well be a source of sin!" (item 21 in *The Pillow Book of Sei Shonagon*)

a just-so story

sea slugs
the reincarnation of
vain monks

come-uppance   *poetic justice*

on the ocean floor   mister dandy
a man of parts no more: still cool, six feet below
hey, sea slug!   a sea cucumber

This *ku* follows explanation of other *ku,* so the readers of *Rise* already know that monks who committed certain crimes – such as seducing a woman or forcing others to drink – would be reborn *limbless* 500 times. As that information cannot be squeezed into *any* translation, five readings are as opaque as one. I confess, it was done for fun. In *Rise*, the five *ku* are in one cluster, as behooves the pentaradial Echinodermata phylum, but the page bottom got in the way.

~~~~~~

廓 の 灯 た ぬ し む ご と く 海 鼠 売　後 藤 夜 半
kuruwa no hi tanushimu gotoku namakouri – gôtô yahan? 1932
(pleasure-quarter[whore-houses] lamp/s enjoy-as-if, seaslug-seller)

suggestive shadows

he seems to love   that slug vendor
the pleasure quarter lights   does he play with the lights
the sea slug man   of the gay quarter

The first reading suggests that the sea slug vendor with his dark goods seeks out the brightest part of the city like a moth seeking light – though, it could logically be explained by the fact that this is where people eat a lot at night. The verb *tanushimu*, however, strongly suggests the vendor is actually enjoying or having fun with the lights. I imagine either he purposefully or accidentally made risquè shadows, against walls or paper windows.

The above *ku,* from the *Lubricious Sea Slugs* chapter, primes the pump for this:

な ま こ 売 つ ま ん で 見 せ て 嫌 が ら せ　武 玉 川
namakouri tsumande misete iyagarase – mutamagawa 13 (1759)
(sea-slug-seller squeezing shows/showing, harasses [someone])

public display   *boys will be boys*

a repulsive   disgusting!
sea slug vender plays   the vender squeezes
with them   a sea slug

<pre>
         time on his hands   let him sell sea urchin!

           kidding women   the sea-slug man
         the sea slug man plays   harasses young women
            with his goods   squeezing them
</pre>

This senryû could, or rather, *should* have been in a collection of haiku, for the depiction is both seasonable and impeccably real. Not only could the man have laid hand on his phallic goods, simulating things we need not mention, but could have actually squirted customers. In the words of Belon, the first person to note the similarity of the sea urchin, sea star and the sea cucumber: *Exangue maris purgamentum!* (Ludwig: Ibid [*Rise*, has a fair amount of un/natural history])

~~~~~~

口つぐむ海鼠質せば一理あり　高沢良一
kuchi tsugumu namako tadaseba ichiri ari – takasawa yoshikazu 2003
(mouth shut-/clam/med-up seaslug investigate/judge-if, one[a kernal/point of]-truth is)

<pre>
         that sea slug   the sea slug
      who kept mum may have   who held his tongue
           had a point   got a bum rap

                                 ~

                         ancient sea slug
                    there is something to be said
                            for its silence
</pre>

Clever paraversing could not make-up for the fact that English has no verb that by itself means "to clarify the rights and wrongs of some matter" as does *tadasu/seba*. Most of the other haiku about *Silent Sea Slugs*, as we shall see in the chapter by that name, are really about *people* – but Takasawa writes about the sea slug, or, rather, the mythological sea slug, itself.

If you recall, the sea slug was lacerated by a goddess for keeping mum rather than pledging allegiance to the gods. Some say the Japanese myths of origin justify the conquering of natives by people from the continent.

~~~~~~

海鼠喰ふこの世可笑しきことばかり　角川春樹
namako kuu kono yo okashiki koto bakari – kadokawa haruki (contemp)
(seaslug[obj] eat/ing this world laughable/funny/strange/ things only)

<pre>
                          eating sea slug
                        the world is just full
                           of funny things

         truth is stranger   eating sea slug
       than fiction: this world   what about this world
           eats sea slugs   is not strange?

                          this slug-eating
                    world of ours: one funny thing
                            after another
</pre>

I had expected the culinary *namako* to be the least palatable sea slugs in this book, for, as a rule – contrary to what good haiku are supposed to be – I prefer meta-physical to physical poetry. *I was wrong*. Most slug-eating haiku are a challenge to describe taste beyond taste, a struggle to cut, then pinch and pick up slipperiness itself, or a head-trip occasioned by chewing or watching someone chew this chewiest of foods. (*deletion*) Ecological concerns aside, some readers may feel regret that sea slug, who has provided us so much poetic joy must end up in our belly; but the sad truth is that if sea slugs were not eaten, they would rarely if ever make it into haiku. After all, one sees as many if not more starfish (called *hitode*, or "people-hands" in Japanese) on the beaches in Japan as sea slugs, yet, I can't recall a single one in the 100,000 or so old *ku* I have perused.

Kadokawa inherited one of Japan's top publishers. Jailed for smuggling cocaine (for his use, not sale), he wrote a far better *ku* than the above, about a sea slug in a tub at mid-day, which I do not give here. Perhaps, one must be in the situation of a *namako,* relatively immobile, to mature as a poet and an artist. This *ku* did not need so many readings, but something demanded I play with it.

~~~~~~

硬 直 の 酢 の も の 海 鼠 勘 弁 な　高 沢 良 一
kôchoku no sunomono namako kanben na – takasawa yoshikazu (2003)
(rigid/stiff's vinegar-thing/marinated seaslug [i'm] sorry[+emphasis])

    my apologies   sea cucumber
for your *rigor mortis*   forgive my putting you
    sea cucumber   into this pickle

soft sea slug
forgive me for turning you
into a stiff!

At first, I thought this an apology for making the pickled slug too hard, but the adjective *kôchoku* is the word to express the *rigor mortis*. The poet kindly explained that the (live) sea slug is dressed with rough salt before it is cut. There is an association here. Heaps of salt are commonly placed outside the door of the deceased, for purification. Some might find the *ku* artificial if not maudlin, but I read it as a poetic expression of appreciation for the sea-slug-as-food, i.e., the life we take to preserve our own. (2nd ed. 蛇足 Dorothy Parker might have apologized for leaving the slug stiff, rather than *a* stiff.)

Takasawa, who has done more for old *ku* with his on-line compilation than any-one since Shiki, has written more slug *ku* than anyone else, too (Shiki came in second place). Obviously, I play more with the *ku* than the poet did. And, let me add that *vinegar-thing* or, Japanese marination, is far lighter than pickling.

呑 み す ぎ て 哀 し く な り ぬ 酢 海 鼠 よ　田 畑 益 弘
nomisugitte kanashiku narinu sunamako yo – tabata masuhiro (contemp)
(drinking-too-much, sad/pitiful/beautiful become/ing, vinegar/pickled-seaslug!)

   in vino sentitas   *pickled twosome*

over-drinking   poor sea slug!
i suddenly feel for   i know just how
the pickled slug   you feel!

It is wonderful how alcohol can make us (all good people, at any rate) feel warmth for all creation, even that which we are chewing on. The poet ties one on and starts talking to – the exclamation *yo* suggests direct address – pickled sea slug. The character used for sadness is a particularly poetic one which puts a classical patina of beauty upon the sadness. [p.s. I have no idea if *sentitas* is real Latin.]

~~~~~~~~~~~~~~~~~

<div style="text-align:center">

我形に蓋をしている海鼠哉　可幸
waganari ni futa o shiteiru namako kana – kakô (1773)
(my/its-own form-on lid-doing[keep secret] seaslug/s!/?/ǿ/the)

the sight of silence

it clams up
its very appearance:
the sea slug

</div>

undercover	*camouflage*
putting a lid upon the way we are sea slugs!	the sea slug its form well hidden by its form

The sea slug with its just-so lacerated mouth can no longer speak up even if it wants to. Ah, but its body, too, without limbs cannot or dares not express itself imagines this poet. Or is he, perhaps describing his own conventional, don't-rock-the-boat nature? This *ku* may as well have been placed with the *Meek Sea Slug* or the *Featureless Sea Slug* [two other of the 21 metaphor-based chapters]. Hiding one's true self by giving up self-expression is the most common form of meekness. At the same time, as the third reading would show, the idea of formless form hiding form is witty by itself.

The original idiom, "lid-doing," or, "putting a lid on," is the one in a dozen idioms that can actually be translated, rather than re-created of fresh words or an idiom of different metaphor. The first and third readings are paraverses.

~~~~~~~~~~~~~~~~~

黙りゐる事のかしこき海鼠かな　青々
damariiru koto no kashikoki namako kana – seisei (1869-1937)
(shutting-up thing's smart/clever seaslug/s!/?/ǿ/the/'that's)

pragmatism	*sublimation*
bright enough to hold its peace: the sea slug	when it's smart to hold your peace eat sea slug!

quiet types

the sea slug:
does it look bright
clammed up?

advice for radicals	*from this talker*
intelligence remains mum: the word is sea slug	sea slug, think your silence makes you look deep?

Hindsight does not allow us to call the sea slug's choice to remain quiet in the face of the gods a good one, nor did fish get caught because of excessive blabbering until recently – ultra-sound devices let fishermen listen in – so Seisei [a prolific poet of *namako* – seven *ku* in *Rise*] would appear to be describing a human sea slug who is 1) not necessarily resigned but bright enough not to get involved in the heated politics of the age or argue with his or her spouse, or 2) sits and eats the food which best allows him to work off his frustration or anger. However, the vague grammar does not rule out further readings. Seisei's first *nom de plume*, Mushin = *no-heart/mind*, artlessness in the Taoist sense, was associated with *playfulness* (opp. *ushin,* "with-heart" *sincerity*) in *waka* that flowed into *haikai* and he was from Osaka, a loudly verbal part of Japan, so it is possible, though grammatically improbable, he was chiding smug silence.

沈黙は金なり海鼠頑に　佐々木正男
chinmoku wa kin nari namako katakuna ni – sasaki masao 1999
(silence-as-for, gold/en is, seaslug strictly/obdurately/absolutely)

stubborn		*kinko*
silence is golden: sea slug absolutely		silence is golden ossified sea slug
	silence may be golden but sea slug's a bonehead	
etiquette		*what i eat*
silence is golden one doesn't talk when eating sea slug		silence is golden i'm a sea slug man confirmed
	(^ - ^) silence is golden: sea slug my mantra	
soul food		*credo*
sea slug: chewed in golden silence		silence is golden: my food sea slug

The original *ku* was truncated, even by haiku standards. The infinite possibilities of silence provoked half a dozen readings. I would bet on the *What I Eat* reading, mostly because contemporary haiku have taken the old theme of the *Silent Sea Slug* and turned it into the silent sea slug *eater*. Indeed, *silence* comes right after *slipperiness* and *chewiness* as a major sub-theme of the culinary sea slug. I was tempted to fuse it with the *Drinking Sea Slug* – not quite a metaphor (*drunkenness* is) – but it that would not have been fair to the *Chewy Sea Slug*, also involved with silence, so I slipped it into this chapter. If the reader rereads the *Chewy* and *Drinking* sea slugs, the un-mentioned silence will be felt more strongly for seeing these clear-cut *Silent Sea Slugs*.

~~~~~~

不思議とふことの一身海鼠かな　萩月
fushigi tou koto no isshin namako kana – hagizuki (2002)
(wonder/ous/mysterious called thing's one-body/life seaslug!/?/ó/the)

an exemplar
of this thing called wonder
the sea slug

slime or sublime?   *interrogative animal*

the sea slug   the namako
a body that makes   its entire being
you wonder   a question

nomination

wonder
thy name is
sea slug

namako teleology   *the esoteric animal*

sea slugs   sea cucumber
have but one end   everything about it
wonder   says "mystery"

fushigichi

do you know
the second wisdom?
namako is it

The *fushigichi* I put in the last translation-reading is the second of the Five Wisdoms belonging to the Buddha (Amitâbha Tathâgata). This Wisdom is the "wisdom whose best part is beyond mental comprehension." Needless to say, it is a perfect fit for the *namako* we have come to know.

c'est moi   . . . . . .

and what is   sea cucumber
this thing called wonder   struck speechless by
asks sea slug   its own wonder

sea slug
its whole life
a kôan

[The title wouldn't fit before the end of the page. Can you guess? Answer: *clapping with no hands.*] I thought the *tou* of the original meant *tou*, or "ask," but the poet told me it was an archaic ellipsis of *to iu*, or "[as] called." But, I left the translations made before the poet set me straight. A *koan* is a question unanswerable by ordinary logic. The " . . . " translation – which isn't really a translation – is my idea for a new *just-so story*, challenging that in *Records of Ancient Things* (*Kojiki*). I dare say Hagizuki will be surprised to see so many readings of her simple *ku,* summing up the essence of *namako* to herself and many other Japanese.

Not only do my ten readings of Hagizuki's *ku* bring out more facets of the original than could possibly fit in a single translation, but they include angles not even considered by the original author. Had I only come up with things the poet intended, this might be called an extraordinarily complex *composite translation*, but the fact is that some of the readings are clearly *paraverses,* though I did not know how clearly that was the case until I exchanged letters with the poet, who confessed to learning of "The Fifth Wisdom" for the first time from my paraverse. Hagizuki-san did not at all mind seeing her haiku multiplied like that and even expressed delight with it – she had never heard of the Fifth Wisdom – but would have preferred I had her gender right, something I corrected in the passage from my book, above, as I did long ago on the on-line *Errata*.

~~~~~~

What torture trying to decide which of the thousand or so *ku* to introduce. I favored large composite-translation clusters giving multi-translations the most play, as such seems most interesting *out of context* – as it forms its own – but double and triple translations are far more common in the book, and there may be better examples of how multiple translation can be used as a standard method of translation between exotic tongues. My modest argument for multiple translation given in *Rise, Ye Sea Slugs!* and quoted with approval by Willliam J. Higginson in a 5 page review in the prestigious *Modern Haiku:*

> Multiple translation is often the only way to translate all the faces of a poly-faceted poem in a witty, which is to say, brief manner, when trying to squeeze all the information into one poem would kill it, and not including that information—and this is, regretfully, almost standard with haiku translation today—would constitute negligence with respect to the intent of the original.

I also push extreme examples here because I feel my technical explanation, or rationalization, is not the whole story. *Something happened* and is still happening to me since I started paraversing, and these examples demonstrate it best. Follow D. Hofstadter in *Le Tonbeau de Marot* from an excruciatingly stiff start to exhilarating freedom as he gradually stretches his mind with each translation (most are not his, but many are and he studies the others they, too, become him) and you have a step-by-step record of the growth (see pg 165-178). Stick with multiple translation, or paraversing and sooner or later one learns to translate out of the box, if it were. And, I would argue that to translate poetry, as poetry, between exotic tongues one *must* do that, and *for* that one must first be there.

Multiple Translations and Exotic Tongues. When Austro-Hungarian writer Roda Roda writes *"a translation is good only when it is better than the original"* (as paraphrased by Knight and cited by Hofstadter (1997)), I think she has exotic tongues in mind, for Hungarian boasts just enough difference – reflected by the Hungarian name order, the same as in the Far East and contrary to most of Europe, which makes her name name an excellent way to avoid affront and confusion! – to be exotic with respect to the major European tongues. Her "good" either means "acceptable" and her "better" reflects the fact that an individual sentence or poem must make up for the loss in cultural context to make good, or it is a tongue-in-cheek criticism of the status quo in translation. Since I cannot count the number of times I have come across utterly boring poems in English or Japanese translation, I imaginethe latter case. To my mind, the translator, editor and others happily reading such translations have either an abnormally low measure of self-respect, far, far too much patience, or low expectations of what they imagine the original to have been (*i.e.,* a paternalistic attitude). Aesthetics and Manners demand something *better*.

Serious Readers may buy my books of translated haiku and senryu and compare my translations with those by others and judge whether or not my attitude and admittedly odd methods have or have not had a positive influence on my work. In my opinion, they *have,* because I am a far from skillful writer and must outdo myself to do justice to the translation. Despite lack of brain-power and a poor vocabulary, I have been finding more and more happy surprises since I began paraversing, enough so that even one of my strictest (and kindest) critics, Professor Lewis Cook of CUNY, who, like William J Higginson, has noticed that I might sometimes make do with one translation if I kept working at it until I hit the nail on the head – which is doubtless, true – had this to say about my 3000 translations in

Cherry Blossom Epiphany:

"It was bad old Ezra Pound, acknowledging his heavy debt to haiku in translation, who affirmed that the first rule of poetry was "Make it new." This is something Gill has done more effectively, as far as remaking haiku in English goes, than anyone else around." (Posted at one of Gabi Grebe's blogs date lost)

Perhaps half of the 3000 *ku* in the book have only one translation, so Cook is not just talking about the composite translation but my efforts to read a haiku and take an educated chance on the meaning when it is called for, or try to retain the ambiguity when that seems right, or slip a wee bit away from the wording of the original to take advantage of the perfect English idiom where none might exist in the Japanese because I know the opposite often occurs and such gains in translation are the only way to balance the losses, or, through some slight adjustment, such as an added title (something haiku usually don't have and when they do it is a *preface* or a *theme*), create something perhaps wittier than the original, or, by using some rhyme (ideally, AAB Dickinsonian vowel-rhyme), snappier. Speaking for myself, I would prefer my poems to be mistranslated so that the readers found me a poetic wit to "properly" translated so that I came off as a prosaic bore. In translation, as in all things, we really should do onto others as we would be done, unless, that is, the other party raises an objection.

p.s. If you buy a first edition copy of *Rise, Ye Sea Slugs!* you will find many multiple translations in the first part of the book are strung out in serial. That began to look *awful* to me midway through the book, as I learned how to make columns better using MS-Word (sheer torture, especially w/ insufficient RAM), but with each page hand-crafted, I could not go back and beautify everything and still finish my other books. I apologize for the ugliness.

iii

<u>Sweet Neglect vs. Benign Art</u>
paraverse as riposte, or a new marvel

> *Still to be neat, still to be drest,*
> *As you were going to a feast;*
> *Still to be powder'd, still perfumed:*
> *Lady, it is to be presumed,*
> *Though art's hid causes are not found,*
> *All is not sweet, all is not sound.*
>
> *Give me a look, give me a face,*
> *That makes simplicity a grace;*
> *Robes loosely flowing, hair as free:*
> *Such sweet neglect more taketh me,*
> *Then all the adulteries of art;*
> *They strike mine eyes, but not my heart.*

In high school, I had Andrew Marvel's poem memorized. His praise of natural beauty greatly appealed for I assumed the love of such a woman was my birthright. Of course, that was not how I rationalized it *then*. Like everyone else, I put down make-up for being contrary to "natural looks." If some women didn't look good without make-up, that was *their* tough luck. A decade or two later, a more forgiving man responded to Marvel and his younger self, as follows:

A Proper Foundation for Lasting Beauty

Take your time, Dear, *Haste makes waste!*
Cover your past with rouge and paste!
Who gives a damn if we run late,
I'd have you in no lesser state:
So do as you *must* do, take an encore!
Return to the mirror and paint yourself *more*.

Aye, pile on the powder, *make* me a face,
That puts Mother Nature back in her place;
With girdle and bra and fanciful dress,
(For only young beauties look good in a mess)
Remake thyself, so the whole world can see:
That thou art *all* art, and all agree!

The best-known researcher on the history of beauty and beauty contests in Japan begrudges the cosmetic industry for trying to convince women that *anyone* can *make* themselves beautiful. If women did not believe looks were something that could be *made*, he argues, make-up would not sell. Thanks to the cosmetic industry, he laments, people no longer admit that beauty is something one is graced with. Rather than appreciating human beauty as we might appreciate other kinds of natural beauty as gifts, we live a lie. The beloved subject of his research – the natural beauty – is belittled by corporations with financial interest in making *plain jane* feel good. With American feminists categorically attacking cosmetic companies for making women feel *bad* about themselves to sell make-up, I found Inoue Shôichi 井上 章一's perspective a breath of fresh air. Beauty is no myth, Naomi.   Its presence, or absence, is *an accident* we must live with.

> *Take your sweet time, my ugly mate,*
> *At home alone we can't be late:*
> *Build your foundation brick by brick;*
> *Beauty made, is no cheap trick*
> *(especially for one not born with it)*
> *And nothing to be laughed at or denied:*
> *Make-up is the original white lie.*
>
> *So, make me a look, make me a face,*
> *The artificial has its place:*
> *Plumpers and girdles, for a start,*
> *Dye for your hair, perfume for farts:*
> *If kitty a dead mouse can bring to life*
> *What cannot be done for man by wife?*

Extraordinarily attentive readers and experienced translators – translation makes attentiveness a habit as, perhaps, does paraversing – will already have noticed that Marvel's "As you were going to a feast" must mean "as *if*" you are going; hence, my youthful riposte (*who gives a damn if we run late*) was either a misreading or laziness (it is easier to reverse the place as well as the position, though contradicting the former weakens the riposte for the latter, as the need to look good in public is more broadly agreed upon than the need to do so in private). I am not being cute. I really do not remember which it was. All I recall is that I was delighted with my first line: *"Take your time, dear, haste makes waste!"* because I liked its comfortable Ogden Nashiness. Some readers may take umbrage, which is to say, cloud their brow, at my "ugly" in the new *stay-at-home* paraverse, but I get tired of hearing every participant in a game show on Usanian television mention their "beautiful wife" and, more recently "beautiful husband." I suppose I share some of the Japanese researcher's feelings. *Enough already with these lies!* The problems inherent in *enormous differences* in face value will not dissappear or even be helped one iota by calling everyone beautiful, nor those in *sex* value by calling every husband a *stud* or every wife an *octopussy* (blessed w/ what might be called a prehensile snatch, a *bona fide* Japanese term: see my book of dirty senryu), nor those of income by calling every household middle class. *Think about it*. Do participants on television game shows ever say "my wealthy husband" or "my wealthy wife"? Yet, many people deserve their wealth while few deserve their looks, so why boast about it? Ah, a *"plumper"* is something old women once used to puff-out their sallow cheeks and old or thin men, under stockings, to fatten their wizzened calves, once a major part of male beauty.

Negative Paraverse

A riposte in kind might be called an *antiverse* or a negative *paraverse*. It is not only fun for all who enjoy argument, but easier than a positive paraverse, for when the original is both excellent and in the same tongue, creating variants is a losing proposition. *Aldous Huxley once complained about teachers asking students to put Shakespeare into their own words.* I cannot recall whether he did not like to see beautiful lines uglified or thought it would do the students better to simply memorize and thus incorporate the lines, but what bothers me is that students are not encouraged to use their imagination as they would if only the teachers would ask them to *play with* rather than summarize Shakespeare's lines. For you really come to pay attention to things only when you start messing with them. Translation is the best place to do this (though most translators need help with escaping from school-room timidity) for "to be or not to be" can be put into your own words in Japanese in countless ways, none of which compete with Shakespeare; but, *in English*, it would be better to have students try take-offs building upon questions like "to pee or not to pee," "to see or not to see," "to eat or not to eat," "to beat or not to beat," or even "to me or not to me,"etc.

Four Clear Exceptions to the No-masterpieces-in-your-own-words Rule.

1) Translation between exotic tongues requires breaking the rule, for without your own words there is no reading.

2) Localized or dialectal paraversing works for it gives you the homecourt advantage. To have a strong command of *any* dialect or jargon, criminal or scientific is to be blessed as a writer. In Japan, people from Kansai (especially Osaka) enjoy taking classics – often English or Chinese philosophy translated into standard (Kantô Yamanote, *i.e.* upperclass Tokyo-area) Japanese, or heavily Sinofied academese, and remaking it in what seems to the outsider an extraordinarily droll manner. Nothing beats their *Tao Te Ching* or Descartes best-known line. In 19c Usania, dialect writing was so popular writers who could not do it faked it, mostly by exaggerating small differences with absurd spelling. People enjoyed a slow read so much, speshilusts in this were featured in top magazines. Maybe people figured they got more for their money when something took forever to get through. Or, maybe they liked to read something puzzling enough to justify scratching their head-lice as they read, I dunno. Today, with everyone rushing to that last page so they can boast about how many books they read, as they do of all the places they visit, so-called "extreme reading" competition favors the *slick 'n' quick.** Still, we find good dialect paraversing in Yiddish, Black, Hawaiin and West Indies English. At present, we have a simultaneous dumbing down in the center and blossoming on the periphery. The question is how widely dialectal variations of, say, *"to be or not to be"* or *The Night Before Christmas* are read and who reads them and *that* I do not know.

3) A masterpiece may always be paraversed without fear by distilling it; say, making a page-long poem by Wordsworth into a haiku, couplet, or whatever

form is your bag of tea. Or, you might take a longer poem and turn it into a series of haiku or a single longer, but not too long, poem. Maybe a sonnet. Or, you might, instead, make aphorisms out of it rather than poems. You will find this more comfortable than competing w/ the original or parodying it. Here is an example of distillation I cooked up, or rather boiled down, when writing an appendum to *Mad In Translation*. The original Donne. We shall start with the 14-line original so the reader, if he or she so wishes, may try to make a (31-syllabet) *kyôka* of his poem *before* seeing how I did it. You might hold a piece of paper over mine below it so you do not see my poem until *yours* is done.

> DEATH, be not proud, though some have called thee
> Mighty and dreadful, for thou art not so:
> For those whom thou think'st thou dost overthrow
> Die not, poor Death; nor yet canst thou kill me.
> From Rest and Sleep, which but thy picture be,
> Much pleasure, then from thee much more must flow;
> And soonest our best men with thee do go –
> Rest of their bones and souls' delivery!
> Thou'rt slave to fate, chance, kings, and desperate men,
> And dost with poison, war, and sickness dwell;
> And poppy or charms can make us sleep as well
> And better than thy stroke. Why swell'st thou then?
>   One short sleep past, we wake eternally,
>   And Death shall be no more: Death, thou shalt die!

Now, look at my mad poem, below. While I have used the word "distill" or "boil down" to describe the process, in retrospect, it would seem my *kyôka-length* rendition *telescopes* the original, so only the ends remain –

♪ Thou, not I! ♪

Death be not proud!
One short sleep past, we wake
eternally. Doubt not

Who shall be no more: Death,
For His sake, thou shalt die!

Pardon my odd enjambing and please rhyme "eternally" with "die." "For His sake" was added partly for a rhyme with *wake* and to improve the wit by presenting the reverse side of the coin (Christ dying that we should enjoy eternal life). On the other hand, we lost the expression of death-as-pleasure. Perhaps a reader who tried his or her hand at this gave that more attention, but I thought Cervantes did that better, so I concentrated, for better or worse, on the message/ wit first done by Donne. Do not think this sort of thing always works. The above-alluded poem from Don Quixote is a case in point. In Ozell's 1930 revision of Herschel Brickell's English translation, it runs 6 lines of 7 syllables: *Death, put on some kind Disguise, / And at once my Heart surprise: / For 'tis such a Curse to live,/ And so great a bliss to die; / Should'st thou any Warning give, / I'd relapse to Life for Joy.* I hoped to cut it by a quarter or a third to turn it into a *kyôka* – I thought it would be easy as it seems like a *kyôka* death poem, – but I failed. Instead, it came out five words *longer!*

Death,

in disguise, come
take me by surprise:
'Tis such a curse to live,
And so great a bliss to die –
Should'st thou any warning give,
I'd jump with joy right up from bed
When I'd rather not be alive, but dead!

As touched as our knight was, we should recall that the real ruler of Spain actually slept in a coffin and carried around a skull, not to mention other relics (pieces of saints) in his last years. Not just the ideals of chivalry but Christianity as it was actually believed in and practiced was satirized here. Cervantes was a brave man. Be that as it may, my failure to equal or better the poem in *less* words tells me the translation is a masterpiece. As for mine, you will have to judge.

4) When your poem is not the masterpiece in your own words or even a parody but only an idea picked up from reading it, who can complain? There is no rule against inspiration. Another example fron *Mad In Translation*. This minimalist AABA 4x7-character Chinese-style mad verse, or *kyôshi,* by Gubutsu 愚佛, or Silly-buddha, titled dog-bite-meet 犬咬合, *i.e., The Dog Fight,* goes *Wan wan wan wan mata wan wan.* / *Mata mata wan wan mata wan wan* / *ya an ka jo ton fu bun* / *shi shû shi bun wan wan wan* (狂詩古今狂歌大全).

椀々々々亦椀々。	*Rough! Rough! Rough! Rough! Again, Rough! Rough!*
亦亦椀々又椀々。	*Again! Again! Rough! Rough! Again, Rough! Rough!*
夜暗何疋頓不分。	*In the dark of night, I couldn't tell the number of mutts,*
始終只聞椀々々。	*From start to finish, I just heard Rough! Rough! Rough!*

The Chinese character used for the barking, or ruff-ruffing does not mean "rough" but "bowl." Be that as it may, if the dogs were barking to be fed so the "bowl" became significant as punning mimesis we would at least have doggerel, but this is not even up to mutterel (Princeton appraises it higher, as proto-Dadaism). With about 15 minutes of work, however, it was easy enough to work the *ruff=rough* idea into a lively mad exchange that, as you can see, has nothing in common with the original but the fact both pun and are four lines:

Tom Cat said, *"Dog, you have such an eeeasy life!*
Your Wives don't scratch, they only bite – Meow!"

"Tom," said Mutt, *"Who is free to play all night?*
I've a Master to obey! I have it rough! Ruff! Ruff!"

An Essay on Man by Alexander Pope. EPISTLE I. ***An Essay on Woman*** attrib. to John Wilkes

Wilkes' take-off on the first Epistle of Pope's famous Essay in heroic couplets (1732) may be found in E. J. Burford's magnificent *Bawdy Verses,* which offers us a far broader and just plain better selection of the same than any other book I know. Wilkes, who was taken to court and acquitted of blasphemy and obscenity charges resulting from the publication of *An Essay on Women* (1764) and was so well known a defender of democratic principles that the phrase "Wilkes and Liberty" came into being, pillories the Establishment's leader, the Third Earl of Bute and mentions the most famous courtesan of the time within this take-off. But, even so, *An Essay on Woman,* is first and foremost a paean to sex from this "member of the infamous club known as the Friars of Medmenham, in whose 'Abbey' the most fantastically lewd behavior was allowed."

Awake, my St. John! leave all meaner things
To low ambition, and the pride of kings.
Let us (since life can little more supply
Than just to look about us and to die)
Expatiate free o'er all this scene of man;
A mighty maze! but not without a plan;
A wild, where weeds and flowers promiscuous shoot;
Or garden tempting with forbidden fruit.
Together let us beat this ample field,
Try what the open, what the covert yield;
The latent tracts, the giddy heights, explore
Of all who blindly creep, or sightless soar;
Eye Nature's walks, shoot Folly as it flies,
And catch the manners living as they rise;
Laugh where we must, be candid where we can;
But vindicate the ways of God to man.

AWAKE my Fanny, leave all meaner things,
This morn shall prove what rapture swiving brings!
Let us (since life can little more supply
Than just a few good fucks, and then we die)
Expatiate free o'er that loved scene of man,
A mighty maze, for mighty pricks to scan;
A wild, where Paphian Thorns promiscuous shoot,
Where flowers the monthly Rose, but yields no Fruit.
Together let us beat this ample field,
Try what the open, what the covert yield;
The latent tracks, the pleasing depths explore,
And my prick clapp'd where thousands were before.
Observe how Nature works, and if it rise
Too quick and rapid, check it ere it flies;
Spend when we must, but keep it while we can:
Thus, godlike will be deem'd the ways of man.

i

Say first, of God above, or man below
What can we reason, but from what we know?
Of man, what see we but his station here,
From which to reason, or to which refer?
Through worlds unnumbered though the God be known,
'Tis ours to trace Him only in our own.
He, who through vast immensity can pierce,
See worlds on worlds compose one universe,
Observe how system into system runs,
What other planets circle other suns,
What varied being peoples every star,
May tell why Heaven has made us as we are.
But of this frame, the bearings, and the ties,
The strong connections, nice dependencies,
Gradations just, has thy pervading soul
Looked through? or can a part contain the whole?
Is the great chain, that draws all to agree,
And drawn supports, upheld by God, or thee?

SAY, first of woman's latent charms below,
What can we reason but from what we know?
A face, a neck, a breast, are all appear
From which to reason, or to which refer.
In every part we heavenly beauty own,
But we can trace it only in what's shown.
He who the hoop's immensity can pierce,
Dart thro' the whalebone fold s vast universe,
Observe how circle into circle runs,
What courts the eye, and what all vision shuns,
All the wild modes of dress our females wear,
May guess what makes them thus transf orm'd appear
But of their Cunts, the bearings and the ties,
The nice connections, strong dependencies,
The latitude and longitude of each
Hast thou gone through, or can thy Pego reach?
Was that great Ocean, that unbounded Sea
Where pricks like whales may sport, fathom'd by Thee?

This preface, on the whole, is boring except for "a few good fucks" – Damn, that sounds modern! – the rose as an example of issueless sex, the "pleasing depths" replacing Pope's "giddy heights," and the last four lines, clever in both the original and Wilkes' semi-parodic paraverse. Part i, with whale-bone corsets turning into oreries and cunts charted to end at sea is as masterful as Pope.

ii

Presumptuous man! the reason wouldst thou find,
Why formed so weak, so little, and so blind?
First, if thou canst, the harder reason guess,
Why formed no weaker, blinder, and no less;
Ask of thy mother earth, why oaks are made
Taller or stronger than the weeds they shade?
Or ask of yonder argent fields above,
Why Jove's satellites are less than Jove?

Of systems possible, if 'tis confest
That wisdom infinite must form the best,
Where all must full or not coherent be,
And all that rises, rise in due degree;
Then in the scale of reasoning life, 'tis plain,
There must be, somewhere, such a rank as man:
And all the question (wrangle e'er so long)
Is only this, if God has placed him wrong?
Respecting man, whatever wrong we call,
May, must be right, as relative to all.

In human works, though laboured on with pain,
A thousand movements scarce one purpose gain;
In God's one single can its end produce;
Yet serves to second too some other use.
So man, who here seems principal alone,
Perhaps acts second to some sphere unknown,
Touches some wheel, or verges to some goal;
'Tis but a part we see, and not a whole.

When the proud steed shall know why man restrains
His fiery course, or drives him o'er the plains:
When the dull ox, why now he breaks the clod,
Is now a victim, and now Egypt's god:
Then shall man's pride and dulness comprehend
His actions', passions', being's, use and end;
Why doing, suffering, checked, impelled; and why
This hour a slave, the next a deity.

Then say not man's imperfect, Heaven in fault;
Say rather man's as perfect as he ought:
His knowledge measured to his state and place;
His time a moment, and a point his space.
If to be perfect in a certain sphere,
What matter, soon or late, or here or there?
The blest to-day is as completely so,
As who began a thousand years ago.

Presumptuous Prick! the reason would'st thou find
Why form'd so weak, so little and so blind?
First, if thou canst, the harder reason guess
Why form'd no weaker, meaner and no less.
Ask of thy mother's cunt why she was made
Of lesser bore than cow or hackney'd jade?
Or ask thy raw-boned Scottish Father's Tarse
Why larger he than Stallion or Jackass?

Of Pego's possible, if 'tis confess'd
That wisdom infinite must form some best,
Where all must rise, or not coherent be,
And all that rise must rise in due degree;
Then, in the scale of various Pricks, 'tis plain
God-like erect, BUTE stands the foremost man,
And all the question (wrangle e'er so long)
Is only this, if Heaven placed him wrong.
Respecting him, whatever wrong we call,
May, must be right, as relative to all.

When frogs would couple, labour'd on with pain
A thousand wriggles scarce their purpose gain:
In Man, a dozen can his end produce
And drench the female with spermatic juice.
Yet not our pleasure seems God's end alone,
Oft when we spend we propagate unknown;
Unwilling we may reach some other goal,
And sylphs and gnomes may fuck in woman's hole.

When the proud Stallion knows whence every vein
Now throbs with lust and now is shrunk again;
The lusty Bull, why now he breaks the clod,
Now wears a garland, fair Europe's God:
Then shall Man's Pride and Pego comprehend
His actions and erections, use and end.
Why at Celaenae Martyrdom, and why
At Lampsacus adored chief Deity.

Then say not Man's imperfect, Heaven in fault,
Say rather, Man's as perfect as he ought;
His Pego measured to the female Case
Betwixt a woman's thighs his proper place;
And if to fuck in a proportion'd sphere,
What matter how it is, or when or where?
Fly fuck'd by fly may be completely so
As Hussey's Duchess, or yon well-bull'd cow.

The first and last stanzas of the sectrion 3 are wonderful. Who would think of that phrase "fly fuck'd by fly"! And Wilkes had the sense to incorporate some of the best original lines as is.

iii

Heaven from all creatures hides the book of Fate,	Heaven from all creatures hides the Book of Fate,
All but the page prescribed, their present state:	All but the page prescribed, the present state,
From brutes what men, from men what spirits know:	From boys what girls, from girls what women know,
Or who could suffer being here below?	Or what could suffer being here below?
The lamb thy riot dooms to bleed to-day,	Thy lust the Virgin dooms to bleed today,
Had he thy reason, would he skip and play?	Had she thy reason would she 'skip and play?
Pleased to the last, he crops the flowery food,	Pleased to the last, she likes the luscious food
And licks the hand just raised to shed his blood.	And grasps the prick just raised to shed her blood.
Oh, blindness to the future! kindly given,	Oh! Blindness to the Future, kindly given,
That each may fill the circle, marked by Heaven:	That each may enjoy what fucks are mark'd by Heaven.
Who sees with equal eye, as God of all,	Who sees with equal Eye, as God of all
A hero perish, or a sparrow fall,	The Man just mounting and the Virgin's fall;
Atoms or systems into ruin hurled,	Prick Cunt and Bollocks in convulsions hurl'd,
And now a bubble burst, and now a world.	And now a Hymen burst, and now a world.
Hope humbly, then; with trembling pinions soar;	Hope, humbly, then, clean girls; nor vainly soar
Wait the great teacher Death; and God adore.	But fuck the cunt at hand, and God adore.
What future bliss, He gives not thee to know,	What future fucks he gives not thee to know
But gives that hope to be thy blessing now.	But gives that Cunt to be thy blessing now.
Hope springs eternal in the human breast:	
Man never is, but always to be blest:	
The soul, uneasy and confined from home,	
Rests and expatiates in a life to come.	

To the extent that Pope's message is be content with your state for it is your fate and expounds the chain, rather than a circle, of being, I can see the champion of democracy justifying his eroticism as parody. Yet, in a grander way, Pope was himself democratic in the broadest and most important sense: he was not only tolerant but what would now be called a Unitarian, which is why, a decade or two ago I was infuriated to find a popular US poet savaged him and his "Lo, the poor Indian!" stanza for cultural imperialism, anti-ecological attitude, etc.. I understood that popularity depends upon being in tune with the bias of the times and with poor Pope being unfairly villified by feminists,* said poet may not have bothered to read him closely or misread him for psychological reasons fully described by Montaigne and Bacon that we now call *cognitive dissonance.* If you believe, you should thank Pope for saving God (The Essay on Man is an *Apologia* ala Leibniz for Him) and thank God for Wendell Berry's coming to Pope's defense against the well-meaning but misguided poet whose untutored mind saw bad in what was good.* That the English, or at least those intellectuals who buy books of bawdy verse, all know Pope, or at least are expected to, is made clear by the fact that Burford did not chance insulting their intelligence by noting what poem *An Essay on Woman* paraversed. Likewise, for the one immediately following it, also attributed to Wilkes, M.P., which many Usanian readers will not be familiar with in the original. I include it because it casts light on Pope's better side – to my mind, Pope wrote to make himself happy (in an age where looks were openly associated with the soul, being notably stunted must have hurt far more than it would today) and did so by vitrolous vindictive, i.e., catharsis, on the one hand and luminous meditations, i.e. images of the ideal, on the other.

THE UNIVERSAL PRAYER.
DEO OPT. MAX.
Alexander Pope (1738)

Father of all! in every age,
  In every clime adored,
By saint, by savage, and by sage,
  Jehovah, Jove, or Lord!

Thou Great First Cause, least understood,
  Who all my sense confined
To know but this, that Thou art good,
  And that myself am blind;

Yet gave me, in this dark estate,
  To see the good from ill;
And binding Nature fast in fate,
  Left free the human will.

What conscience dictates to be done,
  Or warns me not to do,
This, teach me more than Hell to shun,
  That, more than Heaven pursue.

What blessings Thy free bounty gives,
  Let me not cast away;
For God is paid when man receives,
  To enjoy is to obey.

Yet not to earth's contracted span
  Thy goodness let me bound,
Or think Thee Lord alone of man,
  When thousand worlds are round:

Let not this weak, unknowing hand
  Presume Thy bolts to throw,
And deal damnation round the land,
  On each I judge Thy foe.

If I am right, Thy grace impart,
  Still in the right to stay;
If I am wrong, oh, teach my heart
  To find that better way.

Save me alike from foolish pride,
  Or impious discontent,
At aught Thy wisdom has denied,
  Or aught Thy goodness lent.

Cunno Opt. Min.
OR The Universal Prayer (1762)
Attributed to John Wilkes, M. P.

Mother of all! in every Age
In every Clime adored
By Saint, by Savage and by Sage,
If modest, or if whored.

Thou first great Cause, least understood,
Who all my Prick confined,
To feel but this, that thou art good
And that himself is blind.

Yet gave him, in this dark Estate
To know the Good from ill;
With God-like Virtue to create
Following his Prickship's Will.

Sound honest Cunts should oft be done;
Unsound, I ne'er would do;
These teach me more than Hell to shun,
Those more than Heaven pursue.

What Seed my God's free Bounty gives
Let me not frig away;
For God is paid when Cunt receives;
To enjoy is to obey.

Yet not one Cunt's contracted span
My vigour e'er shall bound;
I'll think they all were made for Man,
When thousand Cunts are round.

If I am clapt, may this Right-hand
Its happy cunning know;
Let [Lest?] rankling Venom, round this land
Brand Pego as a foe.

If he goes right, thy Grace impart
Still in the right to stay;
Oh! may he ne'er from thee depart
To find the Primate's Way.

Save him alike from foolish Pride
Or impious discontent.
If greater thickness be denied
Or thirteen inches lent.

Teach me to feel another's woe, To hide the fault I see; That mercy I to others show, That mercy show to me.	Teach me to feel a Virgin's Woe; The maiden Gore I see In sacred drops from Hymen flow, Be kiss'd, and wiped by me.
Mean though I am, not wholly so, Since quickened by Thy breath; Oh, lead me wheresoe'er I go, Through this day's life or death.	Mean though my Prick, not wholly so, Since stiffened by thy breath. Oh, lead him where he ought to go In this night's Life or Death.
This day, be bread and peace my lot: All else beneath the sun, Thou know'st if best bestowed or not; And let Thy will be done.	This night be thou, black-haired, my lot; Or else beneath the Sun. God knows if best bestowed or not; But let thy work be done.
To Thee, whose temple is all space, Whose altar earth, sea, skies, One chorus let all being raise, All Nature's incense rise!	To thee, whose fucks throughout all space This dying World supplies, One Chorus let all beings raise, All Pricks in reverence rise.
No God, no geese! So let Him know We're happy to be here, down below.	Bucking's the end and cause of human state, And Man must fuck, or God will not create.

This time Wilkes, if it is Wilkes, went *long* rather than *short*. The last two lines of Pope's are mine. Pardon my joke. This is better: according to Burford, the title of Wilkes' antithetical paraverse comes from "The inscription along the frieze of the great phallic Temple at Lampsacus." If that is so, could we see Pope's title as a parody of *it*, in which case, he is as good as acknowledging (cryptically) what really lies at the bottom of things and Wilke's is only making it explicit? I joke again. Chances are the inscription on "the great phallic temple," *Cunno opt.min.* (To Cunt, the best, the smallest) is a parody of *Deo opt. max* (To God, the best, the greatest) which itself might be a parody of . . . As noted in *The Woman Without a Hole* one can never tell what is an original. A Japanese folk-song researcher believes many if not most of the clean folk songs that we parody (Japanese, at any rate love to sing dirty parodies of folk-songs) were themselves originally dirty before being cleaned up – funny, the clean remakes are never called parodies – in early-modern times. This paraverse is more uneven than the other, but the conscientious promise to masturbate if afflicted with ghonorhea is exceedingly well-put – I am reminded of the rare Japanese term *tebobo*, or "hand-cunt" – and both the penultimate and final verses are just beautiful! Looking at the large picture, Pope's broad-minded unitarianism and Wilkes' deification of the cunt *delight* me. Perhaps, the only problem with the content, aside from the mandatory macho stanza ("Yet not one cunt") is Wilkes' kneejerk attack on the Primate,* which is to say Pope (not Alexander): the reference is to sodomy.

~~~~~~

> A more talented poet would have managed to mirror more of Marvel's original in his or her translation yet maintain a more consistent style. Mine only go to prove that even one without much time or talent can have a good time playing with poetry.* I added Wilke's Pope to help you recover after reading my amateur effort! If you *can* do better with Marvel, Pope, Jonson or anyone, please *do*, and send it to me. If I agree, you will be in the next edition of this book or another.

★ *Paraverse* (& *Paraversing*). When I wrote this book, I thought *paraverse* natural enough to define itself, but before publishing it, I did another book on *kyôka,* mad, or comic Japanese poems, and realized I needed a comparison to *parody*. The initial *para* and *par* are the same, meaning alternative &/or beyond. The *ody,* originally meant "song," the *verse a turn* or *line of poetry*. Each Japanese poem, usually written in one line could be called a *universe,* but joking aside, *paraverse* is more useful than "parody" because time has narrowed the meaning of the latter.

♪ *International Perspective.* There are many ways books on human beauty can be improved by an international perspective. Edward S. Morse commented about a fair-skinned Japanese girl who used white make-up powder because not doing so would make her seem conceited when other girls had to do it. (For more on white powder make-up in Japan, see the items #2-15 and #2-66 in *Topsy-turvy 1585*). Cosmetics can level the playing field, up *or* down!

♪ *The Accident of Beauty,* is a phrase coined by Oliver Wendell Holmes and will be the title of a book on ideals of personal appearance and the ways various cultures cope with individual and group difference that I hope to finish/publish when, or if I am graced with students who can, as co-authors, help me to finish it. Despite my love for natural looks, I was a sensitive boy, who both researched and surveyed attitudes on ideal personal beauty in Junior college in 1968-9. I concluded we needed to diversify our ideals enough that most women would look beautiful and most men would look handsome. I invented the phrase "the myth of beauty" when Naomi Wolf, who would surely look fine without make-up, was in diapers (I also sent it to her agent JB, not knowing her book was in the works, but I do not think he/they borrowed it, for the phrase is such a natural and her writing so immature that it was a natural, as it once was but no longer is for me.

♪ *Mentioning Black English*. Paraverse would publish a collection of Metaphysical and Cavalier Poetry in re-created in black English. Anyone commanding Black English who can appreciate those salacious logic-mongering English poets, please, please try it! If you are a black wordsmith yet oddly not familiar with this genre, start with "To His Coy Mistress" and "On Julia's (liquifaction of her) Clothes." Most of the best-known poems and many that are not may be found at a wonderful website called Luminarium. Though able to write books in witty but imperfect Japanese, I envy and admire people who command a dialect and are bilingual *in their own language/s*. That I cannot do.

♪ *On the simplification of writing* No, it did not begin with the computer. I blame Modernism. Complexity died with Ogden Nash, whose flourish was its last flowering (like most fireworks – damn, this would be so much better in Japanese, where "fireworks" are "flower-fire"! – it was a dramatic end. True, Nash as a free-verse poet was very 20c, but his long poems exemplify the *we-have-all-the-time-in-the-world* freedom of 19c humor.

That is *half* of the reason for the mind-numbing simplification of style. The other may, paradoxically, be the complexity of our culture. Until the mid-20c, most leading poets could write a dozen variations on a theme, each in the style a different poet, and most literate readers could follow it. Such stylistic paraversing is no longer possible as a popular art because our interests are too disparate and poets too many for us to follow.

♪ *Of course, gender discrimination* in Pope's time was horrendous. Property and inheritance law was gynecidal. Still, moderns do not understand what fun the sexes had railing on one another (see Angeline Goreau's *The Whole Duty of a Women* for women who gave as good as they took and better). Pope even took *both* sides, riposting his own poem that put-down women as changing clouds (with rain as micturitive rhetoric) from the woman's view!

♪ *Lo, the Poor Indian!* I wrote a venerable English scholar (*Sir* Keith Thomas) I highly respect for giving his readers plentiful primary passages rather than summing up in the Usanian fashion to see if my doubts were justified, and was assured they were. Before finishing the article I had little hope of publishing, I received an advance copy of a book in which Wendell Berry did a more thorough job of defending Pope than I could have (though I could have made it more entertaining). Among other things, Pope's passage is a grave reflection on the loss to human happiness brought by scientific hubrix, the immorality of slavery and the torment brought to others by the Christian greed for gold.

iv

Translating Gods and Demons
◎ or how to multiply an aphorism ◎

If we seek the Buddha outside the mind, the Buddha changes to a Devil.
— Dogen tr. R. H. Blyth

Dogen (1200-53) is the Japanese Zen master best known for his good advice to people intent on storming heaven:

> *Rather than striving to become a god*
> *Strive to become human*

Near the end of one of Montaigne's last *Essays* (III), *Of Experience* (1587-88) there is a quotation attributed to AMYOT's PLUTARCH which says more or less the same thing in a less constructive way:

> *You are as much a god as you will own*
> *That you are nothing but a man alone.*

Montaigne's comments that follow would have made him as beloved by Zen Buddhist's as he is by all free-thinking (liberal) souls in the Occident:

> It is an absolute perfection and virtually divine to know how to enjoy our being rightfully. We seek other conditions because we do not understand the use of our own, and go outside of ourselves because we do not know what it is like inside. ᶜ Yet there is no use our mounting on stilts, for on stilts we must still walk on our own legs. And on the loftiest throne in the world we are still sitting only on our own rump. (trans. Donald M. Frame: *The Complete Essays of Montaigne* (1943, later, Stanford University Press: 1948/71/76). *Buy it!*)

The less famous statement at the head of the chapter, which we will examine in some detail, suggests Dogen found the desire to find (a) god/s out there as misguided as trying to become one. Doubtless, the word translated as "mind" is *kokoro*, also translatable as "heart." In surveys about the relative popularity of various *kanji* (Chinese characters), this character 心 always comes in first place. To a Buddhist, the Buddha is "God/Savior/Godhead," a historical figure, but also something to be re-joined, which makes Buddha also "Enlightenment" and "Heaven." So we need not stick to "Buddha" when translating 仏. Moreover, since Japanese has no number, we are free to chose singular or plural.

> *If we seek the Buddha outside the mind, the Buddha changes to a Devil.*
>
> Dogen, translated by Blyth

For all my paraverses, I follow Blyth and choose the singular, for it fits the conceptual nature of the aphorism: But I adopt *God*, rather than *Buddha,* in a big way, for two reasons. First, "a Devil" cannot help but stink of sulfur, which is to say, Christianity, so, saving Him, requires a likewise tainted word, God. (Yes, we could ditch the "devil" for a "demon," but demons are not necessarily bad, so the connotation is off). Second, God is a monosyllable, and we know what the soul of wit is. If we happened to call the Buddha simply *Boo,* while God had to be the two syllable Yaweh, I might have chosen the former and dropped the devil, though for what I do not know.

> *God sought without is the Devil within.*

The *naru* in the original can mean *to become* or *turn out to be* and if it what is found turns out to be the devil, in my opinion, it is as good as saying the devil lies within, even if he enters through the open portals of the eyes.

> *The God found without, becomes the Devil within.*
> *Seek God outside and the Devil will come in!*
> *Seek God without, find the Devil within!*
> *To go out for God, is to bid the Devil in!*
> *To look out for God is to look up the Devil!*
> *When we shop for God, the Devil waits at home.*

There is *some* humor in black and white contrast, for the world is hardly so clear, and sudden clarity astounds us, as does paradox, where that which *seems* at odds is actually one. You might call paradox, the rhetoric of magic. But, that is not enough for those of us who demand a double dose of wit. We also want the magical blessing – or, should I say, *validation?* – of the right rhyme or perfect pun. Eventually, I found the latter, though the result strays so far from the original (assuming Blyth was faithful to it, as I have yet to read it), as to be a fresh aphorism:

> *Look out for the Devil! Look in for God!*

Have you noticed something missing from these paraverses? Yes, Blyth's "mind" is absent. Because our "mind" was a bit too narrow and square (?) for what had to be the original word, *kokoro,* or *mind/heart/feelings,* etc., I found it made more sense to drop the *word* for the larger concept it contained: something *within.* But I did make explicit reference to *kokoro* in one translation, arrived at with the help of rhyme.

> *To seek God apart is to give the Devil your heart!*

If we seek the Buddha outside the mind, the Buddha changes to a Devil.

Dogen, translated by Blyth

I leave it to quibblers to decide whether seeking A outside the mind is to give the anti-A your mind or whether that is the same as saying that seeking A outside the mind is to turn A into anti–A.

To seek your Savior without, is to turn Him into Satan.
The Savior sought without, turns Satan within!

Faith alone was thought to save people in some major schools of Buddhism and there was a Hades – indeed, Japanese paintings of it make "our" fire and brimstone speeches seem tame – with its boss often (mis)translated as Satan. But, as much as I love the alliteration, these words in English are too damn Christian to describe a Buddhist thought. The Buddha was a "savior," so that word is fine, better, perhaps, than God, for the Buddha is not a Creator. But Satan is completely wrong, for the Far East has nothing even close to the powerful force for evil we call the Devil. A true translation can not use Occidental terms, here.

Seek Buddha without, find Yama within!

A dictionary will explain that Yama (Enma) is the King of Hades, but it will not say that his role of judging those who die is more like that of the Christian God (or, his proxy, St. Pete) than the Devil, and that he, himself, is not at all interested in encouraging evil behavior, but punishes the bad to give them their just reward and discourage bad behavior by the living. Moreover, he feels so guilty over the pain he gives to those he must punish that he tortures himself by swallowing molten metal I forget how many times a day (dying is easy, Yama suffers for our sins over and over and over again). Thus, Dogen could not mention Yama, but an *oni* or *akuma* ("bad-demon"), something we just cannot say in a word.

To seek God without is to be without God.

One solution for the problem of translating that "Devil" is not to do it but instead settle for a simpler antithesis of god/no-god. But, it really is not the same, for finding *evil* is worse than simply losing the good. Another solution is to find a substitute for *both* Buddha/God and Akuma/Devil:

Seek Heaven outside ye, and find Hell within be!
Leave yourself to seek Heaven and you will find yourself in Hell!

I would have liked to do one with a Buddhist vocabulary. Say, *Seek the Pureland outside yourself and you will find a cesspool.* But I would doubt Dogen, as a Zen Buddhist, was of the Pureland sect and his *Western Paradise* would be hard to make into an aphorism. But, Heaven/Hell *may* be improved:

If we seek the Buddha outside the mind, the Buddha changes to a Devil.

Dogen, translated by Blyth

~~~~~~

Leave yourself to find Heaven and Hell will find you out.

Leave yourself to seek Heaven and you will go out of your mind.

The second of the above does not mention Hell, and I do not claim that dementia is equivalent to it. It is not, for we have all known senile or otherwise demented people who are radiantly happy.

> Times like this are when I feel fortunate to be Japanese. "The Buddha," "the devil" are just so hopelessly monotheistic! （日本人で良かったなと、こういう時は思う。The Buddha, the Devil とはまさしく一神教の世界になってしまうのだから。(角田　尚子　(特活)ERIC 国際理解教育センター)

I had forgotten *when* I first played with Dogen's/Blyth's words until I came across the first and only unfavorable review of my 1987 (and four or five times reprinted) book 誤訳天国 – ことばの PLAY と MISPLAY (Goyaku Tengoku = *Mistranslation Paradise* – wordplay and misplay) I have ever seen on a blog at a center for international understanding. The reviewer noted my espousal of "parallel+multiple translation" (「平行多訳」), read Blyth's translation and my handful of paraverses of it and got so upset she stopped reading right then and there. You will note she not only took umbrage at the Devil but "the" Buddha. In Japanese, Buddha is a vaguer word including "the" Buddha, "a saint," "sainthood," Buddhist statues (obviously, not the case here), and even if "the" Buddha is intended, there is generally no concept of a concrete reunification beween believer and Buddha, as in the Christian heaven. When I commented on the blog that I was surprised to find someone that excited about what I had only intended to encourage more creativity in translation, her reply was a long, not bad but no longer aphoristic explanatory translation:

> To expect Buddha, the enlightenment of life, outside youself is already the work of Devil, doomed to fail. (Commented by eric-blog at 2006-03-15 13:05)

I like her attitude – people should qustion translations and I do not mind being kicked around to make a point even if I deserve better – but, unfortunately, Buddha without "the" still seems *that* Buddha while Devil without the same oddly enough makes no sense. English can not be Japanesed at will. Like Hearn, Blyth's translations – especially of poetry – are seldom much to speak of, but they are in good, sometimes beautiful English and his explanations, always witty and occasionally outrageous (especially concerning women), usually make up for what cannot be translated. This makes his translations perfect game for paraversing. So saying, I have found another version of the same attributed to Blyth and one by Suzuki Daisetsu on–line, respectively, "As Dogen said, outside the mind, the Buddha changes into a devil," and "If we seek the Buddha outside the mind, the Buddha changes into a devil." And, speaking of the Buddha/devil problem, Kawabata Yasunari's quintessentially Japanistic 1968 Nobel Prize speech* included the words, the quoted part of which came from calligraphy by the maverick Monk Ikkyû.

> There can be no world of the Buddha without the world of the devil . . . . . "It is easy to enter the world of the Buddha, it is hard to enter the world of the devil." (Seidensticker trans.)

We shall skip discussion of the meaning. Suffice it to say that Seidensticker must have put much thought into how to translate 魔界, literally "demon/devil-world," before settling on an uncapitalized but singular "devil," which doubtless tries to express what English cannot. Thinking of half of the pair, *The Demonic* would be better than "the world of the devil" but then what would the contrary be? The Buddhist? The Sacred? The Good? *The Enlightened?* In that case, the proverb I was playing with . . .

> *Seek Enlightenment without and you'll find the Demonic within.*
> *Seek your angels without and you shall find your inner demons.*
> *Seek to be blessed if you would be cursed.*
> *Blessed without is blasted within.*
> *Good sought without turns bad.*

And *there we go again*. Returning to the Nobel speech, it also included the Zen advice 逢仏殺仏 (meet-buddha-kill-buddha). Like me, you might have run across it somewhere and wondered. If the Buddha sought without impedes rather than speeds Enlightenment such advice makes perfect sense. The following phrase advizes us to kill the founder of the faith. Better, it goes without saying, to build upon our *first-heart* 初心. This is precisely contrary to the reasoning of Dostoevsky's Grand Inquisitor who would kill the returning Savior lest people lose their blind faith in the Church. But none of that solves what has no solution. I did play fast and loose with Dogen's proverb, but when you consider that there is no truly satisfactory translation, while there are many good paraverses, why not do it, or, rather them?

There is, however, one thing that troubles me. Dogen's words are not well known enough to have become a proverb in Japan. They are not in a couple large books of *kotowaza* or sayings I own. Neither Googling nor the scholars I wrote could find me the original. Since Blyth, bless him, usually supplied that, if only I were not stuck in the woods but esconced in a library, maybe . . . So, I cannot even say for sure whether I have enlarged a short phrase such as the above *meet-buddha-kill-buddha* or shortened a longer sentence. Usually, I *do* know. Most of my aphoristic translations have been incidental to my translation of haiku, *senryû* or *kyôka* (mad poem). My favorite concerns the *when* rather than the *where* of H*e*aven & H*e*ll. I shorten a 31-syllabet mad poem into a haiku-length proverb. You will find it leading the *Mad In Translation* chapter (pg. 221). The original Romanization and gloss follows so you can try your hand at translation, first. If you do so, do not immediately check out my version, but give yourself some time.

gokuraku-mo jigoku-mo ikite-iru uchi zo shinde-no-ato-wa nani-ga aru beshiki
paradise & hell, too, living-while[+emph]! Dead/dying's-after-as-for, what! is-ought.

PLEASE TRY ONE OR MORE TRANSLATIONS YOURSELF!

♪ **Nobel Speech.** Kawabata Yasunari's books make as much sense as most books do in Japan and can be translated as well (or poorly) as others, but that speech was another matter! Some of it seems purposefully abstruse and obtuse, as if the novelist wanted to torture the poor interpretor or translator. Never one to be stymied by small matters, Seidensticker whipped it into shape; i.e. made it as clear and plain to read as all his translations. The only question is whether he *should* have. Take that title, for example: *utsukushii nihon no watashi*. It literally translates as *"Beautiful Japan's Me."* One cannot just make it the odd but natural-sounding "Beautiful *Japanese* Me" because that would have been too easy to write otherwise in Japanese: ~ *nihonjin no watashi*. In other words, the novelist is not boasting of his genes but exalting the beauty of the country and culture that bore him. Reading such, I think of Descartes and things like *Japan is beautiful, ergo me*, or *The Beauty of Japan Made Me*. But, the beauty can also apply to the "me" and combining that with the low confidence of 20c Japanese abroad (at least in the Occident), I came up with *In Japan I am beautiful*, and considering the mindset of a Japanese writer, *In Beautiful Japanese, I am*. Such "translations" would. however, require the permission of the author. So what did the translator do?

Japan, the Beautiful and Myself.

Seidensticker did not try to approximate the untranslatable in English. He removed the links between the adjective, noun (minus "language") and pronoun to link them by sequel, proximity alone. That, too, is a sort of paraverse. I think it a good solution though it might not have been mine. Regardless, it is *settled* now; for we have Oe Kenzaburo's 1994 Nobel Prize Speech punning on it: *Japan, the Ambiguous and Myself* (trans. Hisaaki Yamanouchi, Kunioki Yanagishita) *aimaina nihon no watashi,* or, in direct translation, *Ambiguous Japan's Me*. That is to say, the Japanese original is a take-off on Kawabata's 1968 title. Or, you might say that Seidensticker mated with Kawabata and the issue has spawned a variation . . .

♪ **Buddha=Butsu Translation.** The problem is not only the connotations of the *butsu* we might capitalize, but those we might not: dead people are so written (though usually pronounced *hotoke*)! Choosing between *those* two *butsu* has often caused me trouble when translating haiku. Believe me, it is no fun having to decide whether flies are on the face of a statue or a corpse. But, my only real regret for the loss in translation is in respect of a mad poem by Sengai punning the might-be-capitalized *butsu*, or Buddha, with the sound of farting. Yet, I am not *butsubutsu*-ing (complaining) about translating Butsu. It is comparably easy to translate compared with *kami,* usually translated as God/gods, but actually running the gamut from God to minor spirits, or **numi-nous** things, good or bad, weak or strong, singular or plural . . . Motoori Norinaga, perhaps the first to seriously consider *kami* as a concept, defined *kami* as "anything which provokes a high degree of wonder." (For more, see Ryusaku Tsunoda, Wm. Theodore deBary et al, comps., *Sources of Japanese Tradition*). Norman Havens (*The Concept of Kami and the Concept of Deity* (on-line)) points out such *kami* are not merely the "countless gods" (*yaoyorozu no kami*) often mentioned, but "countless phenomena capable of arousing the recognition of powerful, non-everyday presence." (Google a phrase for more if you wish).

V
Can One Hundred Frogs All Be Wrong?
◎ why the most translated poem of all cannot be ◎

There are well over 100 translations of Bashô's famous frog-ku in Hiroaki Sato's *One Hundred Frogs*. I was surprised to find the first on the list was by Shiki:

"The old mere! / A frog jumping in / The sound of water."

I will not give any other translations for many can be found on the world-wide web and there are hundreds of libraries with Sato's book. As far as I know, however, no one has thoroughly explained why the *ku* cannot be perfectly translated, so that is where we will start. First, a word-by-word rendition:

~~~~~ *furuike ya   kawazu tobikomu mizu no oto* ~~~~~
old/ancient pond!/?/a/the/Ø: frog/s jump/leap-enter/s/ing water-/water's sound/s

The problems for a translator who knows both English and Japanese well (which, I am afraid, rules out almost all translators of haiku) are as follows:

1) *Furu,* with its patina, seems less literal (opp."new") than "old." Its "o" *sounds hard*, when it should evoke a soft, tranquil ambience. *Ancient,* on the other hand, sounds overwrought, and "ole" cannot help but conjure up Southern (USA) kids fishing in it. Spelling it *auld* would help but . . .

2) *Ike* is well matched by *pond,* though a darker? *mere* would be better if it were not obsolete. *Hearing* "the auld mere" today we might expect a horse.

3) *Ya* is a *kireji.* These "cutting-letters" generally Englished as "cutting words" or "cutting terms" – *caesura* by eggheads – were originally few and always found at the end of a *ku* to separate it from other *ku* in a sequence. Sato, quotes Harold J. Isaacson to the effect that "they have a meaning that lies in themselves as sounds, and in that way are as meaningful in English translation as they are in Japanese" (not quite) and points out that, by this time, eighteen such *kireji* had been recognized and Bashô himself wrote elsewhere that "every sound unit is a *kireji*" (precisely). Depending on the way the words cling together (depending on sound, syntax, and semantics) a *ku* can break, that is encourage the reader to pause without any recognized *kireji.* Sato also emphasized the *conjunctive* nuance of the *kireji* as a colon both separates and by equating, joins phrases, i,e., *"An old pond : a frog jumps in — the sound of water."* But the most common *kireji* (*kana* and *ya*) also may be emphatic, exclamatory, and/or interrogative. In English, it is enough to break the line, and the biggest question becomes a choice Japanese lacks: whether to use "a" or "the." I prefer the "the," indicating a specific pond, for being more evocative.

4) *Kawazu* is a literary term for *frog* (more commonly *kaeru,* which I happen to think the more poetic because it and "return" are homophones). As Japanese does not require distinction of number (singular/plural), generally, the only time it becomes an issue for a poem is in translation into a language like English that demands such a distinction; but, as Sato points out, Japanese have debated the number of frogs in this famous *ku* and most critics have concluded *it* is singular because a) Bashô has a painting showing just one, b) it seems more Zen, and c) it is "matched" with another singular frog (floating on a leaf) in a 1686 book called *Kawazu awase* (frog-matches, or frog-matching). This, despite circumstantial evidence favoring multiple frogs because Bashô was in a house owned by a fish merchant with many ponds, making *"it hard to imagine . . . the pond . . . as the exclusive residence of one hermit frog."* (Sato: Ibid). I would add that the Korean essayist Lee O-Young (i o ryon) argues that the phenomenon described by Bashô's *ku* is best imagined as neither singular nor plural but *single events occurring repeatedly over the course of time.* Why? There already were many Chinese poems about a sudden sound in a quiet place and Bashô being a genius who would not just dish out more of the same . . . ("Why did the frog jump into the old pond?" *Kawazu wa Naze Furu Ike ni Tobikonda ka* Gakuseisha: 1993).

5) *Tobikomu* is a compound verb *"jump+enter,"* which in English can only be matched with a general verb, "jump," supplemented by "into." Sato writes that *"kawazu* is the subject of" this verb, which "as happens in Japanese grammar, [is] at once the conclusive and the noun-modifying form." These well-put words hint at but do not sufficiently explain the reason why no good English translation is possible, namely that in English, an active present-tense verb cannot modify a noun. Again, Sato's translation: *"an old pond : a frog jumps in — the sound of water."* Do you see? He went with the conclusive reading alone. In his head, Sato may read his second phrase as modifying the third, but it does not work that way. One thing happens, then, another. We will return to this in the text, below. Note that Japanese haiku are generally 17-syllabets and break (though seldom published parsed) after the 5th, 12th or 17th (if the end of the *ku* can be so called). Some have a second, minor pause. This one breaks after the 5th (the *ya*) and barely slows after the 12th. If I were asked to describe it simply, I would call it a 5-12 split.

6) *Mizu* is "water." Water is water, but years ago, I thought I detected a pun: "seeing-not" (the sound not seen). Unfortunately, Japanese never hear it.

7) *No* is possessive, like "of" or "'s," but both stronger and weaker in the way it binds words: *stronger* because it can bind two words into one (Eg. *hinode* = sun's appear = sunrise), recognized as such by dictionaries, in the manner that a hyphen does more rarely in English, so that the *"sound of water"* may be thought of as the *"water-sound;"* and, *weaker* because it keeps them far enough apart that the noun which becomes the modifier is still free to link as a noun to the noun-modifying verb without necessarily passing on the connection to the modified second noun, the *oto,* or sound, in this case. In other words, the *jumping-in* verb *tobikomu* can link to water, sound or both.

8) *Oto* is "sound" and, as Sato points out, *"mizu no oto* (water's sound)" is "not, as sometimes translated, onomatopoeic."

The only way to really *connect* all of the last 12 syllables of the original *in English* would be "*[the old pond –] the sound of water into which jumps a frog*" or *"the sound of water into which a frog jumps."* Leaving aside the ugly swarm of articles ("the," "of," "into which," and "a") that English needs to tie things together, the *sound* (*oto*) which comes to a head *at the end* of the original is replaced by the frog/s or jump. As long as it must come out backwards, then, why not just put the old pond at the end? One of the translations given by Sato *did*. Variation III of Ten by William Matheson (one of two reprinted by Sato) ends *"In thyss olde Bogge."* The "In" appeals not, but the "e" on old does. I like the rhyming *bogge*, but knowing Bashô was in a tame setting must forgoe it. I will give you three paraverses which are like, Matheson's, out-of-order:

    A poet passes,   *~ water-sound ~*
frogs riot and once again   *a frog has jumped into*
    the pond is quiet.   *the dark pond*

a frog's plunk:
how the silence fills
the old pond!

The impossibility of doing justice to Bashô's *ku* led me to write dozens of paraverses. This was maybe twenty years ago, mind you, before buying Sato's book, for books are my file cabinets and had I not already lost them, they would have been glued or taped inside the cover. The first above is one of them, as close as I can recall. The idea of adding the poet (probably borrowed from *senryû* Englished by Blyth) is found in a number of translations in Sato's book, without the ridiculous *riot* which was, of course, arrived at by reason of rhyme. The second is an effort to skirt some of the problems enumerated above. The "dark" works, but the overall structure too explanatory to be poetic. The third, also *ad hoc*, is, like the first, more along the lines of an expansion upon the original than a translation. "Plunk" has more *gravitas* than the hollow "plop," more profundity than the shallow "splash" (the two most common mimesis used in "translation" of the *ku*), and is softer than Ginsberg's harsh and corny *kerplunk* (that would be perfect for some *haikai* link-verse, but not *this*). But let us get serious and consider a translation that is one of the closest if not the closest to the original of those I have seen, for it will help to see the limits of translation more quickly.

the old pond
a frog jumps in
water's sound

tr. William J Higginson

One of my lost translations had the frog plumbing the water *to prove it sound*, for, to me, the sound is less an open-ended splash than a *capsule*, created when the water seals over the hind-legs of the frog. It speaks, or, rather *demonstrates* the solidity(?), or *soundness* of the body of water. It makes good sense to allow this English idiom some play, as it can add poetry not in the original to compensate for some of that lost in translation. It is one reason I like Higginson's translation, though he might not have intended the pun – Likewise for his apostrophic predecessor Suzuki Daisetsu, who wrote: *Into the ancient pond / A frog jumps / Water's sound!* (in Sato *ibid*). The more important ambiguity in Higginson's translation, also found in Shiki's, one of D. Keene's and some others (see Sato's book), is that which allows us to put the frog's jump *within the sound of the water*, if it were. I like that, because the scene *as I imagine it* is this:

> *an old pond*
> *in the sound of water*
> *a frog leaps*

For if Bashô did not see the frog, but imagined it *from* the water-sound, or *-note*, as some music-minded translators put it, such is the reality. Indeed, one of the explanations in Makoto Ueda's *Bashô and His Interpretors*, has him seated in his hut across from Kikaku when the sound is heard, so I am not the only person who does not have the poet sitting or walking by the pond. Yet, one thing is wrong about these readings: in the original, *water* is what is jumped into plain and simple, *and* the sound is *of* that water. True, the Japanese possessive *no* allows a reading where the "water's sound" can be jumped into, but it is not so read by 99.9% of Japanese readers. There is only one way translators can keep the original word-order *and* significance of the last 12 syllabets of the original more or less intact in English, and, I am sorry, but it is *ugly*:

> *The old pond . . . a frog-leaps-into-the-water sound.*

Why? Because, when the original is read through to the end, *everything* that comes after the cutting-letter *ya* modifies that *sound*, not the *water*. Readers familiar with my other books should immediately recognize what I call the "Japanese style" of poetry, where an entire poem can be nothing but one long modified subject. Here, the poem is 2/3 that. I wish hyphens were not so damn ugly. Phenomenologically speaking, I feel such a sound means this (a clear exposition of what I put more poetically above) is what happened:

> *the old pond*
> *i see that frog jumping*
> *after the plop*

Until this chapter made me work on it, I was unsure *what* made me like Bashô's *ku*. Now, *I know*. It is that the *apparent* order in which things happen is *wrong*, yet still seems right. In other words, we do not just experience quiet paradoxically brought out by noise, which, as Lee O'Young pointed out, was old hat in the Sinosphere, or the new idea of repetition at natural intervals that he hypothesized was what made the poem good, but something I would call *dream reality*, which can preface an actual sound with a sequence of events – a whole dream! Cognitive scientists have studied the way our perception can act like the television or radio censors and edit our reality without our being aware of it within the space of a split-second delay (I read a whole book about it from Basic, the champion publisher of badly edited books by brilliant scientists, a decade or two ago). Well, my dreams can do the same *and* squeeze in a whole story, to boot.

The body-clock, knowing the alarm clock will ring explains only a portion of such dream-events, for many happen despite the outside stimulous being a one-time event. I doubt I am an anomaly, so I dare to think at least a part of my readership will follow my reading of Bashô, inspired because I recently *had* such a bass-ackward dream. Nevertheless, my last translation is off, for our perception, *right or wrong*, is our reality and the ultimate source of poetry!

☆ Forget Sato's *Frogs!* Read Ueda's *Bashô and His Interpreters!* ☆

There are probably a score of books ★ treating multiple-translation in English, though only the half-dozen that are mine use this form of translation *for translation itself,* rather than for the sake of collection and comparison; but there is only *one* book I know of dedicated to showing just how many *interpretations* a single poem may have: Makoto Ueda's *Bashô and His Interpreters – Selected Hokku with Commentary* (Stanford:1992) has over 400 pages with thousands of interpretations by scores of fellow poets and critics for 255 *ku*, all translated (just one translation!) by the author from the Japanese. These include thirteen *interpretations* of the famous frog-*ku,* spanning three long-pages, which tell us far more about Bashô's *ku* than all the translations ever made! If the limits of language intrigue you, read Ueda's book, the *only* haiku-related book I am completely satisfied with (other than wanting it expanded). It should be *much, much* better known than it is. ★

★ ***The Matter of Line Order.*** All translation must trade-off 1) original order, 2) original flow/linkage and 3) something hard to sense, which might be called right-feeling; and, nothing makes this so clear as three-line translated haiku. The second two lines of Bashô's frog-ku are good at bringing out 1) and 2), but, despite the Matheson translation and my paraverses, the *old pond* seems so natural at the head of the poem that we do not have to consider whether it might not seem more natural at the tail. With many haiku, however, that is the case. Something seems amiss if we do not reverse that order. One might say the original order should be respected, but is that respectful to the original if keeping it kills the poem? I would love to have a linguist (one could make a thesis of it) go through Blyth or my translations (we both do not hesitate to reverse the order to get the right feeling and we both give the original, so you would not need to look it up) and try to find out what factors are involved. *Order* vs *flow* problems are relatively easily understood as coming from the difference in syntax (SVO vs SOV) and other matters related to right and left-branching languages. It is something psychologically subtle, hard to pin down. I only brought it up here, at the risk of boring most readers – for which I apologize! – because I just received HAIKU, TRIKU, TANKA AND MORE – *Fifty Years of Japan Inspired Fixed Form Verse* from Harold Wright, and his *"triku"* offers a new tool for thinking about that hard-to-sense order problem.

One day, while writing conventional haiku in English, I was trying to decide which of the two images that I wanted to come first. I wrote *"My legs are asleep"* and *"A temple bell rings"* then I reversed the lines. Then I realized that if I wrote a poem of three lines, all of equal length, perhaps five syllables each, then I could read the poem in any order. . . . My first one was:

My legs are asleep
A temple bell rings
My mind is a well.

Which is, of course, also:

My mind is a well
*   A temple bell rings*
*   My legs are asleep*

Or

A temple bell rings
*   My legs are asleep*
*   My mind is a well*

Or, whatever . . .

"Whatever" means there are three more permutations. If I had the first two lines, or better yet the experience, it would probably have gone altogether elsewhere:

the big bell's boom
my legs are asleep: i taste
shiki's persimmon

(All haiku-lovers know of Shiki hearing the big bell as he bit into a persimmon.) But, not to get off-topic, Wright offers other examples of which I think this the best by far: *She has gone away / I can hear the fan / For the whole summer.* If you try this one in various orders – six, if I am not mistaken (and if you put it into your computer, decap and center balance and it is much easier to create all of them) – you will be able to experience a variety of nuances. *Wait! I'll save you the trouble after these notes end.* Let me just say that thanks to the way "for the whole summer" links with the proximate line, there is combinitive variety not found in Wright's first effort, where each line is absolutely independent. Most haiku do not break completely in three, but tend to be like this "For the whole summer" poem. I think when you look at the six renditions, you will see that the last one or two lines are what seems to count most. One reason is because we cannot help but expect a punch line or resolution at the end. This makes a difference in another way, which, as far as I know, was first pointed out by me, in another book, after my all-too-common juggling of the syntax (line order) was kindly challenged by the late William J Higginson – *kindly*, for it was in a personal letter after he praised *Rise, Ye Sea Slugs!* in print. There are reasons why *the context* in which a haiku appears favors one or another word order. If a poem *with*, or *on* a sea slug is a stand-alone or mixed in with poems about other subjects, its appearance at or near the end is a surprise and improves the wit; but, if that same poem were to be read along with hundreds of sea slug (*namako*) poems, the sea slug would be anticipated and the poem deprived of what would have been its snapper. Perhaps, the only solution would be to translate all such poems in composite, with a *for-this-book-version* on the left with a surprise at the end for the reader to see first, and a *stand-alone version* keeping the original order even though the snapper will not surprise. Perhaps, I should name this practice. *Situation-appropriate order? Context-dependent translation? Context-dependent syntax-reversal?*

★ <u>Wright's *triku sextet* is on the next page.</u>

★ ***I do not include smaller publications***, such as chapbooks or magazines. This matters because Liz Henry, a young software engineer has a site called compositetranslation.com (as of 2007/3 = in what seems to be a state of suspended animation) dedicated to the creation and publication of composite translation. As noted in the introduction, she may have invented the term *composite-translation*. Here is a description of her magazine:

> *Composite* features one poem in each issue. The poem in its original language is printed on a page that folds out from the back cover. Inside, various translations of the poem into English or other languages will be printed together.

Because the original may be viewed together with each translation, I understand why Henry uses the word "composite," but, for me – both because my memory has a hard time holding together poems on different pages and the nature of the readings – she just presents multiple-translation, including what I call *paraverses* (she welcomed freestyle contributions) in a practical way. I say "just," but it is a great idea. Hofstadter's *Le Ton beau de Marot* also has the original on the leaf of the book jacket but not on the inside, where it might be folded out and better seen (that is where he keeps his private treasure, the delightful paraverse by his late wife). For right or wrong, I consider some of my clusters of haiku, senryû and kyôka readings the only true composite-translation (excepting some examples of untranslatable *kyôka* by Blyth and others showing the straight reading on one side and the punning reading on the other), and poems arranged serially as multiple-translation. Regardless, I credit Liz Henry for coining the expression unless/until someone else claims prior use of it. I may have used it myself, but lacking time to search my scattered or lost papers may recall what I *wish* rather than what *was*, for had I appreciated it enough, I probably would know for sure.

from HAIKU, TRIKU, TANKA AND MORE – Fifty Years of Japan Inspired Fixed Form Verse from Harold Wright

she has gone away
i can hear the fan
for the whole summer

she has gone away
for the whole summer
i can hear the fan

i can hear the fan
she has gone away
for the whole summer

i can hear the fan
for the whole summer
she has gone away

for the whole summer
she has gone away
i can hear the fan

for the whole summer
i can hear the fan
she has gone away

You may note that when you actually try it the grammar does not mesh perfectly for the last three. Let me do them over now, cheating only enough to naturalize the poems. This is similar to the problems one faces in translation when one stays to close to the original.

i can hear the fan
for the whole summer –
she has gone away

for the whole summer
(she has gone away)
i can hear the fan

this whole summer
i hear the damn fan –
she has gone away

I trust you can see how *triku* and *paraverse* and *composite-translation* all come together in such play. Adding "my" (it was composed at Bashô's hut) to warm up the old pond a bit –

my old pond
a frog jumps in
the water sound

my old pond
the water sound
a frog jumps in

a frog jumps in
my old pond
the water sound

a frog jumps in
the water sound
my old pond

the water sound
a frog jumps in
my old pond

the water sound
my old pond
a frog jumps in

Or, starting basic, then playing –

the old pond – / a frog jumps in / water-sound.   one naturally follows the other
the old pond / the water-sound of frogs / jumping in.   making its sound as they join it
a frog jumps / into the water: sound out / the old pond!   an old pond left to itself is lonely
a frog jumps / into the water: the sound of / an old pond. that sound is not that of any pond
a water sound / only the frog's feet still / out of the pond   imagine catching only the webbed feet
a water sound / how long frogs, how long / this old pond? call it irregular tick-tocks or testing both
a frog sound / how many plops of water / in the old pond? would "left" in the last line be too clear?
a water sound / the life of a frog and / the life of a pond   not quite the same idea, but much better.
a water sound / the old pond gobbles up / another frog   ever heard of Jinny Greenteeth?

Besides the basic choices, the variety of articles and number required by English make for not six but scores of choices of which we have only seen a part and, with paraversing . . .

The old poem mistaken? New Words from Oxford.

I just found something new to me about the old pond *ku* among Susumu Takiguchi's remarks at "a conference at Oxford" repeated in a "Speech at the First International Contemporary Haiku Symposium, 11 July 1999 Tokyo," called "Japan Has Embarked on Her Voyage to World Haiku," among the Appendices to his book *The Twaddle of an Oxonian* (2000). After claiming this most famous *ku* was "also the most misunderstood and mistranslated," he noted that of the 170 translations he saw only three had "frogs!" And, speaking as a Japanese, added that "it is not our usual experience to see a single frog in early spring in Japan" and that "the sound of water is not normally a single plop or splash." If the Korean essayist Lee Oh Young argued for multiple frogs over time from the relationship of Bashô's *ku* to Chinese poetry and Sato from Bashô's particular circumstances as noted in the main text, Takiguchi argues from realism, which is, for better or worse, general. As I *had* a small pond with a hermit frog and I know there are always preternatural times of day when even coconuts don't fall (I grew up in such a plantation), I tend to hear that one frog. But plural is possible, and I would only take issue with Takiguchi when he implies that "we Japanese" read the poem differently than non-Japanese readers with respect to the number of frogs, for, as far as I know, most Japanese imagine one frog, and all the Japanese commentators, including famous haiku poets and top haiku editors quoted by Ueda in *Bashô and His Interpreters* imagine *a* frog. Of course, *he* could have mistranslated, but from the context in almost every case, only the singular makes sense. But, wait, I did not add two pages to this chapter to criticize Takiguchi, but to praise him, for I was delighted with his next statement.

> More importantly, the haiku depicts a cheerful and merry scene whereby frogs are noisy and there's life everywhere . . . far from the standard interpretation of a world of tranquility and eternal stillness. If my interpretation is correct, most of the English versions of this famous haiku have to be mistranslation and mistakes. [sic]. (Ibid)

Yamamoto, the greatest of modern haikai editors in my opinion, has this *ku* articulate "a sense of existential melancholy" (trans. Ueda: Ibid) Needless to say, that implies one frog. Or, at least, one at a time. But, if one imagines a "cheerful and merry scene," lots of frogs makes sense for the first time. One of my many (mercifully) unpublished translations of the *ku* made the frog's splash a bracing tonic slapped on the face of the old pond. That is silly. But many frogs would make an old pond come alive in Spring. And Bashô was supposedly with Kikaku at the time; he was hardly one to be melancholy with. The only problem, as I see it, is that if Bashô intended that, he would not have specified the sound of water or the jumping in. There are other ways to describe such a scene. Still, I am grateful for Takiguchi, as his wholesome modern interpretation – I think of Kyoshi getting cheer from the white top of a mountain over a barren winter field (one of Takiguchi's favorites), where Issa would shiver from the added cold of the image, sunlight or not – adds something to the reading of the poem. However, I can not guess what he wants of the English translation. If "frogs" was chosen by all but three translators, most Japanese critics would call *that* wrong, would they not? Unless frog/s jump/s – which is to say, hitherto not permitted ugliness can English ambiguous number, or the composite translation I advocate is resorted to, choice and the resultant argument are unavoidable.

vi
F*ly-ku!*
◎ <u>normalizing composite translation</u> ◎

I did not write *Fly-ku!* from an attraction to flies, or of flies to me. I am not like the English gentleman obsessed by their supposed ability to breed from sweat who carried out some of the first modern-style scientific experiments in history (Find him in *Aubrey's Lives*). Mostly, I wanted to point out the fallacy of the so-called *pathetic fallacy*, with some help from Issa's famous *fly-ku*, which in Blyth's 1952 translation reads *"Do not hit the fly! / See how it wrings its hands, / its feet!"* The first chapter introduces 15 translations by 14 translators (two by Blyth) and explains in detail how they cannot help but differ from the original, where flies *rub* their *hands and feet*, as said rubbing is simultaneously a fact and common idiom for *begging for mercy* or *praying*, and the vocabulary for *hands* and *feet* only unnatural in English, because the first happens to be reserved for primates. Pedagogically speaking, that single chapter is worth at least two of Weinberger's *Nineteen Wang Wei's* (a whole book), for the attentive reader will leave it wiser in the way that translation *must* distort and understanding why we should be careful about judging others to be naive, artificial, maudlin, or precious. And the reason I decided to finish the book before I finished others of the dozens of partially finished book-to-be's was because I discovered something about the origin of Issa's *ku* (a *senryû* connection) and wanted to publish it. But, such matters I leave to *Fly-ku!* Here, let us concentrate on the composite translations.

~~~~~~

築山は人の手つたふわらびかな　千代
chikusan wa hito no te tsut[d]au warabi kana – chiyô d.1775
(chiku-mt.-as-for, people's hands transmit/pass-along bracken 'tis/!/?)

> bracken pass
> from hand to hand
> mt. chikusan

mt chikusan
the bracken lend a hand
to people

mt. chikusan
we climb hand over hand
like bracken

> mt chikusan
> hand to hand men
> and bracken

Compare, if you will, the various readings against the gloss: "Chiku-mount-as-for, people's hands transmit/pass-along bracken 'tis/!/?" Had I dared go further and allow the mountain's place in the syntax to be disturbed in order to pick up on more meanings of the *"kana"* glossed as *"*'tis/!/?,*"* I would have needed more translations:

what bracken!
here on mt chikusan they
lend us a hand

is that bracken
lending a hand to humans
on mt chikusan?

Chiyo's *ku* plays on the literal meaning of the idiom for help, *tetsudau,* hand-relay and the composite translation allows that to be expressed in English. *Fly-ku!* has a whole chapter on bracken hands, for the trope was developed earlier than *fly* hands. *What am I talking about?* What English calls a head, as in the fiddle-head fern, Japanese calls a *hand*. They come out looking like fists and then open, as hands can do. Because these "hands" are broken off (to eat), there are many pitiful old *ku* about young bracken (*Adiantum*, also called *kujaku-shida*, or "peacock fern"). Chiyo's *ku* adds a sweet feminine touch to Teitoku's *"Bracken hands / Outnumber centipedes / on Mt Kurama"* (*mukade yori warabi-te ôshi kurama-yama*), which plays the myriad hands against the 100-legs/feet of the bug. Note that still more readings might might be needed if we guess that Chiyo was playing on the mountain's name, and if we consider the fact that this bracken can be a girl's name, any number of alternative readings come to mind, though I did not use *that* many in *Fly-ku!* for it took us too far off the subject.

mt construction
here the maiden ferns lend
all of us a hand

~~~~~~
I have expanded on Fly-ku! above. What follows is straight from the book.
~~~~~~

つままれて手をする蝿の命かな　嘯山 葎亭
tsumamarete te o suru hae no inochi kana – shôzan d. 1801
(pinched [between fingers], hand/s-rubbing fly's/flies' life/lives!/?/'tis)

where there is life . .
a fly already pinched
rubbing his hands

the pitiful bug

the fly
i pinch, wrings its hands:
dear life!

the pitiful thief

pinched, he rubs
his hands for life is life
even for a fly

Whether read as metaphor or description, this poem, antedating Issa and his *fly-ku* by almost a century (Shôzan was long-lived), contains much in common with it. The *inochi kana* is a fine phrase which can be translated in many ways: "life 'tis!" "oh, life!" "it means my/its life" "it'll be the death of me/it." I think Shôzan means it is *a matter of life or death* to the fly, which it is. As I cannot imagine a fly pinched between fingers would rub its legs together, I also suspect my first translation is correct, though it is wrong for not maintaining the "fly/flies' life/lives." As usual, it is hard for English to keep the ambiguity of a life possibly both the fly's & the poet's. The entire *ku* is a modification of the "life" (*inochi*) which cannot be kept properly linked together (i.e., *the life of a fly rubbing its hands while pinched!*) in English without reversing the life-comes-last syntax.

蝿一つ打てはなむあみだ仏哉　一茶
hae hitotsu utte wa [utteba?] namuamidabutsu kana – issa d.1827
(fly one, hit-as-for[or, if/when] *"namuamidabutsu"*[part of a sutra]!/?/'tis)

each fly
that i can kill
i bless

namuamidabutsu　　　　　　　　　　　　　　　　*the good death*

each fly　　　　　　　　　　　each fly
we swat gets　　　　　　　swatted earns
a blessing　　　　　　　　　a *sutra*

for each fly
we kill, another *na-mu-
a-mi-da-bu-tsu*

When the protagonist is unclear the general rule in haiku is *assume the first-person*. In that case, we have Issa swatting and blessing, as per the first and last readings. ["can" was added with knowledge of Issa's *ku* about missing] But a general rule is not a law; it does not rule out other possibilities.

namuamidabutsu!　　　　　　　　　　　　　*namuamidabutsu!*

each fly　　　　　　　　　　　each fly
she swats receives　　　　i swat enjoys
my blessing　　　　　　　her blessing

namuamidabutsu!

a benediction
for every *musca maledicta*
we swat

When someone sneezes, they get a *gesundheit*, whatever *that* is. We stick with this phrase we cannot spell, much less understand, because a concrete blessing for so trite a tragedy – if the loss of a bit of breath and snot can be so called – is overblown. Better to use a foreign phrase. This *na-mu-a-mi-da-bu-tsu* is based on Sanskrit and written in Chinese characters beginning with "south-not" (*namu*) and ending in "buddha" (*butsu*). The in-between part is not so easy. We'll skip it. Suffice it to say that it is chanted syllabet by syllabet and the whole phrase can be translated (from my Kenkyusha dictionary): 1) "I sincerely believe in Amitabha. 2) "Save us, merciful Buddha! 3) "May he [his soul] rest in peace! 4) "Glory to [whatever sutra name is inserted]. My first six translations of Issa's poem all assume the third of these meanings, where the nebulous phrase blesses the dead fly. Many Japanese I have asked think the second more likely:

sinners

with each fly
we swat, we cry
god save us!

mea culpa

for each fly
i swat, a prayer: may
god have mercy!

old testament buddhism

each fly hit
is chased by a prayer, god
don't hit me!

a killer's prayer

for each fly hit
a plea: heaven have
mercy on me!

cowardly killers

with each fly
we swat a prayer for
our next life

Or, maybe it is better not to think the prayer is for either the fly or the fly-swatter but for both and all in our killing-field-of-a-world. As two correspon-dents point out, since part of Pureland belief is that we and others are ultimately one, blessing the fly (that its soul speeds over) is good for the karma of the swatter, too. I leave further interpretation and poetic permutation of "I," "he," "she," or "we," as you like, to the reader. The *"God save us!"* may be Japanned to "Merciful Buddha!" or Englished all the way to "Sweet Jesus!" There is no end to the creative paraverse.

引導を渡して呉れと後れ蝿　痾窮

indô o watashite kure to okurebae – ∀Q 2001/08/27
(pull-road[death instructions] give please [says] dying/defeated-fly)

a benediction
please, says the dying
musca maledicta

finally swatted
a brave *musca maledicta*
gets last rites

please give me
the *coup de gráce* says
the dying fly

An *indô* is "the last words addressed by the priest to a deceased person's soul at a funeral;" this "for guidance in passage to the other world." Such words would be wasted on me, for I cannot remember directions alive and hardly think death would improve my memory! The *indô* can idiomatically mean the *coup de gráce*. The Japanese conjunction to serves to indicate something was said without using the anthropomorphic verb "to say." Still, this is a silly *ku*. It's bad enough for a fly to talk, but a dead fly? 痾窮 *aka* ∀Q, says it is his early-stage work, *i.e.*, juvenilia. I suppose it out of place, but if ∀Q was brave enough to post it, I could hardly not include it here.

So long as we have a bit of space at the top of the page, let me remind the reader that he or she should not be thinking about flies but whether multiple translations, at least for some haiku, are good or not, and whether or not the use of clusters to present them as a composite whole is appealing.

~~~~~~

人間の道徳蝿と相容れず 剣花坊
ningen no dôtoku hae to ai-irezu – kenkabô (19-20c senryû)
(humans' morality: fly/flies-with meet/blend-include/accept-not)

Flies / Are excluded / From human morality – trans. Blyth

incompatible   *why we need zen*

human morality   flies make
has no place   a mess of human
for flies   morality

I un-parse Blyth, for he is off the mark. The *senryû* is clearly about incompatibility (not *exclusion*), and is a quite sophisticated statement. It is not that flies do things humans cannot countenance, but that flies, by annoying people, force them to swat out and that is a stain on a moral system where hatred and the taking of life was officially frowned upon. *Flies make us betray ourselves.* They make it almost impossible for a Buddhist to be a good Buddhist. Issa, as we have seen, wrote about striking a *hotoke*, a statue of Buddha or a corpse, while swatting a fly. Keigu paraverses in a more purely philosophical vein including Kenkabô's idea:

蝿打てば即ち仏打ちにけり 敬愚
hae-uteba sunawachi hotoke uchi-ni-keri – keigu
(fly-strike-if/when, namely, buddha hit [emphatic/perfect])

when we swat
a fly, we swat the face
of buddha!

~~~~~~

蝿ハにげたのにしづかに手をひらき 柳樽
hae wa nigeta no ni shizuka ni te o hiraki – yanagidaru bk 16
(fly fled/escaped-though , quietly hand[obj] [he/she] opens)

opened with care
his hand shows the fly
is not there

This senryû is from the same series that I believe gave form to Issa's famous fly-*ku*. I use the third-person because when the subject is explicit in *senryû*, it is almost always that person [unlike haiku which is generally first-person]. A simple translation, true to syntax, might be "the fly escaped yet he quietly opens his hand." Blyth's translation was sober yet hyped up with a double adverb: *"The fly has escaped / But he opens his hand / Very, very slowly."* I prefer to play around with the *idea*. More paraverses:

fly gone
he carefully opens
his hand

a fly is
seldom found in the hand
slowly opened

the emptiness
of a hand that should have
held a fly

his slowly
opened hand reveals
no fly

The first paraverse is in a straight *senryû*-style. The next is aphoristic, a style rarely encountered in senryû or haiku. If you have experienced that emptiness, you know that the third could be a haiku. The last completely reverses the syntax of the original, changing it from a description of how men act to a logical joke. Strictly speaking, it is neither haiku nor *senryû*. I think I got the idea from reading of a North Florida toe-bidding party where a man, finding the dish he hoped to eat gone, quipped that he was not interested in chicken-*was* but chicken-*is* (or something like that in Zora Neale Hurston's ethnographic and literary masterpiece *Of Mules and Men* or autobiography, *Dust Tracks on a Dirt Road*. [Additional: What *is* a "toe-bidding party? Sorry, I won't say. You must read her nonfiction books!]).

老の手や蝿を打さい（へ）逃た跡　一茶
oi no te ya hae o utsu sae nigeta ato – issa d. 1827
old/elderly hand!/: fly/flies hits-even-though, fled after/spot

my old hand
hits the very spot
the fly was

Let's face it, killing flies is not like killing mosquitoes or (with a trap) mice. We have a moving target not only live but lively enough to manifest a *there!-not-there!* quality worthy of quantum physics. Would I be wrong to guess that for all people who did not enjoy the satisfaction of hunting, fly-swatting must have been the game in the days before video and other electronic skill-games. In fact, we might call fly-swatting the prototype for all that Sony et al come up with. The first Gamestation© was the fly-swatter. It, too, was able to command the total mindfulness=mindlessness of the player. Now, the one rule for all games is that we cannot win all the time (This has been tested on all sorts of birds and beasts: they are more persistent if they are not allowed to succeed every time). In other words, if we never missed, fewer flies would be swatted. Yet, there are not as many misses recorded in haiku as one might imagine. Issa boasts the lion's share of them. But before I cough up another, let me play a bit more with the last:

You try: old/elderly hand!/: fly/flies hits-even-though, fled after/spot –

my old hand
even when it takes a swat
the fly is not

the old hand		*an old hand*
when it swats it swats		*swats the fly, all right*
the fly that was		*where it was*

my old hand
not that it misses the fly
just moves!

this ole hand		*right place*
don't miss – it swats right		*wrong time – an old hand*
where fly was		*after a fly*

I am not just trying to be clever with my "was" stuff and other shenanigans. A peculiarity of English is responsible for my forced translation. In English, an animal (or machine) has a trail or a track, or leaves a mark. The Japanese term *ato* (homophonic with another heterographic ato meaning "after/following/next") is more versatile, for it means all of these *and* also can mean something we can only describe as "the place where something was." In other words, the fly was *there,* but not *then.* I am guessing the slow hand is Issa's, but it could be someone else's. [Let me add that the center reading is my favorite, for the fly moves when you read the *ku* from being the object of the verb "misses" to the subject of the verb "moves" – did you notice? – something that is common in traditional Japanese poetry, especially *waka* (5-7-5-7-7) which puts that pun/pivot in the middle 5.]

~~~~~~

<div style="text-align:center">

うつ手を感じて街の蠅うまくにげた　山頭火
utsu te o kanjite machi no hae umaku nigeta – santôka d.1940
(hitting-hand/s[obj] feel/sense/s town-fly/ies[subj] skillfully fled/escaped)

city slicks

the flies in town
skillfully read and
beat my hand

</div>

The past tense – in ordinary vernacular, something rare in haiku – may mean the wandering poet has just passed through a town and, finding a fly that does not flee so quickly, looks back on the flies in the city. A few more paraverses: [Why *"more?"* Note the "read" rather than "sense" and "beat" rather than "escaped."]

literacy	*adaptation*	*sophisticate*
reading my hand	sensing hands	the town-fly:
the town-fly makes	town-flies are adroit	an adept in the art
a great escape!	at escaping	of escape

Familiarity may not breed contempt, but it does create caution. We all are very aware of the difference between animals familiar and unfamiliar with man. Unless tame, those that know "us" flee, and those that do not are curious, then dead, usually.

生き残る蝿がわたしをおぼえている　山頭火
ikinokoru hae ga watashi o oboeteiru – santôka d. 1940
(living-remain/surviving fly/ies-the me[obj] remembering)

*the flies
that survive
remember me*

Santôka's *ku* do not come to a head with the fly/flies, in the manner of many more traditional *haiku* [or *waka*] where everything else in the poem would modify the same. Paradoxically, by turning the fly into the subject of a prosaic sentence and, instead, focusing on the behavior, Santôka avoids making the fly the subject of the poem, ending it with the verb, as done in ordinary Japanese speech, without so much as a nod toward haiku convention (which would, at the very least, put a haiku-esque conjugation on the verb). His second *ku* about "the flies that survive" appear to hypothesize upon the mechanism for the natural selection of smart city flies in his previous *ku*.

I would have thought twice before shortening *another* poet's *ku* as I did the above *ku* by Santôka. The reason is that he composed many under-length haiku. This was not one of them, but I had to do as I did to follow another of Santôka's idiosyncracies. He used exceptionally natural language. Any padding added would have betrayed his style. I am unsure what to call such a translation.

~~~~~~

<div style="text-align:center">

とく逃げよにげよ打たれなそこの蝿　一茶
toku nigeyo nigeyo utare na soko no hae – issa d. 1827
(quickly flee! flee! swat/hit-get-not! hit- get-not! over-there's fly)

</div>

caveat musca		*hey, you there!*
beat it! flee! don't get yourself killed, fly!		better flee! quickly, fly, fly! don't die!

<div style="text-align:center">

♪ *if the swatter
don't kill you* ♪

flee, fly, flee!
fly away and live
until you die!

</div>

unsafe here		*a last plea*
quick, fly beat it! don't die for me.		flee, fly! don't make me kill you!

If Mother Goose
(rather than Kiku)
had a fly-swatter:

Flee, fly! Fly away!
Come back to play
another day!

I was tempted to guess "don't let *him* (or *her*) kill you!" Issa could have been laughing at a bloodthirsty friend or an extermination campaign by his spunky wife Kiku. This seems more likely than warning the fly against staying near to him (unless he wrote this under the influence). Moreover, Issa has a similar *ku* where he tells an escaped bird to quickly get lost in the spring mist. [New: Quickly flee! / Flee! Don't get hit, / Fly, over there!]

~~~~~~

さはぐなら外がましぞよ庵（の）蝿　一茶
sawagu nara soto ga mashi zo yo io no hae – issa d.1827
(disturb [others] if, outside is better [+double emph.]!/: hut's fly/flies)

ultimatum	*house rules*
if you want to horse-around, then, housefly, leave!	if you want to zip about, housefly, go out!

if you would
horse around, outside's better
fly of my hut

the bouncer	*house-mates*
act rowdy, fly, and you'd best get out!	act up, fly, and, by god, you'd best get out!

The rambunctious fly mentioned is probably one type that sometimes comes into the house and rips about like a racing car on a basketball court [Additional: in Hawaii, we called it a *banzai fly*]. I don't know if housefly is right. "Hut's fly" doesn't work, as can be seen from the middle translation, "fly of my hut" is too long and ludicrous. [the double emphatic "by God"

As already clear to readers of *Fly-ku!* Issa was remarkable for addressing flies even when they were not on the point of dying. I think the mark of a healthy anthropo- morphism, if you insist that a relation real or imagined with an animal that is not human be labeled, is that it is as likely to be *scolding* as *loving*. I think we all know that, though we might not be aware of it. If people (poets or not) are often challenged for anthropomorphism, the pathetic fallacy, it is for the pretentiousness, maudlinity and so forth when they express affection for these creatures, but seldom if ever for giving them a piece of their mind or booting them in the ass . . . no, tail!

~~~~~~

夜の蠅人を忘れて何処へか　之房　新選
yoru no hae hito o wasurete izuko e ka – shibô 1773
(night's fly/ies, people[obj] forgetting, where to?)

a mystery   *the question*

forgetting men   flies at night
where in the world do flies   where do they go
go at night   without us

flies without people

Where
do our flies go
at night?

This poem did not *need* many translations. The idea is so simple and, I think, good that *any* translation would work. Yet I did many out of love for the poem and fear that I might fail to select the best possible reading. There is a fine line between paraversing out of strength and weakness. Your translator does not know whether he does it because he is blessed with more imagination than most translators or cursed with worse judgment.

But, look at the titles. Only the last, which incorporates part of the poem in the title is needed. Yet, each creates a diferent and completely different mood. It just occurred to me that if I did not mind the waste of paper, I might reprint a single haiku every other page with a different title and a different explanation. I may just do just that some day on the world-wide web where the carbon footprint will be minimal.

vii

Stopping the Cry-Monster
in paraverse, a literally charming lullaby

天皇皇地皇皇・我家有個夜吠郎・過往君子念三遍・一家睡到大天亮
heaven-emperor-emp. earth-emp-emp // my house has one night howler // pass-go gentleman/men intone/wish three-times // one-house sleep reaches big sky bright

If Roland Barthes is right, the sandman would have a hell of a time in the Far East, where *"the eye is flat (that is its miracle), . . . it is the smooth slit in a smooth surface . . ."* He would have nowhere to pile his sand. It would slip right off. Then again, following Barthes, his services would not be needed – *"with so few morphological elements, the descent into sleep . . . remains an easy operation: without a fold of skin, the eye cannot 'grow heavy,' it merely traverses the measured degrees of a gradual unity, progressively assumed by the face: eyes lowered, eyes closed, eyes 'asleep' . . ."* (*Empire of Sounds* trans. Richard Howard).

Sad to say, neither sandman nor eyelid fold have a wit to do with falling asleep (All Chinese know *that* is caused by the Zzzz bug which crawls into your ear). The ease with which Japanese dozed off in the trains – Barthes' evidence – had more to do with long work-hours and starchy diets than anything else. Oscar Wilde had words for Barthes' exotic Japan/ese before the French savant was even born: *"there is no such country, there are no such people."* Ordinary Japanese had to be *"extraordinarily commonplace and have nothing curious or extra-ordinary about them."* The nursery rhyme we will play with treats an ordinary matter, sleep, more precisely, avoiding sleep-deprivation. The scene is not Japan. It is China. Baron Guido Vitale penned the first English translation+explanation:

> *Heaven is imperial! – The Earth is imperial! – I have at home a young gentleman who weeps during the night – Let all the gentlemen who go by read these words three times – and all the family will sleep till broad daylight.*
>
> This small rhyme is sung by mothers to get children [to fall] asleep and to break the evil charm which forces them to be awake. The Chinese paste [it] on the walls of the town and even in places of which no mention need be made, some words which, read three times, are thought to exert a very favourable influence on the events of the day as regards the reader . . . . . This spell is jokingly composed as if it were intended to be pasted on walls and not to be sung beside the cradle of babies.

Despite the (accidental?) rhymes, Vitale, an Italian, did not even *try* to make his translation scan *as a poem* in English, but he does a thorough job of explaining the original. Readers who would try their own hand at versifying had best *do it now,* before turning the page and seeing verses by I. T. Headland and the author.

天皇皇地皇皇・我家有個夜吠郎・過往君子念三遍・一家睡到大天亮
heaven-emperor-emp. earth-emp-emp // my house has one night howler // pass-go gentleman/men intone/wish three-times // one-house sleep reaches big sky bright

A LULLABY

The heaven is bright,
The earth is bright,
I have a baby who cries all night;
Let those who pass read what I write,
And they'll sleep all night,
Till broad daylight.

– I.T. Headland (*Chinese Mother Goose Rhymes:* 1903)

Vitale was not well-served by whoever advised him on English when he turned the wailing baby into a "weeping gentleman," but his translation does *end* properly, with a sleeping family. Why, then, does Headland, who read Vitale, put his *readers* to sleep? A *typo* is one possibility. While "we'll" is hard to misread as "they'll," it would be easier for a helpful proof-reader/typesetter to mis-correct the pronouns to match the person of "those who pass" than guess that strangers reading a verse would help its author sleep! In a later book on Chinese children, Headland provided background for some of the rhymes, but *Chinese Mother Goose Rhymes* was a typical nursery rhyme anthology with no prose other than a general foreword. Were the rhyme titled THE SPELL rather than A LULLABY, a proof-reader *might* have had a chance to ascertain what was what. As is, only someone who read the original or Vitale could have understood. But, Headland's book has no other typos that I can recall (a few mistranslations, but that is a different matter) and it is very rare for a book to have only one. So, there is a good chance the mistake is not a mistake but a paraverse, an alternative version of the original *deliberately* created. Why? First, Headland may have found such magic antithetical to his Christian sensibilities. He was, after all, a missionary in China. And, second, after testing out "we'll sleep" and finding it did not work, he may have felt it wiser to switch to more familiar rhetoric sure to amuse his audience. Perhaps, he took a hint from a fellow Parson who went by the name The Dean:

> I differ extremely from other writers, and shall be too proud if by all my labour I can have anyways contributed to the Repose of mankind, in times so turbulent and unquiet as these. Neither do I think such an employment so very alien from the office of a wit as some would suppose. For, among a very polite [civilized] nation in Greece, there were the same temples built and consecrated to Sleep and the Muses, between which two [sic] deities they believed the strictest friendship was established." (Jonathon Swift: *A Tale of the Tub*)

Possibly, but less likely, Headland found the couplets of Esther Lewis, who was born two years after Swift died and, stylewise, foreshadows the sassy asides of Byron, who was born a year before she died, in character.

天皇皇地皇皇・我家有個夜吠郎・過往君子念三遍・一家睡到大天亮
heaven-emperor-emp. earth-emp-emp // my house has one night howler // pass-go gentleman/men intone/wish three-times // one-house sleep reaches big sky bright

~~~~~~

> 'This for her poems may be said
> They're mighty good to lull the head;
> For nothing there piquant you'll find,
> To raise a laugh, or rouse the mind.
> No doctor's opiate can exceed 'em,
> Whene'er I want a nap I read 'em.'
>
> (From *"A Mirror for Detractors,"* a multi-stanza poem, including these stunningly witty lines giving what others say about her: *"Why, with men, as I've been told, / She'll paper conversation hold."* and *"I see no difference in the times, / The world's not mended by her rhymes."* In Roger Londsdale ed., *Eighteenth Century Women Poets*: 1990)

In other words, Headland might have fused a time-tested ploy, the author's self-deprecation, with a lullaby. True, the second half of Headland's translation does not flow logically from the first, but Chinese nursery rhymes, like ours, included nonsense – some created and some evolved – so who is to say that the disconnect poses a problem? But that particular nursery rhyme made sense to Chinese readers and I would like to see if it may be translated so as to make sense to English readers. Toward that end, I will offer eight translations of my own.

> *Lord above, Lord below – wherever You may be,*
> *A Cry-monster in our house is torturing the family!*
> *Won't you send a preacher, who knows how to pray*
> *So we can sleep in peace until the break of day!*

The original's repetition of Emperor twice after Heaven/sky and Earth is the first problem for a translator. Headland's *"The Heaven is bright, / The earth is bright"* may be a way to remove non-Christian religious elements, but it also seems to read 皇皇 or, *emperor-emperor,* as 煌煌, or *bright, bright*. In handwritten Japanese, such abbreviation is common, but I find it hard to believe that the thorough Vitale would have missed it. Not knowing Chinese, I can only guess that Headland seized upon such a possibility as an excuse to drop the deities for "bright-bright." If *my* Christianization bothers you, "bonze" may be substituted for "preacherman," but you will lose the alliteration. Either way, the sense is far from the original's appeal to *someone in the street* who would read the posted lullaby. My goal above was a verse that could be read alone.

> *Cry-monster, Cry-monster! We have a real beauty!*
> *She cries without stop; she thinks it her duty!*
> *Won't someone call a preacher to pray all night,*
> *That we may keep sleeping until broad daylight.*

天皇皇地皇皇・我家有個夜吠郎・過往君子念三遍・一家睡到大天亮
heaven-emperor-emp. earth-emp-emp // my house has one night-howler // pass-go gentleman/men intone/wish three-times // one-house sleep reaches big sky bright

Here, the preacher idea was reworked to make *his* duty clear while making the cry-monster's activity seem cuter (?) by calling crying *her* "duty." Another

> *God above and God below!*
> *The Cry-monster is killing us, you know!*
> *So, pray, fulfill this short request –*
> *that our house may with sleep be blest!*

This brings back the God/s and links the same with the prayer for help. That is a clever way to skim over the problem of a stranger reading a charm or a preacher out of his element.

We Have a Howler in Our House

> *Ye Gods above,*
> *   Ye Gods below!*
> *How loud he cries,*
> *   I'm sure you know!*
> *Pray, when you hear,*
> *   this stranger's voice,*
> *Let baby sleep,*
> *   and we'll rejoice.*

Here, the "cry-monster" has been replaced by "howler," a closer approximation of the original. Let me give a belated explanation of why I felt justified to use the former in my previous readings. First, I did not pull "cry-monster" 泣怪 from the air. It is a common Chinese idiom for babies that just won't stop crying. Second, though babies *do* howl or wail, English does not recognize it but "crier" would be too weak. Spelling out what was happening above allows the reader to guess what "howler" means and the setting in the "house" *sounds* right.

> *Master of all the Air,*
> *   Master of all the Land,*
> *A Cry-Monster is after us,*
> *   We pray you understand!*
> *Please heed the passerby*
> *   Who kindly reads my words*
> *And let our family sleep*
> *   until the singing of the birds*

>天皇皇地皇皇・我家有個夜吠郎・過往君子念三遍・一家睡到大天亮
>heaven-emperor-emp. earth-emp-emp // my house has one night-howler // pass-go gentleman/men intone/wish three-times // one-house sleep reaches big sky bright

If you feel *birds* are too much, here is a different ending: *Please heed the passerby / who reads my words tonight / And let our household sleep / until the broad daylight.* "Tonight" brings us back to the question of where the prayers were posted. Vitale mentioned walls and restrooms. Starfield adds that in some places they were on red paper and stuck on trees, in others, they were fastened to the road itself. If they could be read at night, we must imagine a well-lit location.

>*Air master, Earth master*
>>*Help us day and night to keep:*
>
>*The little howler in our house*
>>*Will not let us sleep a peep!*
>
>*A stranger and a gentleman*
>>*Had better read this rhyme*
>
>*So we can all remain in bed*
>>*Until the proper time.*

The original mentions no stranger; we take it for granted that a "passing" person is not an acquaintance – and fortune being fickle obviously would favor such – but it does specify a man of good upright character, or gentleman. That is important because the character of the petitioner has much to do with the success of a prayer. Even in Christianity, doesn't one saintly supplicant's prayers work more good than an entire churchfull of sinners? So, the double description is defensible, but I would like to tighten up for my last three readings.

>*God above and God below*
>>*We have a night-howler, so*
>
>*Please read this thrice, good passing sir*
>>*That none of us till dawn will stir!*

Obviously, the link between lines two and three is tenuous, but why should we worry about little things when the original is at odds with itself in a more basic way: *How can it be both instructions for a charm and the charm itself? Logically speaking, it cannot.* But, if it is sung as a lullaby, and helps a child fall asleep . . .

>**Calling Morpheus**
>
>*God in Heaven! God on Earth!*
>*We have a baby who's cried since birth.*
>*Won't someone take pity and repeat what I write*
>*So my family can get some sleep at night!*

天皇皇地皇皇・我家有個夜吠郎・過往君子念三遍・一家睡到大天亮
heaven-emperor-emp. earth-emp-emp // my house has one night-howler // pass-go gentleman/men intone/wish three-times // one-house sleep reaches big sky bright

I am happy with "cried since birth," for it suggests the baby has some problem a spell might help, but unsure about the "pity." Morpheus, Greek God of Dreams was the son of Hypnos the God of Sleep. He, not Hypnos is the original Sandman and the sand, well, let us just say it was not sand.

A Charming Request

Lords of the Land!
*   Lords of the Sky!*
Our house is home
*   To a little Sir Cry*
Pray, stop, upright man,
*   And three times recite*
That we shall at last
*   Know sleep tonight!*

A bold switch in order between land and sky gave birth to rhyming "little Sir Cry." Unlike Vitale's "weeping gentleman," it is clearly a baby. "Our house is home to" is sheer invention. It is not the sort of thing one would want a translator to do for, say, a scientific essay, but it is exactly what is needed to revive poetry or song in an exotic tongue. It was harder to settle between "thrice" and "three times." *Thrice* has a magical mood, while *three times* improves the echo of the previous line. This has all but the "broad daylight" (a translation so fitting for "big-sky-bright" that I was amazed Vitale came up with it, and fully understand why Headland borrowed it). It would have been easy to have rhymed it in above, but "~ at last / know ~" was more dramatic, so I went with it.

Spell or Counter-spell? and other Associations

Enough translations of *Little Sir Cry*. I am not confident *any* of mine beat Headland's, even if his was wrong. I have hardly begun to share the lullaby's *associations*, which fill about fifty pages of *thousands* of Chinese Mother Goose translations+thoughts (all scribbled in pencil) that will, after rewriting, become a large series of short books, if *any* of my other books *sell*, bringing me the wherewithal to settle, get married and raise a child to test my translations upon. Objectively speaking, that means unless the Goddess of Good Fortune owes up to her past mistakes, and brings me *my* due *soon* (at 58, I am a pauper and have not even seen a doctor in 5 years), the books will die with me. Anyway, here are some more highlights from those fifty pages that will probably never see the light of day.

> *The Nightmare is a noble beast,*
> *but dentists like her not the least . . .*
> *For thanks to her we save our teeth,*
> *by avoiding sweets before we sleep!*

I wrote this ditty after re-reading a 4 x 4 character Chinese rhyme introduced by my co-author of the Japanese version of Headland's *Chinese Mother Goose*, proving *Little Sir Cry* was not just a nursery rhyme, but an instance of *a type of poem* requesting a good man to read a charm to help the author: *"Heaven-lord -earth-lord / night-dream-un-lucky: / gentle-man-come-see, / change-be-good-recite."* To put Chinese nightmares in perspective, I must quote Japanese polymath Aramata Hiroshi (or his cartoon-book character):

> *If one holds the belief that there are only so many horrors floating around the nöosphere, we should be thankful to the (famously sweet-tooth) Chinese for graciously accepting more than their fair share.* (lost source, but translation is mine)

Nightmares in themselves are unpleasant, but, for a people who took dreams seriously, the fear must have survived waking; not surprisingly, the Chinese had many ways to cancel out or reverse bad dreams.

> *O Sleep, O Sleep, O thou beguiler, Sleep,*
> *Beguile this child, and in beguilement keep,*
> *Keep him three hours, and keep him moments three,*
> *Until I call, beguile this child for me.*   - Skelton (Lost Source.)

The above poem is rare. If charms seem natural in China, in the West, they bear the stigma of the supernatural. They remind us of witches and magicians and, *sleep spells,* in particular, were identified with burglars more than parents. So saying, *Little Sir Cry* was not a sleep spell in the sense that a baby was being beguiled. The idea was closer to exorcism. The charm was to remove whatever it was that made the baby cry, that turned it into a night-howler. What lullabies we did have relied more on tone than word (*Rock-a-by Baby*, with the cradle, *baby-and-all* falling(!), gives nursemaid or babysitter her revenge even as she tries to sing the cry-monster asleep). With the exception of Skelton's *O Sleep,* above, the few I know of addressing the problem, address the baby directly:

> *Sleep, baby, sleep,*
> *Thy father guards the sheep;*
> *Thy mother shakes the dreamland tree*
> *And from it fall sweet dreams for thee,*
> *Sleep, baby, sleep.*

This anonymous Mother Goose rhyme is brilliant. Not only do we get our homemade sleeping medicine, visions of sheep, but a tree I have found nowhere else. Now, a poem by a poet who was well-known a century ago yet seldom mentioned today. As we become familiar with Chinese poetry – or, if the current economic trends lead to interest in Chinese culture as it did for Japanese culture when Japan was "number one" – we might do well to note her style:

> *Lie a-bed*
> *Sleepy head,*
> *Shut up eyes, bo-peep;*
> *Till daybreak*
> *Never wake: –*
> *Baby, sleep.*

Christina Rossetti, with her poems about irresistably loveable babies, was the first to write nursery rhymes in English as sweet as those found in Chinese. This last poem in her *"Sing-Song"* enlists sheep by mentioning Bo-peep.

~~~~~~

♪ ***Headland's Foreword*** describes the Chinese as the world's premiere nursery rhyme superpower. That is not surprising as the Sinosphere was a paradise for little children compared to the Occident where parents were not generally as patient. I simplify. See chapter 3 of *Topsy-turvy 1585* (2004) for a more complete picture.

♪ ***Bad Dreams?*** Chinese also enlisted the aid of a fictional Tapir-like animal to gobble up Nightmares when the dreamer was asleep. See ch.13 of *The Fifth Season* (2007) for haiku examples of the same in Japan.

♪ ***Starfield is Hoshino***, a young Japanese man who translated the original Chinese in Headland's *Chinese Mother Goose* into Japanese and supplied some additional related poems and explanation, partly at my prompting. I wanted my general essay of each nursery rhyme and his explanatory notes to be treated equally but the publisher insisted on giving me the larger space and font as I was a fairly well-known writer. Today, Hoshino-san is a professional lute- (to be precise moon-lute, or biwa) maker. He has a website treating Chinese *Mother Goose* and goes by the aka CZ, or Charlie Zhang. Feeling somewhat guilty about being involved with a book about something I really did not know enough about, I over-compensated by eventually preparing a couple thousand notebook-pages of Chinese nursery poems + essay (mostly comparative anthropology). Were I wealthy enough to get a home, get married, stay put and become a parent, I would have done a series of *Chinese Mother Goose* poems before doing *Rise, Ye Sea Slugs!* and other haiku translations. Finishing a book of nursery poems equally charming for parent and child is among my top-hundred unfulfilled dreams. Come to think about it, my paraversing probably developed more over the course of playing with those nursery rhymes between 1996-8 than they did with Issa's haiku before that. Why? Because I could feel more at ease rhyming in an area of poetry where it was expected than one where it was suspect.

viii

From Journal to Haiku
◎ <u>haiku distilled from nature essays</u> ◎

wintering flies
is that star dust we see
on their wings?

Looking for a John Muir quotation in my so-called *daihyôsaku,* or "representative work" in Japanese, *Han-Nihonjinron* (anti-Japanology: *a touch of nature* 1984), I discoeved I was already playing with what would later develop into paraversing decades ago. I did this translating *into Japanese* to bring out the poetry in unedited passages from Thoreau's Journals. This passage was one:

> The flies are for a long time in a somnambulic state. They have too little energy or *vis vitae* to clean their wings or heads, which are covered with dust. They buzz and bump their heads against the windows two or three times a day, or lie on their backs in a trance, and that is all, – two or three short spurts. (1850 Nov. 8)

deep winter
flies walk in their sleep
on six legs

creeping slowly
winter flies . . . all hares
now tortoises

november fly
in your next life, perhaps
a tortoise?

wings so still
could my winter fly be
timothy tortoise?

winter flies
can now rub[pray w/] neither
hands nor feet

flies in winter
butt the window pane w/
little conviction

flies in the winter
some pretend to want out, some
lie on their backs

Four of these: the six-legs, improved by punning the Japanese expression for crawling on all fours, *yotsunbai,* into *mutsunbai,* "all sixes." The tortoise, but no hare, despite *Aesop's* being one of the first Occidental books translated into Japanese, and no Timothy, whom I just now added (If Annie Dillard can have a lost Polar expedition flow down Tinker Creek in a spring-thaw flood, can I not reincarnate Gilbert White's familiar charge?*). Speaking of which, the star-dust seen in the chapter-lead is also brand new for this book. The odd rub/beg refers to Issa's famous *fly-ku* (not anthropomorphic if rightly understood) with flies too weak to [appear to] rub/beg for mercy.

winter starts
house-flies race about
on all sixes

the winter flies
too listless to launder
their own wings

Does the "race about" and focus on the wings, generally clean from being used, help bring back my paraversed Thoreau into his native tongue? In Japanese, I had the fly too tired to launder because *doing laundry* in Japanese also means playing when the cats are out. I cannot substitute a *bird,* for birds are generally out. Maybe:

the fly-swatter out
of sight and mind, winter flies
behave themselves

the fly-swatter
no longer needed: flies
in the winter

when the last
fly-swatter is lost, the flies
finally behave

no flyswatter
i blow warm air on the fly
to make it fly

I only learned to warm up bugs with my breath a couple years later, again reading Dillard, who did it for a butterfly. In Japanese, I did not wander offtrack like this adding my own poems as I had a clear aim: to put Thoreau into a form that might help Japanese to feel his closeness to the natural world by selecting, distilling, or rather, abbreviating his prose. Still, there was a point I failed to pick up on because, at the time, I had not yet read enough haiku. And that is Thoreau's finest observation, one which sets his passage apart to others. It is where he specifies *two or three short spurts* of energy, "and that is all." A Japanese woman (now a well-known translator) who translated the literary passages for me did not care for my haiku and I thought it was because she felt haiku had to well-up naturally from the poet and making it from another's prose was ridiculously artificial, but now I think my lack of awareness partly to blame for her negative response.

my winter flies
try the windows, two, maybe
three times a day

That may not seem like much, but it tells us a world about Thoreau and his wintering in. No clever school boy or girl or adult intent on writing a haiku could ever come up with it. You will find plenty of numbers in good haiku, for close observers cannot help but take the measure of time and space.

> The fly is entangled in a web and struggles vainly to escape, but there is no spider to secure him; the corner of the pane is a deserted camp. (ibid)

winter's come *a winter fly*
a spider no longer here *struggling to escape*
catches a fly *an empty web*

prisoner of
a spider's deserted gaol
my winter fly

It is too much trouble trying to locate other passages I played with in the Japanese book, because I did not bother to date them (in Japan, there are many books for intellectual readers that do not try to pass for dissertations). So this will be all of the Thoreau from *Han-Nihonjinron*. At the time I wrote the book (about 1980), I did not yet have Thoreau's *Journals*. The passages came from selections made by others. Once I bought my own Thoreau, I quickly – within a half-year – read through the *Journals* and found enough facets to the man to divide the best passages into five Thoreaus, each of 200 pages. I am not sure if I can manage to pass off my *Surreal* Thoreau, *Phenomenological* Thoreau, *Symbolic* Thoreau, *Social* Thoreau and *Ecologist* Thoreau as different people as the biographies of a single man imagined by Jorge Luis Borges, but I want to try. And I will not reread Thoreau until I am ready to complete those five books – which will be when I can afford to hire someone to scan in the pages – so I can read and edit it at the same time, thus making good use of my time. Meanwhile, I would love to see others haiku Thoreau. A number of people belonging to a book or haiku club might try to compose a *Mount Merrimac, Walden, or Cape Cod in One Hundred Ku*. Or, considering the fact that Thoreau already did some distilling (it's called editing) for those books – more in last two than the first – instead work on his *Journal* entries (much of which may be found on line). If the results merit it, I would be happy to add the best to a future edition of this book. And it need not be Thoreau. Birdman Burrough, Mountainman Muir, Holistic Hudson (W.H. of Green Mansion fame's essays in Argentina and England) or even grumpy – and often rightfully so – Mrs. Trollop on the tree-stumped landscape of America . . . Or, you could try something modern:

> The mockingbird that nests each year in the front-yard spruce strikes up his chant in high places, and one of those high places is my chimney. When he sings there, the hollow chimney acts as a sound box . . . He sings a phrase and repeats it exactly; then he sings another and repeats that, then another. – Annie Dillard (*A Pilgrim at Tinker's Creek* ch.7 Spring)

mockingbird sings *a new song*
present after present flows *of the mockingbird a new*
from my chimney *song of the*

The mockingbird's invention is limitless; he strews newness about as casually as a god. He is tireless, too; toward June he will begin his daily marathon at two in the morning and scarcely pause for breath until eleven at night. I don't know when he sleeps. (ibid)

*strewing about
newness: this god called
a mockingbird*

*mr mockingbird
most of the time he only
mocks himself*

*the mockingbird
sleeps three hours if he does not
sing in his sleep*

When I lose interest in a given bird, I try to renew it by looking at the bird in either of two ways. I imagine neutrinos passing through its feathers and into its heart and lungs, or I reverse its evolution and imagine it as a lizard . . . (ibid)

*changing birds
into lizards i would hold
my attention*

You may read *A Pilgrim at Tinker's Creek* for a detailed transformation. Personally, I have never lost interest in a mockingbird. They may lose interest in me, but me, them? Never. Even silent, they astound. I can waste hours watching them jumping sideways like lemur when engaged in courtship duels on the ground, or alternating between helicopter and acrobatic biplane mode in the air (often, one plays helocopter over the head of a large blackbird, while its mate fix-wings in from the side). The males do indeed possess vocal chords of steel. They will sing as long as the sun or moon shine. But, as far as the lizard link goes, I have a different bird in mind:

*those pelicans
why do i feel a dynosaur
looks at me?*

*look a pelican
in the eye and you will see
a million years*

*diving pelicans
each splash leaves a crater
on the moon*

*pelican fly by
ten stories high: and i
think of shale*

*pelicans: how
can birds so old fly by
in formation?*

Pelicans have perfectly good bird-brains, but their eyes do not show it. They are strangely distant and, to me, seem to lag their hearts by millions of years. Maybe it is because they are not clear and alert like the song-birds, but I see them as dyno-saurian. I do not know how this can be, or if anyone else feels the same.

I have not done enough distillation+paraversing to confidently sum up the pros and cons of taking on *good* vs. *bad* prose or poetry, other than saying that, for me, it is easier to work with *bad* originals. I might have done more of it here were not the bulk of my library back in Japan. With Annie Dillard or Josephine Johnson's (pg. __) prose, and even some of Thoreau's *Journal*, the poetry is already there. I find myself *selecting* rather than distilling and, then paraversing wildly to create something inspired by yet completely unlike the original. I think this is because when I sense my words do not improve something, I quickly move from the real to the surreal to distance myself from the source. But, this can not be done unless you have something of your own to contribute. Dillard's mockingbird did not just morph into a pelican. Those pelicans had roosted in my head for decades. Somewhere in a scrapbag of haiku, if it survives, I have a *ku* about the day the pelicans turned my mom's condominium into Burgess shale or some other wall of strata (how depressing to juxtapose stories of a condominium tottering on the edge of the sea with natural formations where each layer represents an ice-age or an eon!); and I think that when I first read Annie Dillard in the mid-1980's standing up in a bookstore in Tokyo (Japanese have a word for it, *tachiyomi*) – every once in a while glimpsing to the back cover at her young and ferociously intent face – that I recalled my old feelings about the pelicans then. *Hah!* I said to myself, *Why bring up dynosaurs with a mockingbird? Save that for the pelican, Annie Dillard. What happens if you run into one in another book and you've already used up your dynosaur transformation? What then!* And, later, in an early 90's visit back home, the daily fly-by had me imagining pelican squadrons against the moon back when months were shorter and it was so near you would think you saw it through a close-eye lens. I cannot recall if those thoughts were ever fixed in paper. Probably not. So, what I would seem to be doing when I paraverse is to push off from another's mind, while pulling from my own. New ideas are created in the process. Those "craters" are fresh. They only date back to 30 minutes ago.

Found Haiku & Waka

Another way to play with good writing is to try to find poems without changing a thing. I can spy two good nature books as I write. *Let me grab them.* I see no lines that haiku well in my favorite, William Bebe's *Nonsuch: Land of Water* (1932) – if Tennyson found a world in a wild flower, Bebe found our globe, the earth, at its genesis, in a Halicystis (a grape-sized single cell the equivalent of "a fifty-foot dog, or a hundred-foot man"). John Baker's *The Peregrine* (1967) is not quite so sublime, but there *are* lines I marked for haiku (17-syllabet/7-8 beat) and *waka* (31-syllabet/12-14 beat) in the 1990's. Here are two:

(october)

a hawk's kill
like the warm embers
of a dying fire

The chapter is *October*. With Japanese haiku, the seasonal element should be imbedded in the *ku,* and those *ku* without it are supposed to be few and far between. With that fire, Japanese might take it for a winter haiku, but I suppose awareness of warm and cold does come to us anew every fall, so, who knows!

(november)

their melancholy
plover voices thread down
through the rain

the sorrowing beauty
of *ultima thule*

I did make two small changes, removing "is" between *kill* and *like* in the first and *threaded* => *thread* in the second. *Waka* do not require a season, though they are sometimes organized by them. However, this *waka* not only holds a season but, to my mind, has to be what it is, a November (or early December) poem, though *ultima thule* points toward the winter solstice.

blue sky
nothing but blue sky
all day long

Sorry for the jump. Yes, that is Willie Nelson and I cannot read the words without hearing his voice! (Nat King Cole, you say? Him, too, but didn't Willie *write* it? Not that it matters, for only Willie can sing happy songs that never sound inane, so if you ask me, he owns them). And, my point is that we need not limit our hunting to nature essays. True, the best collection of found poems – no, the only collection of found poemsI have seen – a small book with well-parsed snippets of Dorothy Wordsworth's prose, concerns nature, and so does the one example from Willie above, but that is just because *my* interest lies there. Yours may well lie elsewhere. And it may well be that the form of the poem we look for differs according to the subject. While word-lovers today are still freer to indulge in their creativity with respect to collective nouns thanks to the Lipton's *Exaltation of Larks,* the venereal game as a game only lasted a decade or so. Considering the variety of subject matter and forms possible for distillation and paraversing, if some major magazines and newspapers were to host ongoing contests, I cannot imagine it *ever* coming to an end.

ix

Nineteen Ways to Kill a Poem in Translation

< 鹿 柴 >

空 但 返 復
山 聞 景 照
不 人 入 青
見 語 探 苔
人 響 林 上

As noted in the introduction, I was not smitten by *Nineteen Ways*. The writing was fine, but the translations, "by scholars of high order" (D. Hofstadter), mediocre, and the ideas insufficient. Finding it again in a two-page note at the back of *Le Ton beau de Marot*, I decided I, too, would nonetheless give it a few pages in the woods with the dolphin. I had *not* noticed or forgotten that Eliot Weinberger's comments about the translations were, to quote Hofstadter, *"often nasty sarcastic and condescending."* Perhaps, that was because I *agreed* with most of them, or because I read the book almost 20 years ago, when I understood less Chinese and Japanese than I do now. Before preceding, I will give the book a once-over and see if it really was *that* rude. But first let us see a gloss of the 1200 year-old original, the vertical lines of which, while lost, presumably started from the right. I rendered them from the *left*, because that is how Chinese characters look best. Once, two or three thousand years ago, they were so written and, someday, perhaps they will be again.

      [title] deer - brushwood/enclosure/park

empty/unoccupied - mountain/wilderness/hill/s - not - see - human/men
just/but - hear - human/men - speak/conversation/word/s - echo/sound
return - light/shine/shadow/scene - enters - deep - woods/forest
re - shine/glow - green/blue/light[hue] - moss - up/on/upon/rise/climb

The hyphens separate the characters per line in the original: five. The slashes indicate alternatives. Details aside, my character-by-character gloss of the poem, part of a 20-poem landscape series, and E.W.'s differ in only two ways. 1) He includes "black" as a possible color. While 青 can be *dark* in contrast to a brightly illuminated light surface or in a shadowy way, the color, ranging from pale-blue to dark green is hardly "black." 2) He also does not consider "up/on/upon" as a verb, "rise," though he has a postscript citing an essay by Peter A. Boodberg that argues just that and Octavio Paz's translation with it (*asciende*).

Rereading, I see DH does not exaggerate! I must have been so impressed with the short and sweet preface that starts "Poetry is that which is worth translating" that I did not notice the nastiness. Moreover, from what he writes, he *was* baited. He received Boodberg's 1½ page *Philology in Translation-Land* from a Mexican professor who accused him of "crimes against Chinese poetry," and Boodberg, on his part, was "devoted to excoriating, in idio-syncratic language, all other translators and scholars of Wang Wei for failing to realize that the last word of the poem, shang . . . had an alternative meaning in the Tang Dynasty: *to rise."* But anger is no excuse for E.W. failing to explain what gave rise to Boodberg's conclusion, namely, that *rhyme gave him reason to expect a different pronunciation of the character* 上 *that had that meaning.* There is *shang* and there is *shang* – Boodberg has different diacritical marks over each "a" giving each a different *tone.* Though *tone* is a layer of rhyme English speakers do not even dream of when reading Chinese poetry in translation, it was, perhaps the most important layer for the Chinese, so E.W. might have investigated further. Instead, he quoted Boodberg's philologically correct but admittedly funny-looking *rendition* (Boodberg did not pretend it was a poem) and chortles, *"To me this sounds like Gerald Manley Hopkins on LSD."* Yet, he did not loose the opportunity to celebrate the poetic eye of his co-author Octavio Paz, that "divined this forgotten meaning and translated the word as *asciende*" for his last, and definitely best, version of the poem (in his *Further Comments* just before the postscript). Let us see some of the translations (deparsed) and EW's comments:

> **Dear-Park Hermitage**   *There seems to be no one on the empty mountain . . .   / And yet I think I hear a voice, / Where sunlight, entering a grove, / Shines back to me from the green moss.* – Witter Bynner and Kiang Kang-hu 1929

Witter Bynner was, according to E.W., "a primary purveyor of Chiniserie translation in English." *Purveyer* is a nasty word. But, *how* so?

> Where Wang is specific, Brynner's Wang seems to be watching the world through a haze of opium reflected in a hundred thimbles of wine. It is a world where no statement can be made without a pregnant, sensitive, world-weary ellipsis.

His proof for this charge? "The *I* even hears a voice where the sunlight shines back to him from the moss." What Weinberger overlooks is the fact that the original – at least as a single poem – is a bit *lacking* without the rising light Boodberg deduced and Paz invented. To imagine the poet hearing or thinking he heard a voice *at the same time* he saw the moss glow in the sun, is to imagine a poet intent upon the world. If Brynner's Wang is high, it would be on caffeine from his tea. Alert, not hazy! Moreover, Wang himself was not *specific*. He is *sketchy*, for Chinese is sketchy.

> Jenyns and other translators come from a tradition where the notion of verifying a poetic image would be silly, where the word "poetic" itself is synonymous with "dreamy. . . . Jenyns . . . was so far

> removed from the poem's experience that he found it necessary to add the following footnote to line 2: "The woods are so thick that woodcutters and herdsmen are hidden."

E.W.'s general complaint is largely correct, though I would caution late-20c know-it-alls that they will find more close observation of nature in the early 20c than they imagine, and that altered states of consciousness induced by dreaminess or drink do not necessarily clash with verification (Weren't Coleridge and De Quincey, notorious on both counts, critical and precise when it came to describing nature?); but E.W. provides not a word of justification for savaging the footnote. I suspect it is wrong not because of the reason(?) given by Weinberger but because the "empty mountain" phrase was asociated with late-fall, when absence of all trace of humans was deemed particularly lonesome.

> Chen and Bullock make some familiar "improvements" : the first-person narrator, the lonely mountain . . .

A Chinese verb, like Japanese verbs, can be active without a pronoun. To choose a person is no more an artificial "improvement" than using the passive, something EW does *not* criticize. Neither does he notice that "empty mountain" or even "empty hills" (Burton Watson) do not have the associations in English that they do in Chinese, so "empty" is as far from the original as "lonely" is. Octavio Paz does well to empty the *empty* from both of his translations, which start off, "you don't see people on this mountain / people are not seen on this mountain." (Why my double Englishing? Because passive is the normal way for Spanish to describe seeing, while it sounds stiff in English.)

> Watson retains Wang's parallelism effortlessly enough (no one / someone) yet he is the first translator to do so.

Burton Watson (1971), following Soame Jennyns (1944), avoided person and passive with: "no one in sight," and followed it with *"only the sound of someone talking."* Now, *I* must be critical because EW is lavish with praise and only praise for Watson. First, I would point out that had someone less illustrious than Watson written of "someone talking," E.W. would probably have pounced upon him, writing something like this: *"Does the translator imagine a madman walking around the woods talking to himself? Wang is not so specific . . ."* Unfortunately, the parallelism itself does not have the snap it does in Chinese because the second line is too long and almost as dull as Watson's last two lines, which are painfully prosaic everyday English ("late sunlight enters the deep wood, / shining over the green moss again"). They do not even rhyme. But rhyme, it seems, is of no interest to EW. That, despite the only decent *poem* translation in his book, the last one, with that ascending light, the second by his collaborator Octavio Paz (in his Afterword), *is* rhymed (aabb rather than abab as in the original)! So, we have one imperfectly framed parallelism to match a poem with maybe a dozen or so (if we include tonal rhymes), and EW is *elated?*

Here, I find myself sympathetic to the first-man of form-firstism, Douglas Hofstadter, who wrote:

> What astounded me about all of these versions . . . is that not a single translator tried what to me seemed to be the totally obvious thing to do: namely, to create an English poem consisting of four lines of five words each." (*Le Ton beau de Marot*)

When I introduced the Cry Monster (ch 7), I failed to note that, I, together with a young Japanese scholar of Chinese, translated into Japanese and essayed I.T. Headland's *Chinese Mother Goose Rhymes*.[1] Some of those were perfect rectangles and I recall noting which characters were different and which were changed in one rhyme of four six-character lines saying that a good child does not try to capture a butterfly, though it may alight nearby, and checking the result against the *I Ching*. Sure enough, the pattern counseled the same thing as the rhyme, though it was not specific to butterflies. (I would give it to you right here, but my book is either in a box in my mother's closet or a casualty of moving). Be that as it may, rectangular poems are indeed *delightful* both for making internal similarities and differences obvious at a glance and for the clean elegance of the overall geometric pattern. And, as D.H. points out, a square poem is fitting, for it contains square characters. I first made perfectly squared-off lines for a *Chinese Mother Goose* rhyme I translated into Japanese that was published in 1984* (that was discovered by a student of Chinese who peddled full-speed for three or maybe it was six miles to show it to his friend, the young scholar who eventually asked me to help with the aforementioned book). But I have never tried a word-for-character translation. After all, many characters are not words but only half-a-word. DH did it for the *Deer Park*, but the results were not much to read so we will skip them. That is not to say, I have done much better, even with fewer restrictions:

deer park retreat

a hollar home to none
but, hark, i hear men
in forest dark the sun
kindles moss again!

in this empty wood,
hearing voices i see
sun to moss restore
its green and leave!

As Burgess wrote *about* his Purple Cow, "Yes, I wrote it *but* . . . . ." Please do *not* quote these. They have no soul. I feel I have too little command of Chinese to take on a serious poem (nursery rhymes are another story) without more information. E.W. does mention Deer Park was a location, like, say, Deer Grove, in Illinois – I'll go one better: *"Deer Park Man Breaks 33-year-old Texas Tarpon Record"* – and that it might allude to "the Deer Park in Sarnath, where Gautama Buddha preached his first sermon." That is helpful. But, unless I missed something, he neglects to supply information about the vantage point of the protagonist. I favor the hermitage idea found in the titles of some translations, for Chinese loved naming places so much that not only a poet's cottage but, if the poet was in a big house, his *study*, generally had a name (placard and all, over the window!). In that case, the mountain has only one clear mark of human presence and it is the poet's cottage. Deer Park/Enclosure/Brush was first written on a landscape painting, later lost. But it was probably discussed and what I want to know is:

Did it include one hut or not? If E.W. had time to explain that one poem's title, *Li Ch'ai* was incorrect – "something like *Beer Park*" – he should have had time for other things that matter. One last square not to quote:

> in woods so wild men
> only cross voices now
> and then – rays of sun
> light the moss and rise
> again the day is done

Another example would be his taking issue with a French translation for titling the poem *Le Fôret* (the forest). I agree it *is* a lousy title; but not because it generalizes. It is because "forest" is already in his translation, so it adds nothing. What E.W. should have told his readers is that "mountain" in Chinese (or Japanese) had, and still has, the connotations "wilderness" or "nature" have in English today – hence "forest" makes some sense – as "desert" did to the classical world and to Europe, where a "deserted mountain" would have meant the same thing as Wang's "empty mountain, i.e., one where human presence was not felt, only a few centuries ago, with one important difference: Europeans had a more negative attitude about such places. E.W.'s unstated assumption that the poet was as truly nature-oriented and objective as the modern haiku poet (here, I use a stereotype I do not fully buy for the sake of argument) is itself naive.

> i
> see
> no men
> on this mountain
> only hear their voices
> while long shadows steal
> through the forest and
> moss glows green
> ascending in the
> light of the
> setting
> sun
> o

Don't bother to criticize my readings, only printed here for the form; I do not pretend to have translated Wang's poem. As far as I can tell, only Octavio Paz has done that. It is not just the ascending light (by no means certain); it is that we feel the mind of the poet in: " . . . *luz poniente / alumbra el musgo y, verde, asciende.*" How so? As Paz wrote explaining his less interesting earlier translation, "*this is nature poetry, but a Buddhist nature poetry.*" To the religious Buddhist – and, in his last years, the poet was said to be deeply religious – the setting sun held all the promise the rising sun holds for Christians, at least on Easter morning. *The light was not just light.* It was, to use the words of one of ours, Jonathon Edwards, "a shadow of the divine."

> "Snyder's explanation [for "*Again shining / on the green moss, above.*" (1978)] is only one moment, the latest, when the poem suddenly transforms before our eyes. Wang's 20 characters remain the same, but the poem continues in a state of restless change." (Ibid)

A *rising* translation is not the only way to raise ones eyes. I would have expected Snyder, a woodsman, to have responded to E.W.'s query by citing his own experience, but he humbly asked and credited his Chinese teacher and Japanese wife for the insight. Evidently some readers of *Nineteen Ways* needed *more* explanation of Snyder's explanation – "illuminating some moss *up in the trees.* (NOT ON ROCKS)" – for I came across the following by an enthusiastic reader of a 2006 book of Chinese poetry by the Santa Fe poet Arthur Sze, "You see, their book *Nineteen Ways* is 19 different translations of "Deer Park," and only Snyder gets that the moss is hanging from a tree, not on a rock. Sze gets it too!" Sze's version, "shines again on green moss, above," may be beholden to Snyder, but the moss in question is not "hanging" – no Spanish moss in China that I know of – but found growing high up trunks and on branches (as well as below), because mountain-side forests are moist, and the sun can indeed peek up Silva's skirt if she is up high enough.

> Changing the passive *is heard* to the imperative "hear" is particularly beautiful, and not incorrect: it creates an exact moment, which is now.

This response to Snyder's "*Yet — hear — /*" is correct. I would only add that I would not be surprised if Snyder echoes Göethe in this.[3] E.W.'s response to the truncated line's continuation, "human sounds and echoes" waxes more enthusiastic yet:

> Giving us both meanings, sounds and echoes, . . . is like most sensible ideas, revolutionary. Translators *always* assume that only one reading of a foreign word or phrase may be presented, despite the fact that perfect correspondence is rare. [my italics]

Always should be "usually." Working as a translation checker, I found double words were not that rare in Japanese translated from English prose. The bigger problem was that translators rarely reduced two English words to a single Japanese one, even when a word with both connotations was available. It is the bigger problem because books tend to grow in translation. Without effort to do what the other language cannot do, the result is bound to bore. Now, *I* exaggerate. Some translators write so beautifully they can get away with it. Octavio Paz's translation, with its poly-syllabic vocabulary is far longer than Wang Wei's, but his Latin liquidity is beautiful *in its own way*. Unfortunately, that could not be said about the other 19 versions.

~~~~~~

To my way of thinking, Weinberger, like most of the translators he featured, was working with a handicap. Like all too many moderns, he failed to appreciate rhyme. He did not come out and say that, but he did. Take his romanization, for example. It is done, by his choice, "from modern Chinese." Here it is minus the plethora of diacritical marks which are only of use for those who can probably read it without them.

> Kong shan bu jian ren
> Dan wen ren yu xiang
> Fan j/ying ru shen lin
> Fu zhao qing tai shang

While I do not know Chinese, I know the Japanese pronunciation of the last words of each line: jin-kyô-rin-jô. Those pronunciations come from old Chinese. This does not mean they are exactly what was. But chances are that the change in the pronunciation was uniform and the original was a crisp ABAB rhyme. Had I written a book about an ancient poem, I think I would have tried to get an educated guess on the pronunciation. If that is, sound mattered to me . . . Instead, we get this,

> Chinese has the least number of sounds of any major language. . . a Chinese monosyllabic word (and often the written character) is comprehensible only in the context of the phrase. . . For poetry, this means that rhyme is inevitable . . . But translators often rush in where wise men never tread, and often may be seen attempting to nurture Chinese rhyme patterns in the hostile environment of a Western language. (from EW's introduction to *Nineteen Ways*)

Rhyme is a way to give lines snap – if Pound did not always need to rhyme, it was because his lines snapped, crackled and popped with energy – but EW *never* criticised a translator for *not* rhyming, for he follows the modern poet's party line which counsels against rhyming because 1) The original is not rhymed, or 2) The original is rhymed. For a finely nuanced, devasting critique of the contemporary tendency to find *any excuse not to rhyme*, see the last three pages of the Introduction to *Songs from Xanadu*. Here, is Professor J.I. Crump's telling crescendo:

> It strikes me that the real reason these translators used no rhyme is that they did not want to be bothered with the added difficulties. Then why not tell us so instead of positing dubious universal truths? Certainly no one would think any less of them for doing *their* work in the manner *they* prefer.

Perhaps, I should add, for EW and others who think like him that Japanese has as few sounds as Chinese (less if the tones are counted), and, with its ubiquituous homophones, has even been identified with "a culture of puns," yet, it is nonetheless famous for NOT end-rhyming. It does, however, have internal rhyme, as noted previously, and I have responded to that by trying to rhyme two of three lines of my haiku translations, but not so clearly as to turn the short poem into a jingle. Had EW attacked me for rhyming Japanese (which I often do) he might have had at least one leg to stand on, but to see translators rhyming originally rhymed Chinese as renegades is perverse. And, did I say the translation by the shining light of *Nineteen Ways*, Octavio Paz, did rhyme?

I apologize to readers for not providing the full text to the translated poems. I did not mean to be coy. It is just that *Nineteen Ways of Looking at Wang Wei* is so tiny a book that I had to be careful not to borrow too much of it. Besides, unlike my work (what I have written in English has ten times more *pages* than readers), EW's book is in *hundreds*, possibly *thousands* of libraries, so finding it and the texts should be easy. But if you are serious about Chinese poetry, you might better try Professor Crump's books, which supply the original in the margins, or check out the enormous *Sunflower Splendor*, with six hundred pages of great variety, unfortunately separated from the originals, which are in a separate book, rare and hard to find. My favorite poem in the latter, which I think infinitely more interesting than *Deer Park*, even in Octavio Paz's illluminating translation, is 韓愈 Han Yü's 盆池五首, which Kenneth O Hanson translates as *"The Pond in a Bowl, Five Poems."* The original five poems, which seem more like stanzas, are each four 7-character lines (the first line:老翁眞個似童児) rhyming AABA. This is Hanson's translation for the first poem/stanza of the sequence:

In old age   *Throughout the night*
I'm back   *frogs croaked*
to childhood pleasures.   *till it dawned,*

A bowl in the ground   *As they did*
Just add water —   *when I fished*
it's a pond!   *as a child in Feng-k'ou*

The italics and double column (to keep them together on this page) are mine, but that is nothing compared to the extremely creative reformating. Note that each line of the original is parsed into three, creating what looks like four haiku for each poem of the five! Thinking it seemed a bit too much, and wanting rhyme if at all possible, *I* tried to make a short four-line AABA translation, but like Hanson's twelve-liners better. A translation may look right for being formally close to the orginal, but if it reads poorly, it is worthless. With translation, the proof is always in the pudding. I wish I could have paraversed it, for then I could have shown you the whole thing – especially the fourth stanza where Han Yü chews out the frogs for quarreling like married couples – without fear of copyright. But Hanson has another I could, with help of the Chinese, do something with. So here is the whole thing, his translation first:

Don't shoo the morning flies away	朝蠅不須驅 morning fly/ies not need chase
Nor swat the mosquitoes in the evening.	暮蚊不可拍 dusk mosquito/es not can slap
Between the two, they fill the world.	蠅蚊滿八区 mosquitoes flies fill 8 districts
So many, should you fight them all?	可盡興相格 can exhaust [emphatic] other?
And yet, how short a time they live.	得時能幾時 gain time active howmuch time?
While they last, give in and let them bite you.	興汝恣啖咋 [emph] you freely suck ?
October, and a cold wind wipes them out.	涼風九月至 cool wind ninthmonth reaches
You don't remember then they ever were.	掃不見蹤跡 sweep not see trail trace

Compare the original and the translation. It is a good example of how much more flesh English needs than the more telegraphic Chinese. Still it is what amounts to a prose poem, rather than a poem poem. Here are two off-the-cuff tries to keep the form, perhaps we should call it *translation ala Hofstadter:*

IGNORE ALL THE FLIES AT DAWN,	CHASE NOT FLIES IN THE SUNLIGHT
SWAT NOT MOSQUITOS AT DUSK!	& KILL NOT MOSQUITOES AT NIGHT.
TOGETHER THEY FILL THE WORLD:	B'TWEEN THE 2, THEY FILL THE EARTH;
WHO ARE YOU TO TAKE THEM ON?	ONLY A FOOL WOULD TRY TO FIGHT.
HOW SHORT THEIR ALOTTED SPAN !	LITTLE TIME THEY HAVE TO STAY:
LET THEM SUCK U WHILE THEY CAN:	WHY NOT GIVE 'EM BLOOD TODAY?
COME NOVEMBER'S CHILLY WINDS	'TWILL BE AS IF THEY NEVER WERE
GONE LIKE THEY HAD NEVER BEEN.	WHEN PLUTO BLOWS 'EM ALL AWAY!

The Chinese has 40 characters, including a few equivalent to our punctuation marks. My short translation has 45 words, the long one 51. Hanson's has 60. I trust that I need not point out my paraverses many faults! It is hard to squeeze English into neat squares. Because the Chinese Luni-solar Calendar wanders about a month, either *October* or *November* is fine, but my *Pluto* is over the line. I considered Bruno for Arctic winds, but thought the God of the underground sounded better though the cultural disconnect is greater. The Chinese provided in the separate copy of *Sunshine Splendor* is in two lines, with parse marks showing each divided in four lines, but no indication if the original was 8 lines in a row or 4+4, so I compromised with a 3-point increase in space between lines 4 and 5.

Did Han Yü really care that much for the mosquitoes? I doubt it. Perhaps he occasionally felt for them. Buddhists and wine-drinkers do sometime. But, the poem is largely logic-driven. It is soft philosophy. Had my awareness that Chinese probably included more and more diverse metaphysical poems – which is to say intellectual light-verse – than English come early enough in my life to make mastering Chinese worthwhile, and if I had pull at the *New Yorker*, I would gather hundreds of those poems and, each week, provide a word-for-word gloss (including all relevant connotations and other polisemy) of just one poem, challenging readers to turn that into something interesting in English. It takes much time, skill and luck to do a good translation of any poem and, it makes sense to borrow the heads of thousands of readers. The sketchiness of Chinese poetry allows contestants to be themselves, and the abundance of brief poems (& aphorisms, etc.) fortunate, for a detailed gloss for anything long would be no fun to prepare or to read. I have no doubt the result would be stunning and give all of us far more joy than what passes for the humor page at the end.

Non satis est pulchra esse poemata, dulcia sunto - *Ars Poetica*

It is not enough that poetry is agreeable, it should also be interesting.

'Tis not enough that poetry be pretty, it should also be sweet

It is not enough for poetry to be beautiful, it should have a heart.

Beauty in poetry is but the start; we want a heart.

It is not enough for a poem to be beautiful, it should be good.

We are not satisfied with beauty in a poem, we want to be touched.

(The first translation was on the world wide web. The others are my instant paraverses.)

That *dulcia*, or "sweetness/interest," is not always obvious, for the heart unlike the face must be opened before it can be read. The question to be asked while reading *Deer Park*, or any poem is *where is its heart?* As a translator, I have come to assume the original has a heart, for we seldom find what we do not anticipate. The clever thing to tell readers would be *it lies in you;* the truthful thing would be *if it has one, you may find it somewhere between the poem, the translator and whatever you have come to know and feel.* The odd thing is that, despite decades of experience as a professional reader (book scout and translation checker), the heart often alludes me until paraversing drops it right in my lap.

Headland's *Chinese Mother Goose* translation. I was going to say we translated the "entire" book, into Japanese, but a nursery rhyme about a blind man who fell into a pond feeding the frogs was deleted by the publisher for fear of being assailed for discrimination against the visually impaired. Indeed, the very word "blind" (*mekura*) was deemed a problem.

My First Square Translation from Chinese was of a dandelion song in I.T. Headland's *Chinese Mother Goose Rhymes* and it was in Japanese rather than English:

タンポポさん　てんまでとぶ
タンポポさん　つちにころぶ
タンポポさん　あたましろい
タンポポさん　こっちにこい

Which means *"dandelion-sir heaven-'til flies / dandelion-sir earth on tumbles dandelion-sir head's white dandelion-sir here come!"* The original Chinese was 6-7-7-7 and had a bit more information which Headland turned into: *"Thistle-seed, thistle-seed, / Fly away, fly, The hair on your body will take you up high; Let the wind whirl you / Around and around, / You'll not hurt yourself / When you fall to the ground."* and I did not English, but will now, as

dandy old dandy-lion, look at your white hair,
hair above & hair below flying through the air
blown up, blown away, blown to kingdom come
if you ever come back down, i bet you are bare!

The Chinese lies in-between, with neither safe-landings nor denuded manes, but that is neither here nor there, my main intent was to show Japanese readers what end-rhyme was and you may find the book somewhere if you look for it. It was in *Omoshiro hikaku bunka kô* published in 1984, and republished in mass market pocketbook as *Eigo wa Konna ni Nippongo* in 1989. Shortly later, I was approached to help do a Japanese version. Perhaps, I should add that I have not encountered anyone else trying to match Chinese form in Japanese.

A Dozen or so Chinese-format translations may be found in my recent *Mad In Translation* (2009).

Shadows of the Divine. The Usanian theologian Jonathon Edwards (1703-58), like many 18c European theologians, combined or excused his interest in natural history with religion by finding deeper significance in various natural phenomena. "Shadow" used to mean "reflection" or "image."

X

Cherry Blossom Epiphany
◎ 740 pages of composite translation ◎

骸骨の上を粧ふて花見かな　鬼貫
gaikotsu no ue o yosoute hanami kana   onitsura
skeleton-upon[obj] dress/adorned/ing, blossom-viewing!/'tis

dressing up
my old bones
the hanami

our skeletons 　　　　　　　　　　　　　　　*all those bones*
well dressed, off we go 　　　　　　　　*decked in robes of silk*
blossom-viewing 　　　　　　　　　　　　*blossom-viewing*

our skeletons
dressed to a "T"
the hanami

This is one of the best-known *hanami*, *i.e.* (cherry) blossom-viewing haiku. It boasts countless translations. The Japanese can be read in the first-person, or *any* person. Such ambiguity is not unknown to English, for the pronoun "you" can be singular, plural, the other, or any person, including the poet; but due to an accident of language elaborated in my book *Orientalism & Occidentalism*, Japanese rarely uses pronouns and, with no conjugation for number as well, allows us to enjoy delightfully person-free poetry impossible in English. As we are not concerned about what a particular "you" refers to, Japanese are not aware of that ambiguity *until they see it in translation* and wonder at the aptness of this or that choice. In a longer narrative, such apparent ambiguity rarely offers choices of interpretation, for context decides. With short poems that lack a determining context, there is no way to tell for sure the person of the subject. As a rule of thumb, haiku is first-person and *senryû* third-person, but I have read far too many haiku with no subject that obviously fit other persons to religiously obey the "rule" in translation. Moreover, the ambiguity that permits multiple readings is precisely what allows the Japanese haiku to be so full of meaning. This poses an interesting problem for philosophical linguistics as it is generally argued that the more possibilities ruled out the more something means; yet, here, we find that the opposite is also true. Style-wise, ambiguity permits a *ku* to be at once a simple personal observation *and* a generality (the latter of which causes some Japanese critics to detest this *ku*).

phantom/s of the hanami

my old bones 　　　　　　　　　　　　　　*blossom-viewing*
dressed up enjoying 　　　　　　　　　*a million skeletons*
the blossoms 　　　　　　　　　　　　　　*dressed to kill*

111

This use of the turn-of-the-century Usanian slang "to kill" (meaning gorgeously here) is obviously not suited for the translation of any haiku that does not itself use slang (some do, but this one did not), but I will leave it and other such fun for I think more readers will enjoy it than not. (2007)

The title *"phantoms of the hanami,"* nods to my book's title: *Cherry Blossom Epiphany*, from the Greek, *Epiphanie*, or "apparition." *Hanami* means blossom-viewing. Halfway through the 740 pg book, I returned to Onitsura's *ku*, placing it at the head of a chapter on *Death in the Bloomshade* (*bloomshade* being my neologism for *hananokage*) and added three more readings:

骸骨の上を粧ふて花見かな 鬼貫
gaikotsu no ue o yosôte hanami kana onitsura
skeleton/s-on-top-of costumed blossom-viewing!/?/'tis

my skeleton
plumped in pretty silk
views blossoms

blossom-viewing
costumes without belie
the bones within

bones, old bones
dressed up like the trees
blossom-viewing

B. H. Chamberlain: *"Oh! flower-gazers, who have decked / The surface of their skeletons!"* Miyamori Asataro, until Blyth the leading haiku translator, wrote, *"Their skeletons / Wrapt in richest silks, / The people are viewing cherry bloom,"* and snorted: "This verse, although very famous, seems to be of little value." The editor of a book of famous *ku* (名句辞典), is harder yet on Onitsura, claiming it is just an application of the Buddhist platitude of men as flesh and skin on bones, where beauty is an illusion. "Not only is this shallow rationalizing (*rikutsuppoi*), but the example used is banal (*chinpu*)." *Bullshit*. The *ku* deserves its fame. The blossom-viewing experience makes us feel our mortality even more strongly than we do in the fall, facing colored leaves; and *who says Onitsura did not experience what he wrote*, did not suddenly *see* skeletons in drag viewing cherry blossoms? We should not forget that many cherry trees have no leaves when they bloom, so we view what are, literally, skeletons bedecked. Note that the original is subtle, as may be surmised from the word-by-word rendition. With scores of previous translations, by others and mine at the start of the book, I felt free to play with the last ones.

~~~~~~

けふもまたさくら／＼の噂かな 一茶
kyô mo mata sakura sakura no uwasa kana issa -1827
today again/too cherry cherry's rumor/gossip/news!/?/'tis

today, again:
sakura sakura grinds
the rumor mill

today, again
talk of the cherries
is in the air

today, again
cherry blossoms are on
all of our lips

Issa plays on a folk-song phrase *sakura sakura* to depict the cherry is on everyone's lips. The rumors probably concern cherries soon to bloom, so I include it with *Waiting-for-the-bloom ku*, of which it is by far the best. *Why is it best?* Because it is light on the ear and cool. I mean, real-ly, do men await the bloom of a tree with bated breath as most of the other olde haiku might have us believe? Issa conveys that interest in a believable manner.

~~~~~~

風吹けば尾細うなるや犬櫻　芭蕉
kaze fukeba obosônaru ya inuzakura　bashô 1654-94
wind blow/n when tail[branch-ends]-thin-become/s!/?/: dog-cherry

facing the wind   *after the gale*
it cowers thin of tail   *what a scraggly tailed*
a dog cherry   *dog cherry!*

when it blows
i feel weak and thin of tail
dog cherry me

The Japanese prefix "*inu*=dog~" combines aspects of our denigrating "horse~" or "crab~" (chestnut, apple) and the more neutral modifier "wild." This *sakura* or "cherry" is not a cherry proper but a "bird cherry" (*P. grayana*) or "cherry laurel" (*P. spinulosa*). It has small flowers little resembling cherry, strung out on thin stems (panicles) liable to break in a strong wind. The flowers diminish in size and have shorter stems at the end. An early *waka* features what might be a one-day flower arrangement or thin tail of a poor cur of a dog-cherry "out in the country" so emaciated it draws no viewers (*yamakage ni yasesaraboeru inuzakura ohibana tarete hiku hito mo naku* anon. 散木寄歌集 1128). Draw (*hiku*) also suggests the leash it does not have, and the *boeru* part of *yasesara-boeru* ("wasting away of thinness") puns as "howl." Bashô's "Tail-thin-become" is idiom for fleeing with one's tail between one's legs and petering-out in a pitiful manner. Unlike my translation, Bashô's *ku* pretends to be zoo-morphic by extending the metaphorical name into an allegory while remaining perfectly natural. Note that it is *stereo*: the image of a maltreated dog with a piteously thin tail, hanging down between its legs, *and* an objective description. Young Bashô writes in the nominalistic Teimon style (playing with the tree for its canine name), but the *caesura* (*ya*) before the dog-cherry allows for the third, self-referential [ergo deeper], reading, too. A generation earlier, Shigeyori wrote:

犬櫻風をばおどす聲も哉　重頼　犬子
inuzakura kaze o ba odosu koe mo gana　shigeyori 1633
dog-cherry wind [emphatic] threaten/scare-off voice [desired/oh, for~]

the dog cherry
if its bark could only
scare the wind!

The "bark" pun only works in English. For once, the translation clearly beats the original! If the bark was effective, watch-dog-cherries could be planted around a grove of blossoming cherry. Another early *ku* rhetorically questions: *"Haven't you leaves=teeth? / Bite the wind, bite it! / Dog* cherry! (*ha wa nai ka kaze o kame kame inuzakura* shôichi 1642). Here, the translator must put *his* tail between his legs, for Englishing the leaf=tooth (*ha*) homophone is hopeless. The dog-cherry, unlike the more valued cherry, had leaves mixed with its bloom, justifying the teeth pun provide.

~~~~~~

すなをなる空になりてやはつ櫻　紫白女 -1719
sunao naru sora/kû ni narite ya hatsuzakura　shihakujo
meek/frank/open-is-sky-become! first cherry/blossom

be as simple
and open as the sky!
first blossoms

ready for cherry　　　　　　　　　　　　　*cherry spring*

be sincere　　　　　　　　　　　　　*when the sky*
and empty of self!　　　　　　　　　　　　*becomes plain blue:*
first-blossoms　　　　　　　　　　　　*first blossoms*

wileless this
clear sky for today's
first blossoms

Sunao describes the mindset Japanese are supposed to hold before their superiors. It is the opposite of *questioning* or *cynical*. The original "sky/empty" is ambiguous. The latter *kû* is a Buddhist concept of nothingness that is beyond good and evil. My last reading assumes a *sunao* sky would be one without much action (few if any clouds, and those relatively still), for old Chinese and Japanese poems about *devious* clouds may have been on the poet's mind.

~~~~~~

人ことの身の何なれやはるのはな　宗祇-1502
hito goto no mi no nan nare ya haru no hana　sôgi
people-each's body/self's what is!/: spring's blossoms

tell me what
is this thing called self
among flowers

what the hell　　　　　　　　　　　　　*what the hell*
is a self or a body!　　　　　　　　　　*are separate bodies*
spring blossoms　　　　　　　　　　　　*in cherry time!*

spring blossoms
have we our own bodies?
have we selves?

How odd this *ku* is not famous! It seems to express something similar to Issa's none-are-strangers *ku* on a more esoteric level though "spring's blossoms/ flowers" suggests it is not about the cherry alone. Forgive my "hell." English has no grammar to make "what is" *emphatic* as it is in the original and lacks an equivalent to *mi*, meaning both "body" and "self."

Issa's famous *ku* about the familiarity of all men under the bloom is treated *at length* as an example of double-negative all-inclusive rhetoric, so I do not include it here. Sôgi's strangely modern *ku* is a challenge because of the *mi,* elsewhere explained as literally "body," but figuratively meaning *oneself.* One reason for four readings here was the problem mentioned above: lack of equivalent words. The other is that *I love Sôgi* and want to make his contribution to meaningful haiku hundreds of years before Bashô, who also loved him, better known. I have no idea which of my translations will strike the reader who might be in the position to help bring Sôgi more attention, so I hunt with scatter-shot.

~~~~~~

何くれと浮世をぬすむ花の陰　鬼貫
nani kure to ukiyo o nusumu hana no kage onitsura 1660-1738
what['s this] "please"! floating-world+obj steal blossom-shade

all's fair in love, war and blossom-viewing?

don't *ask* for it,
take your fair share of
the bloomshade!

what's this "please!"
under the bloom you *steal* your
place in the world

Is this advice to someone too shy to barge his way into a lightly populated bloomshade? The wealthy have retainers go early and obtain space which is staked out and guarded until they appear. For others, it is not so easy. The poor could not get away with "stealing" space.

The title I just added is not in the original *ku* or my book, while the "floating world" is in the original *ku* but not the translations, as it means this *world of woe,* yet *also* has some connotations of what might be called *the cool lifestyle.*

~~~~~~

花に来てはや欲ばるや居所　梅室
hana ni kite haya yokobaru ya iridokoro baishitsu 1768-1852
blossoms-to coming already desire/covet/want! be/sit/stay-place

*to see blossoms
is to desire to be
among them*

*as soon as i see
cherry blossoms, i'd be
here with them*

*as soon as you
reach the bloom you crave
your own spot*

*as soon as you
arrive, you want a place:
the bloomshade*

The original is vague to say the least. There is no English word for "being-place" or, *a place one is*, so I had to be inventive. If you compare the above to the translations in the book, you will notice some changes. It took a while to come up with loose readings for "being-place," such as "among/with them."

115

うかれ立人遣り過し遅ざくら 素丸
ukaretatsu hito yarisugoshi osozakura somaru 1712-95
floating/excited-leave/ing person/people let-pass[by], late-cherry

the excitable
crowd is motioned by:
slow cherries

letting all with
ants in their pants go by,
the late-cherry

Somaru's ku has two compound-verbs: *ukare-tatsu* = rushing out of the house in an excited frame of mind, exhilarated from being in love or whatever; and, *yari-sugoshi* = letting others pass one by and go ahead. The original *ku* lets the link between human behavior and plant nature remain vague.

騒しき世をおし祓て遅桜 一茶
sawagashiki yo o oshiharatte osozakura issa -1827
tumultous/agitated world[obj] push-banish/sweep-away late-cherry

pushing aside
the tumultous world
a late-cherry

While D. Lanoue's *"the cure for / this raucous world . . . / late cherry blossoms"* is a fine paraverse, I am too stuck on the active verb in the original to let it go. Makoto Ueda is yet more active, bringing out the exorcistic nuance of *haratte* as Issa wrote it = 祓: *"pacifying / this clamorous world / late cherry blossoms"* (*Dew On the Grass*). His Issa humorously makes the tree *"into a god that has pacified all the clamor."* To me, the late-cherry is a miracle, a stone holding solid in the rapids. Issa's rhetorical question to faster, i.e. normal blossoms (*"What is wanting that you rush to fall?"*) suggests he favored a way of life slower than that of fast-paced Edo. The trees back in the mountains of his Shinano – a place-name he punned as "do-nothing" – bloomed as late as the "Trees-do-nothing" Fifth-month, i.e., mid-summer! (*miyama ki no shinano satsuki mo sakura kana*). Another Issa *ku* gives what may be the late-cherry's active attributes:

信濃・短夜をさっさと開く桜かな 一茶 希杖本
shinano // *mijikayo o sassa to hiraku sakura kana* issa -1827
(short-night/s [+obj] quickly[mimesis] open/bloom cherry/ies!/'tis/are)

shinano

short nights
cherry buds opening
lickety-split

our cherry trees
make short work of bloom
summer nights

rushing to bloom
in the short night
shinano *sakura!*

the night short
cherry blossoms make haste
one by one

I borrowed the "rushing to bloom" (which I wished I had written first) from DL. Note that Issa also had grasses blossoming one after another, dewdrops hastening to cover leaves, and amazingly complexly crafted wild-flowers created in the short night. The brief time to do such "work" (Issa saw a world of work) is half of it and the mood created by the contrast of such activity with the slow pace of the hot days the other. Were Issa's *ku* not titled "Shinano," I might have thought it a Spring *ku* and played it, say: *"Shortening nights: / Who can get any shut-eye / they bloom so fast!"*

山姥の遊びのこして遅櫻　蕪村
yamanba no asobi nokoshite osozakura buson 1715-83
(mountain-aunt/hag/witch's play/freedom leaving/remaining late-cherry)

the mountain hag
left them for her last dance
these late cherries

the mountain hag
did her dance and left us
these late cherries

late cherries
the mountain witch still
plays around

the mountain hag
has some play in her yet
a late cherry

the old witches
still have a place to go
late-cherries

The mountain hag . . . is a Sinosphere construct, a demon woman, or witch, who wanders about begging (rewards/curses doled out to all she meets: standard folklore stuff). Buson plays with a popular song that had her migrating from cherry to cherry but the *ku* may also be read to mean the late-cherry is not only her handiwork but her personification. Like the *ubazakura* (ch 7 [grandma, or babushka cherry]), she was old but sexy. . . . .

行春の逡巡として遅櫻　蕪村
yuku haru no shunjun to shite osozakura buson
(departing-spring's hesitantly being/acting, late-cherry)

(my trans)

she hesitates
while leaving: the spring's
a late cherry

the spring
hesitates while leaving
late cherry

(blyth trans)

departing spring
hesitates
in the late cherry blossoms

(hass trans)

(behn trans)

the end of spring
lingers
in the cherry blossoms

spring is almost gone
so now this silly old tree
decides to bloom!

(combined)

    departing
    spring lingers
    late cherry

~~~~~~

花も幾世春をくらさん遅櫻　宗祇
hana mo iku yo haru okurasan osozakura　sôgi 1420-1502
(blossom/s, too, how-many[countless]-ages/reigns spring delay-would/try late-cherry)

floral alchemy

late-cherries, too
how many generations tried
to slow the spring

would blossoms, too　　　　　　　　　so flowers, too
forever keep their spring,　　　　　have e'er tried to hold spring?
  my late cherries?　　　　　　　　　late-cherries!

over generations

how much spring
have you flowers saved,
my late cherries?

The "too" alludes to our, human desire to stay youthful. The first reading is a beat too long in the middle, yet, even with a title, cannot quite translate the entire original. It misses the general *blossoms*, of which the late-cherry is the example. The second reading catches them, but turns the generations into a vague extension of spring. The third needs no comment. The last recalls the great artic explorer Steffansson's remarks about the *"years of happy belief in Santa"* saved by his helping import reindeer to fool children.

春しはし抱て居たり遅櫻　　一黛 堅並
haru shibashi idakite itari osozakura　ichiyo ( )
(spring a-while embraces/sleeps[with] stays late-cherry)

i'd just keep
embracing spring a while
a late cherry

late cherries　　　　　　　　　　　the late cherry
they would embrace spring　　　　would stay a spell longer
  a while longer　　　　　　　　　　in spring's bed.

not yet ready
to let go of her spring
the late cherry

Daku means "hug" and "embrace." Since people in Japan have never embraced each other as a greeting, it has far more erotic connotations than in English. Hence, my "bed." I am not sure how to pronoun the poet. *He, she, we, they,* . . . The last translation sidesteps the problem.

夕ざくらけふも昔に成にけり 一茶
yûzakura kyô mo mukashi ni narinikeri issa -1827
(evening-cherry today, too, past/ancient-time-into become[+fin.])

twilight blossoms
today is already once
upon a time

blossom dusk
today, too, is long ago
and far away

dusk blossoms
suddenly everything
is long ago

For a beautiful depiction (*". . . lanterns glimmering here and there, the trees no longer trees but blossoms suspended in the air above us and around us . . ."*) and gushy metaphysical commentary (*". . this feeling of time is intensified . . ."*), see Blyth (*Haiku* Spring vol: pgs 617-618) who translated Issa's ku as *"Evening cherry-blossoms: / Today also now belongs / to the past."* His "belongs to" is a fine creative translation. Voices seem to come from a distant place, not this one. After a long day drinking under the bloom without sunglasses, something changes. Keigu has his own memory of a magical evening where, as Buson put it, *"Days lengthen / until we are way back / in the past"* (See IPOOH: Spring I).

花さくや目を縫れたる鳥の鳴 一茶
hana saku ya me wo nuwaretaru tori no naku issa
(blossoms bloom:/! eyes[obj] sewn bird/s cries/cry/singing)

cherry blossoms –
chickens with eyes stitched shut
are clucking

trans. lanoue

♪ ♪ ♪ ♪

cherries bloom:
a bird with sewn-up eyes
sings and sings

David G. Lanoue writes: *"Jean Cholley notes that in the poultry market in the Muromachi district of Edo (today's Tokyo), the eyes of the doomed birds were sewn shut to keep them immobile while being fattened in their cages"* (Cholley, Jean. *En village de miséreux: Choix de poèmes de Kobayashi Issa.* Paris: Gallimard, 1996.) in his *Simply Haiku* article "Master Bashô, Master Buson ... and Then There's Issa" (Autumn 2005). Checking Issa's *Journal*, I see an editor's note to the effect that the eyes were sewn shut *on birds used as decoys.* My reading is based on yet another cruel practice, that of sewing a bird's eyes shut to make it stay put and sing more. . . .

A multiplicity of explanations calls for the same with translations. If a chicken is involved, a "bird" would not do, for English does not call chickens *birds* any more than it calls humans *animals,* though we know they are, and we are.

たのしみよ胡蝶も花に一勢　有貞女 玉藻
tanoshimi yo kochô mo hana ni hito-ikioi　yûteijo 1774
(pleasure [it is]! butterflies, too, blossoms-to one-power/force)

cherry blossoms

what a joy
the butterflies also
out in force!

this is pleasure!
the butterflies also
coming in waves

blossom-viewing
what fun to find crowds
of butterflies, too

The suggestion of collective energy in *ikioi* (power/force) is perfect for describing an assault of butterflies. Watch enough butterflies up close and you will find some so full of nervous energy – even twitching! – they are *spooky*. If only the word "butterfly" were not so damn long, blossoms might have fit into the first two readings. The *"too/also"* is what makes the poem.

~~~~~~

彼岸とて慈悲に折らする花も哉　重頼 犬子 維舟等
higan tote jihi ni orasuru hana mogana　shigeyori 1601-1680
(equinox/paramita-as/because mercy-for break-let blossom wish-for)

breaking her would be
a blessing: how i long for
an equinox cherry!

equinox cherry

oh, for a flower
that even i could take
for mercy's sake

equinox cherry

oh, for a flower
who would give herself
out of mercy

equinox cherry

for mercy's sake,
won't anyone break off
a blossom for me!

The Equinox in Japan is the Enlightenment, that is, the time to celebrate the translation from our wretched bank of the proverbial river (or sea) to the other shore, the *higan*, which is homophonic with 悲願 a sad plea, i.e. a prayer for the sake of mercy, and includes the connotation of a cherished goal. The poet plays with all of this and more, for a song 謡曲＜田村＞ mentions "the merciful blossom/s of spring" (大慈大悲の春の花). By the common law of synchronicity (no Jung needed in Japan!), dying in that period (like a blossom's life, seven-days) made it easier to know Nirvana, so this *ku* can be seen as both a plea on the behalf of the poet and a rationalization of the act of breaking a bough as mercy for the blossoms. The poet's wish is practical in one sense, for there was and still is a cherry variety called Higan-zakura. Blyth's translation (*"It is the spring equinox; / The compassion of Buddha / Allows us to break the flowering branches" History of Haiku*) and explanation that, on this day, "The Buddha is merciful enough to let us break the Buddhist law together with the branches, for the sake of beauty" overlooks something: the *mogana*, a classical emphatic signifying *desire for something* (usually a member of the opposite sex) that one lacks and is not likely to get, i.e., wishful thinking, and, with it, the poet's chuckle. Perhaps, I should add that in his *History of Haiku*, Blyth gives over a page to Shigeyori (also called Isshû), but only includes one of his *ku* in *Haiku*. I feel Shigeyori deserves better; but, for all of his love for zany, or should I say, Zeny nonsense, Blyth followed the Japanese lead and shortchanged the playful Teimon school in favor of conventional Bashôism.

~~~~~~

ちるはなの中にたちたる此身かな　成美
chiru hana no naka ni tachitaru kono mi kana   seibi -1816
(falling blossoms among standing-is this body/self!/?/'tis)

blossoms fall standing among them by god, it's me!		blossoms falling who stands amid them? *c'est moi*, seibi

among the blossoms
falling, something stands:
it is this poet

Since neither "this body" nor "myself" worked for *kono mi*, we get "this poet" and *c'est moi*, both perhaps more affected than the original. Something draws me toward Seibi's *ku*. The "by god" in the first reading sounds right, though it is Occidental. Again, *English has a problem:* it needs religion – the big G or the big D or variations there of – to emote.

新古今集 *Shinkokinshû* (1205) poem #131
~~~~~~

山たかみ岩根の櫻散る時はあまの羽ごろも撫づるとぞ見る　崇徳院御歌
yama takami iwane no sakura chiru toki wa ama no hagoromo nazuru to zo miru   shûtoku-in   skks

when petals fall from the rocky heights of the mountains *i see down rubbed off the wings of angels*	*when petals float down from rocky heights in the mountains* *i can see it: those wings of angels brushing earth*	*when petals fall from the rocky heights of the mountains* *i almost see them brush the wings of angels*

What an extraordinary *waka!* Only the middle reading is correct, though the others would be as good a guess as any if you did not know, as I did not know, that "the rub/stroke/brush of heavenly feather-robes" alludes to something happening slowly, *"longer than the time required to wear down boulders covering forty square leagues brushed once every century by an angel's wing."* [More on kalpa in Mad In Translation]. Are petals from mountain cherries fluttering down very slowly because of the heat rising from the ground?

~~~~~~

窓の雪にさきつく花の光哉　紹巴　大発句帳
mado no yuki ni sakitsugu hana no hikari kana   jôha 1523-1602
(window-snow-in blooming-link/continue blossom-light/shine!/'tis)

the well-read cherry   *enough to read by*   *a scholar's spring*

what fine light   how they glow!   illuminating
from blossoms opening to   my cherry blossoms succeed   indeed! blossoms born
window snow!   the window snow   of window snow

The proverbial Chinese scholar studying by moonlight, magnified by snow piled by his window, inspired millennia of bookworms. The first reading assumes a budding branch newly blooms in a window, which snow piled up outside to reflect sunlight hatched (?). The central reading imagines a tree outside in the moonlight and captures the idea of a succession from snowshine to bloomglow better than the others. Illuminating / indeed: bloom follows / window snow! The third reading puts the glow inside the scholar. Buson (-1783) would later exchange the snow for the leading Chinese tree blossom, in Harold Stewart's translation (*A Chime of Windbells*) *"The pear-tree blossoming in the moonlit night, / A lady reads her letter by its light"* (*nashi no hana tsuki ni fumi yomu onna ari.*).

~~~~~~

花の木の持て生たあいそ哉　一茶
hana no ki no motte-umareta aiso kana   issa 1822
(blossom-tree's having-born[natural] amiability!/?/'tis)

blossom smiles

is friendliness   oh yes, they are
something blooming trees   born to be charmers!
are born with?   cherry trees

my cherry tree
in bloom: natural
amiability

born to bloom   *free blossoms*

cherry trees   what charm
so sweetly natured   is born with every
by nature!   cherry tree!

This is *sympathetic* rather than *pathetic* fallacy, and I liked the *ku* so much I introduced it twice, giving it six readings split into two clusters of three translations in the book. Here I combined them.   Some of the commentary:

Who knows if Issa is praising trees, reflecting on women or fondly recalling his dead daughter Sato. A couple years later, after his wife, Kiku, dies and he remarries, Issa recycles the *ku* with a small change: *amiability* became *good fortune* (*aisô* =>*kahô*). It is on a card he gave to his new bride's relatives. In Ueda's words, "The tree in the *hokku* must stand for Yuki who the poet thought looked as beautiful as cherry blossoms." *Perhaps*. But the marriage only lasted about as long as a tree blooms. So there is some *woman-as-tree* [a chapter in the book] in Issa. Be that as it may, Lafcadio Hearn, wondering what could make Japanese cherry blossoms so dazzling and luscious, draws out the *tree-as-woman* metaphor:

> Is it that the trees have been so long domesticated and caressed by man in this land of the gods, that they have acquired souls, and strive to show their gratitude, like women loved, by making themselves more beautiful for man's sake? Assuredly, they have mastered men's hearts by their loveliness, like beautiful slaves. (*Glimpses of Unfamiliar Japan*: 1894)

As I may have already pointed out elsewhere, cats, not women, make themselves beautiful (by plentiful grooming) when they are *loved;* women do so when they *love*. Hearn's "slave" is not a felicitous metaphor, but, that aside, he does bring out a kernel of truth in Lowell's contrast, for no Japanese writer would lay on their anthropomorphizing with such aplomb.

* Hearn partly follows Percival Lowell who described the way people celebrated plants' birthdays rather than humans' and how blossoms drew vast crowds of admirers despite the lack of "a social loadstone," i.e., a personality in *The Soul of the Far East* (1888).

~~~~~~

いや／＼ん芝居やふりの遅桜　末祐　犬子
iya iyan shibaiyaburi no osozakura　matsuyû 1633
(no, no-ooh! play [drama] breaking [ending] late-cherry)

boo-hoo, spring's over!

our play-house
is finally emptied by
the late-cherry

auld lang syne　　　　　　　　　　　　　　　*that ends well*

oh no, noooo!　　　　　　　　　　　　the curtain closer
blossom-viewing's over:　　　　　　we applaud with wet eyes:
the late-cherry　　　　　　　　　　　　the late-cherry

Shibai-yaburi, literally "play-buster," is an act intended to get the audience to leave the playhouse, or the last act, usually the best, called that because, after it finishes, people leave. In Japan, where plays could go on all day – different play acts leapfrogging one another! – dozing off was probably common and called for a grand and loud finale. The ambiguous *iya iyan* is a translator's nightmare. A shout of approbation used by the play-goer, close to *Iya iya*, literally *"No! No!"* but *also* a coy put-off *and* something yelped by women nearing orgasm. The "~n" gives a plaintive tail to the begrudging *hurrahs* and suggests a largely female audience, also the case for late-cherry-viewing! *Bravo!* or *"The last hurrah: / The late cherry brings / down the curtain!"* would be too buoyant. My initial reading was a fine mistranslation: *"Late cherry / no more of that "No!" / "No-ooh!" act!"*

xi
Ghost Crabs & Man-o-war
◎ how to make long poems good and short ◎

I have never written a how-to and I am not going to start, but if you have not tried to make good short poems out of bad or mediocre long ones, you may learn something from this chapter. If nothing else, you will begin to read poetry differently and *seek what is good in other's poems* rather than simply saying *"yuck!"* and turning your head on the basis of your overall impression.

Sand Crabs

> *Sand crabs skittering*
> *sideways over wet hot beach*
> *into unseen holes*
> *spitting round bubbles*
> *as they watch me watching them*

This, from *Braille Me – A Beyond Seeing Experience,* by Jean Poos Brady, came to my attention because it was published by my mother's Grapetree Productions. 5-7-5-5-7 syllables, it aims at a *tanka's* 5-7-5-7-7, or another Japanese form, as proven by a missing "the." As a whole, it does not work for me. How about –

ghost crabs,	*boiling over*
spitting bubbles, watch me	*ghost crabs watch me*
watching them	*watching them*

The descriptive "sand" is dropped for the correct name for this crab that foams from the mouth when confronted by curious people, as it adds to the mood. Needless to say, crabs walk sideways – *crab-walking* (蟹の横這い) is idiomatic in Japanese – and if anyone can blow square bubbles I want to know! But, my distillations, while good as are, miss things. The "wet hot" has me puzzled. The gulfstream, shallow water near the beach and color of the sand create warmth, but the dry sand, even if it is lighter in color, is hotter yet except in the winter when the wet sand is warm but never *hot*. About all I can do with the puzzling heat is this (on the left):

ghost crab, do	*watching crabs*
you boil over? where is	*blowing bubbles i think*
your cool hole?	*about their holes*

Which brings up the "unseen holes" (on the right) and the temporal element they bring, also missing from my distillation. I imagine the poet as nearsighted, for growing up on the beach with good eyes for every distance, the holes were always "seen." What was comparitively rare was to watch a crab come out of its hole. Like the moon, a crab is hard to catch coming out – unless you stake out a likely hole or walk down the beach peeking at and into every one, taking care not to cast a shadow on them as you do so – but easy to spot zipping into them. The last time I was on a beach (over a year ago), I left gifts from the sea by the entrance of the holes walking one way and, on the way back, saw some of them had been investigated. If I had a camera, I would have photographed each hole first, for the variety of ways a crab will toss out and/or bundle-up the sand is amazing. If I had the thousands of lives I desire, one would be spent entirely on the investigation of patterns of sand around crab-holes (I can be a bore, but I can never be bored and find it hard to understand how most people have to think up things to do, or if they are writers, to write). Anyway, if you do not stick with that crab, the minute you look away, it will be gone, not because you loose it like the skylark when you blink but because its little stalk-eyes notice the instant you stop stalking it – it would not help for avoiding animals that sniff-out prey, but the waking crab's nemesis is the hungry bird (at night, I imagine the racoon and rat – if there are such beach rats – would come for them).

the ghost crab
after you foam over
where are you?

unseen holes
of the ghost crabs i see
bubbling over

So far, I have more or less followed Jean Poos Brady's lead. But let me add some purely from my own recollections – I am sure I have a dozen or two ghost crab haiku, but my haiku are in a bag of scraps or scattered through hundreds of books, whatever I had with me at the time, which is to say they are as good as lost, so it is far easier to t try to remember and write afresh:

the ghost crab
foams and i imagine it
is really mad

ah, ghost crab
i'm afraid your bubbles
backfire on me

I suppose that when a crab starts to foam from the mouth it is preparing for flight, unless I misread and it is really pumping up its testesterone like a tail-wagging cat or gecko, but my gut reaction is, *uh, oh, keep away from its claws! It is mad!* And, I must confess that I deliberately harassed ghost crabs – got between the crab and its holes or lightly poked it, etc. – in order to see it do that. (But if I were to make an objective guess, I would bet the foam has some acrid or otherwise off-putting quality, but who knows?)

stuffing a cork
into a crab-hole new year
at high tide

Walking on the beach, I found a champaigne cork and stuffed it deeply into a crab hole. I *imagined* it popping up as soon as enough water filled the hole and wrote a haiku about it which may or may not be better than the above.

Warriors

> *Man-o-war strewn like*
> *blue balloons across the sand,*
> *tentacles like string –*
> *deadly poison sting –*
> *how deceptive their beauty.*

Again, a 5-7-5-5-7 syllable poem by Jean Poos Brady. The best word here, after the name, Man-o-war, is the "strewn." For what other living creature is *strewn*? A jellyfish might be, but its tentacles are not red like those of the Portuguese Man-o-war and tend to shrivel up, so they are comparitively less strewsome.

> *dark red strings*
> *on purple-fringed blue balloons*
> *why portuguese?*

> *the man-o-war*   *man-o-wars*
> *corpses on a beach-head* *strewn across the sand*
> *booby-trapped*   *shades of 1588*

> *man-o-war*
> *who says that beauty*
> *is deceptive?*

> *man-o-war*   *man-o-war*
> *i take it your beauty*   *dangerous if you don't*
> *is a warning!*   *know beauty*

> *man-o-war*
> *dying on the beach who*
> *can hate you?*

Am I too pushy? The poet, despite her advanced age and background in behavioral science, takes a childish perspective. My thoughts on bright color cannot help being informed by biology. While my personal bent in poetry shies away from description, I would like to see some Portuguese man-o-war, blue balloon with sunset gradation purple frills and reddish purple tentacles reproduced as *giant floats*, with symbiotic fish hanging from the tentacles to liven up the surprisingly poor parades of Miami. Speaking of color,

> *gallantry lies*   *dead gallantry*
> *dead on the beach: portuguese*   *litters the beach: beware*
> *man-o-war*   *the man-o-war*

I almost forgot to deal with the "Warrior" title of the original. When you see the bodies on beaches in WWII, you see khaki, khaki, khaki. It is not about camaflogue, either. Every side in that War bought into the Great Sartorial

Renunciation (Pflugel), whereby manliness was defined as being dully dressed, every man keeping his individuality hidden, every man proud to be a nondescript corporate slave, a sign of his more highly developed social sense compared to women who, protected, and lacking social shame, could afford to indulge their idiosyncracies. We no longer explain it that way, but even today, women have much more choice than men in the Occident. Once, when soldiers, especially mercanaries, dressed like peacocks, this was not true. A battlefield would be covered with colored silk and pretty ribbons. And, since only a confident man would dare flaunt his expensive silks – which he neatly slashed to show off his sharp blade, add frills to the decoration, and keep cool on marches and in battle – this sartorial lifestyle was called *gallantry*. When the Portuguese on their man-o-wars ruled the sea, the man-o-war would have fit right in.

I will end this short chapter of shortened poems with my version of *Me*, which, like each of the other poems in *Braille Me*, takes up a full page, as most poems in English do today. I do not want to give it a page, so, with apologies to the poet: *"Salty swells / slap the seawall / sounding out / my sense of belonging. // So long / I never knew / Now dispelling forever / Where is home. // The scent / the sound / the persistent sea wind / all I recognize // As creating / the parts / to make me / me."* In a *ku* written after a quick read:

last visit home

the slap of waves
against a seawall, thanks
i needed that!

Clever, perhaps, but I am the one who needs the slap for misplaced flippancy. The original is confusing, unnecessarily wordy and plagued with ~ings. But, still, I think I can recognize what is happening:

dispelling

How long have i heard
those waves slap against
the seawall and that scent
and the persistent sea breeze
that, leaving, i recognize as me?

27 words, including the title. The original has 41. Distillation-wise that barely makes port of the wine. There is another way and that is making the poem mine. Did you notice Brady's "Sounding out my sense of belonging"?

waves slapping
the seawall . . . i think of
bashô's old pond

Growing up only a hundred yards from the beach, I took for granted the thump of the breakers on the shore, but returning to the beach as an adult, the constant pounding or the whack of waves on a seawall fill me with awe. Away from the sea, the only similar experience I know of is a bamboo forest at the time the sprouts are pushing up and the earth around throbs with energy day and night.

~~~~~~

Lest the poet take umbrage with what I have done to and with her poems, I should add that she is not my only victim. I have done the same (and worst) to the *tanka* of a very famous, and much beloved early 19c Japanese poet:

秋来れば・恋ふる心のいとまなさよ
夜もい寝がてに雁多く聴く　　啄木
~~~~~~~~~~~~~~~~~~~~~~~~~~~~~~~~

うるさいや、妹許ならぬ雁がね床

枕うかぶ雁が音きけば恋もさわぐ

雁が音や寝コイも起こす罪ぶかさ

コイ乱す雁がネ落つる「心」の池

I won't bother trying to English myself, here; Japanese readers will have enough trouble with it　蛇足：　「寝こい」は、寝る恋と鯉の掛けに「ねごい」つまり「なかなか起せない方」。心の形くをした池もあった). Let us just say that punning on carp and alluding to heart-shaped ponds, I made four witty 17-syllabet versions of a 31-syllabet heart blue with love finding it hard to sleep below migrating geese.

xii
*D*istill *Y*our *O*wn
an appeal to my readers

Unlike, the poems and aphorisms which I paraversed as a matter of course, I have not done the same with prose. Once upon a time, when I was scouting out fine nature essays for translation into Japanese for two publishers, I recall finding many not worth translating *as a book*, and thinking that even they had some good observations or ideas which merited gathering and one way to do this would be by turning them into the poetry I was then researching on my own, haiku. I never did it. Instead, I spent most of my spare time experimenting with flipbooks and one-string instruments, making discoveries that would have changed the world of music and art had I only had the money to hire others to complete what I started. At about this same time, or slightly later, a man whose name I cannot recall had a column in the *Japan Times* in which he described how he boiled down books, movies, practically anything into a single haiku holding their essence. It sounds great but I am afraid I was not impressed with his overwrought explanations or the final product. The words "making a mole-hill out of mountain" come to mind, but I may have been jaundiced because, I was toying with the idea of doing the same and he beat me to it. If he happens to read this, I apologize for my rudeness (please note that I am equally rude to myself): I would like to see a few of his best columns, in case I was unlucky enough to have seen the worst.

My distillation of Muir's prose, done specifically for this book was supposed to be here. But, I chickened out. Two people read it. One said it was OK but offered no particulars, while the other found my composite-translations *far* more interesting and Muir *too long*. If something is really good, it is *never* long. I will still print it after another cyle of multiple translations, composite translations and paraversing poems, which is to say as ch. 16, because the concept needs more fleshing out than provided by Thoreau's winter flies in ch. 8. Someone will surely find it as lacking as I found the gentleman's distillations in *The Japan Times*. But, for this edition, I see no other solution.

Hopefully, before the next edition, my readers will take pity on me and supply me with better examples of their making. And, please remember that you can play with a whole book, a chapter of a book, an article, or whatever you wish to, and the distillation or essence of it need not be a haiku or series of haiku. It could be couplets, sonnets, rhyming free-verse after Ogden Nash, any of those many fancy forms whose names I can never remember though I read Hollander three times over . . . as you like it. It can be anywhere from 1-20 pages in length. It can be utterly off the wall, like say: one couplet each containing the soul of one hundred books or *shibui*, which is to say, subdued as can be.

132

xiii

Minding "One Head" of Poetry
◎ from the <u>Hundred Poet One Poem Anthology</u> ◎

hyakunin isshu (13c)

Title first this time. Any English word-lover cannot help wondering what exactly *"hundred-men-one-head"* means. Actually, it is nothing exotic. "Head," or *shu*, is a counter. If we can count *head* of *cattle*, Japanese count *heads* of 31-syllabet songs/poems (but never *haiku*, which are counted as *ku*), which are, after all, collected by the editors of anthologies as assiduously as head-hunters seek their prizes. This 13c anthology is the most popular selection of poems in Japanese and, perhaps, *world* history. One finds its 31-syllabet *waka*, often together with the stylized painting of the seated poet on everything from kimono to decks of *uta-garuta,* or "song-cards." The cards came in two decks, one with the entire poem in mixed characters and hiragana phonetic script, the other with only the last stanza (14-syllabets) of the poems written in *hiragana* alone. The first is read by a third party as competitors try to grab for the card with the correct ending as soon as they can, or dare – a wrong one gets you a purple penalty card – with the object being to get rid of one's cards. These cards take some getting used to for non-Japanese. A grab-card (*torifuda*) I saw on the internet had the *hiragana* arranged *kakeshiyaso / tenonuremo / kososure*, precisely like this:

```
こ    て    か
そ    の    け
す    ぬ    し
れ    れ    や
      も    そ
```

This, mind you, is what in English is usually called "the last two lines" of the poem, but Japanese, who usually write it in one line, are not hung up with lines any more than they are with words, which they separate in their heads rather than on paper. In the above case, a word meaning "sleeve," *sode* （そて in old style, with the diacritical marks そで left to the reader to imagine, which seems to say *sote*) has been split between the first vertical line (on the right) and the second. Why not just shrink the font and parse the words right? I would guess the 14

133

syllabets are written as large as possible to be fair to people with bad vision and because it was often played in dim light. As *fuda,* cards were first popular among nobles from the 15c and became popular with the masses in the 17c after having picked up the name *karuta* from the Portuguese, who started a craze for gambling with their *carta* in the 16c. Because *waka* poetry is a link with the ancient past the game became a form of entertainment proper to the New Year, the season for re-creating the world and reaffirming the culture. Women, though comprising only 21% of the poets represented, were the most active card players – or became so at some point in history – and still are. Are men less excited than women by what are largely elegant seasonal and love poems said to be assembled by Fujiwara Teika in the 13c from the major anthologies of poetry? Or do they prefer not to compete with their word-quick minds and deft fingers?

~~~~~~

Joshua Mostow compiled ten translations of each poem in *Pictures of the Heart: The Hyakunin Isshu.* (U. of Hawaii Press: 1996). Judging from the examples in a *Japan Times* review by Hiroaki Sato – I have yet to see the actual book – the translations are too similar to each other to be called "composite translation" (Liz Henry), "variations" (Douglas Hoftstadter), or *paraverses* (rdg, me).

> *1) I have watched weeping through the night,/ Deserted, desolate, alone./ Till now hath broke the morning light / I almost deemed forever gone, / So slowly by / The creeping hours seemed to hie.*
>
> *2) How think you, sir, / the lingering hours of night-time / I have slept, lonely, / from dusk to dawn deserted,/ in solitary sorrow.*
>
> *3) Sighing and weeping,/ Waiting for the light of dawn / As one lies alone, / Have you ever thought at all / About how long this can seem?*
>
> *4) When one lies alone / lamenting the whole night through / until the break of day, / how slowly the time goes by – / ah, but yes – you wouldn't know.*
>
> *5) The span of time / that I sleep alone, sighing, / until night lightens – can you at all know / how long that is?*

This, the 53rd poem in the *Hundred Poets,* by 'the Mother of Michitsuna,' was, in Carter's words, *"sent to her husband . . . when he complained about being kept waiting outside her gate after coming late one night."* The first two translations of this *waka,* are by Dickins, the first to English the anthology (1866/1909), the third by Galt (Princeton: 1982), the fourth, Carter (Stanford:1991), and last, Mostow, himself. Sato presents them properly parsed in his review. I did not bother, because none seemed worth presenting *as poetry*. The hyperbolic "almost . . . forever gone" in the oldest translation deserves *kudos* for *something*, and the third by Galt deserves credit for the bitter "Have you ever ~," but the only really poetic phrase in the lot is Carter's acerbic "you wouldn't know." It, at least, is clearly alive. Not content to leave bad enough alone, Sato added his own translation. I shrank the font a half-point to squeeze it into one-line, for Sato is so in/famously insistent about not parsing that he probably avoids eating parsely:

134

嘆きつつ独りぬる夜の明くるまはいかに久しきものとかはしる
ナゲキツツヒトリヌルヨノアクルマハイカニヒサシキモノトハシル
nageki tsutsu hitori nuru yo no akuru ma wa ikani hisashiki mono to ka wa shiru
lamenting-while, alone-sleep-night's-dawning-space-re. how long thing etc. know!

The night, aggrieved, you sleep alone, you know how long before the day breaks.

So saying, Sato deserves credit for doing something here that is all too rare in translation. He made good use of the inclusive English "you," that is the *you* that means *"I"* while not being insistent, allowing the reader to identify with the writer *and* raising personal complaint to proverbial truth (though it is too restrictive to call the transpersonal "you" merely "proverbial")* while preserving the tasteful ambiguity of the pronoun-less original that is so short it is done before you feel it is trite. I joke, but we cannot help wondering if a thought so simple, even beautifully expressed, is a poem at all. Following the above translations and the transliteration, I might have translated, say,

*Lie alone and blue
the whole night through
and you will see*

*just what you have taught me:
How slowly comes the dawn!*

~~~~~~~~~~~~~~~~~~~~~~~~~

*When you lie alone and worry until the sky grows bright,
then, you, too, will really know how long a night can be!*

~~~~~~~~~~~~~~~~~~~~~~~~~

How long it takes for day to break while one waits up all night, worrying when and if he'll show – but that *you* wouldn't know!

But, I still would not think it poetry. There is something else I want. A critical scholar responded to my question as to whether there might be some evidence to justify my heroic efforts to save – that is make a witty translation of – another *Hundred Poet* poem by warning me that many of those old poems *really are as boring as they look:* expectations were that low and the wit *I* want might have been considered out of order. And the proof is in the poems chosen for some anthologies. I cannot argue with that, but only hope that some poems are indeed wittier than they look. And this poem by Michitsuna's Mother may be a good example. Who can say how much of the following paraverses is mine or hers!

blue winter	perspective
the night *you lie alone, love*	*together* *we always found it brief*
you know how long *a lover's short night* *can be!*	*passed by* *i lie alone, and weep* *all night long.*

135

aggrieved

last night, no doubt
too short for you,
was very long for me

you had little time for sleep
i had far too much!

Granted, the original poem is not so cavalier or metaphysical as my readings which come close to being paraverses are; but consider the circumstances. It was common for a husband to have more than one wife and lover. Noblemen in Japan remind one of Tom Cats making their rounds! Assuming she was upset for being kept waiting earlier that night or the night before by her husband who passed her by to visit someone else, might not such thoughts have been on her mind? And is it not possible that the Hundred Poet editor, Teika, read the same parodoxical wit into it or out of it that my paraverses make explicit? With Japanese lovers, including spouses, typically parting at dawn, *there were many poems about the all-too-short night*. Is it not possible the unstated contrast between the stereotypical short night of the lovers and the long one of the complaint by Michitsuna's mother – fitting the season, for the poem (from her *Gossamer Diary*) was in the Winter – made the poem interesting? For me the poem read without that contrast in mind is nothing more than a good line in a drama, but as poetry, it is as good as dead. I speak of the original, but I am afraid that such lifelessness might not even be recognizeable in English, as it is all too common a condition of *waka* translated from Japanese.

~~~~~~

Today, many Japanese readers would not get the point either. But, if I am not mistaken, not long ago, it would have been too obvious to explain. Even the father of modern haiku, Shiki (1866 – 1902), who was supposed to be upright to the point of being prudish (but seems to me quite the rascal) could not resist one poem about the shortest night of all, as I cannot resist sharing it with you:

<div style="text-align: center;">

短夜のまことを知るや一夜妻　子規
mijikayo no makoto o shiru ya hitoyotsuma – shiki
(a short night's truth knowing: one-night-wife=husband)

</div>

short night	**nox brevis**
no room for doubt	you want to know
what real *noc brevis* is about!	how short the dark can be?
a one-night stand	try a one-night stand

<div style="text-align: center;">

first-hand trope

a one night-stand
i finally experience
the true *noc brevis!*

</div>

The length of nights is a far more salient topic for the Japanese than for us. As is often the case with translated poetry, we lose the wit that lies between the lines – or, *words*, if you think of haiku as I do, a single line in the original – unless the translator brings it to our attention. Because this can be done in many ways, it is hard to settle on a single translation; but we need not go quite so far as Mostow, who declares that no translator should be interested in producing the *"definitive translation,"* for a *"definitive translation is a murdering translation."* I love that bold and beautiful statement which is not all wrong; but, I say if a translator can do a poem good, so good that no one else will touch it with a ten-foot pole, kudos to him or her! But, *as a matter of fact*, this hardly ever happens. It is so rare that the greater paraverse – the constellation of possible readings of all poems – will not miss the loss. Rather, we should celebrate the poem's fortunate apotheosis!

I am afraid, I skipped forward to Shiki before proving my claim that Michitsuna's Mother was playing with conceits already old in her time. Let the following less well-known *Manyôshû* (9c) poems suffice for evidence. Both are translated by Cranston (Waka I, #1370-1), but I prefer to do them myself, just borrowing his *"Ah, how heartless(!)."* We will skip the Japanese, for it is not significant in the case of most *Manyôshû* transcriptions. The poems were two of three related poems, Manyôshû #2301-3, #2302 and #2303, respectively.

Aru hito no ana kokoro na to omouramu aki no nagayo o nesamefusu nomi

Some think 'Ah, how heartless, we need more time'
while I lie awake alone the whole long autumn night.

Autumn nights are long, or so they say; but, for spending
my love built up and stored, they are too short in ending!

Aki no yo o nagashi to iedo tsumorinishi koi o tsukuseba mijikaku arikeri

Yet, thanks to the Mother of Michitsuna's *Gossamer Diary*, we know she was not only playing with such conceits, but specifically addressing her husband. That Fall was when she gave birth to Michtsuna and in early Winter, after finding a letter he addressed to another woman in his out-box, she put a tail on him when he left that evening to learn more about her competition. At this time, he was absent several days and on his return in the morning, she would not unbar the gate. He went back to his lover's house. That was when she decided to send him the poem. Some think the "lightening/opening" of the night in the poem includes an allusion to the gate, usually opened in the early morning, which he was forced to wait by. In other words, there is a slight "now, I have tried to give you a hint of what it is like to wait" nuance between the words of the poem.

Anyone with Mostow's book and particular insight into one or more of the other poems that none of the translators did full justice to is welcome to double the length of this chapter. I have, for the time being, seen enough of the hundred famous poems, having had to deal with a score of them, plus parodies and other sorts of take-offs and comments by *kyôka* poets, in *Mad In Translation*.

For a contrast with the usual five-line – and my occasional two-line – format, I recommend readers see Peter McMillan's recent *One Hundred Poets One Poem Each*. His translations, while more or less standard length when it comes to the beat, are freely parsed and vary from four to eleven (!) lines. I can imagine some might find the inconsistancy of form terribly unsettling and readers familiar with my uniquely symmetrical presentation might think I would not approve; but, far from it, I find McMillan's free parsing shares much with my two-line style (most fully developed in my latestest book, *Mad In Translation* where most of the poems are *waka* length), which is often a single-line with enjambed rhyme only appearing to be a couplet. The reason is that free parsing permits the poet to ensure readers enjoy natural clusters of words *as Japanese readers can*. Not parsing does not ensure the same, but it encourages it, as readers, or at least *good* readers, can, with occasional help from punctuation, do the job themselves.

Five-line fixed syllabic parsing, on the other hand, tends to become an excuse for less than poetic translation and un-natural reading. True *waka* did have a fixed number of syllabets and a tendency to break 5-7-5-7-7, but aside from the most common 17-14 split, we are only talking about possible breaks, often only as slight as not splitting a word in two, and not the clear-cut break suggested by line change in English. There is good syllabic poetry – usually eight or ten syllabets per line – written in English, but the beat is controlled, lines break naturally or are rhyme-justified. Shorter lines of fixed-syllable, un-attentive to beat and not rhyming are, as a matter of fact, rarely deserving of the word "poetry."

Japanese poems are read in a natural manner which does not require clearly separate lines. That is why they may be found in single lines in many printed books yet brushed on cards or with pictures may be broken up into any number of lines. To quote the last line of my appreciation for the new form McMillan pioneered – which I crammed into what was a blank page between the text and the aftermatter of *Mad In Translation* –

Delicate nuances demand a fretless instrument.

I have not yet seen how McMillan did the poem by Michitsuna's Mother as little of the book was viewable at Google Books.

---

* **The worst syllable-counting I have seen**, by Henkenius and Rodd (*Kokinshû*) has big spaces showing breaks within lines and false enjambment, by which I mean ending a line with "the" merely to make that syllable count! That the current dean of Japanese literature in translation Donald Keene lauded their translation tells us something about the state of translation twenty years ago! I was pleased to see Keene recently wrote an enthusiastic foreword to McMillan's book, which shows he can recognize the superiority of a radically different method, but cannot help wondering if he really understood *why* the syllable-based method he was evidently happy with before was wrong-headed.

xiv

The Fifth Season
◎ <u>normalizing composite translation</u> ◎

長閑さや皆我家のみよの春　宗因　三ふえ集
nodokesa ya minna wagaya no miyo no haru sôin 1604-82
(calm/tranquility! all[everyone] my[their own] house's realm's spring)

<blockquote>
how tranquil!
each house tending to
its own spring
</blockquote>

<blockquote>
what tranquility
the spring of the realm
in every home
</blockquote>

<blockquote>
a tranquil realm
everyone thinks spring
visits *his* home
</blockquote>

<blockquote>
a peaceful time
who doesn't lay claim
to this spring!
</blockquote>

English must throw up its hands before "everyone my-home's realm's spring." The use of "my/mine" as *third*-person as well as *first* in Japanese allows *my-ism* to be universally applied (personal computers are called *maikon* (my computer), etc.). The "my" used here, *waga*, warrants comment, for Japanese has many ways to say it (Indeed, the "my this and that," once awkward but now ubiquitous in Usanian English, may have begun in Japan, where "our" *mai* was adopted for product naming). *Waga* is egoistic yet warm. That, however, is only a start at reading this simple *ku* by the top haiku-master of the Osaka school. The first reading between the lines is Confucian: the non-action of everyone keeping to his own house, the microcosmos of the larger polity, brings peace. The second reading credits the peaceful reign with a situation where every home is able to enjoy the spring. The third imagines people so content with the calm day that they each think Spring pays special attention to them. The fourth combines and exaggerates the second and third. This calm of the first day, which we encounter in many New Year's themes, may not have existed as a New Year's theme in its own right until modern haiku turned it into one: *hatsunagi* "first-calm," or, more loosely, *nodokesa/nodokasa* "calm" (either pronunciation) on the New Year's.

I just changed the fourth translation from *"everyone lays claim"* to *"who doesn't lay claim . . . !* The next time I quote myself, I may change it back, for I would seem to belong to the school of Humes, who, the anonymous author of *Curiosities of Literature* tells us, *"was never done with corrections; every edition varies with the preceding ones."* (vol.IV 1823)

正月言葉皆軽薄の世界哉 未存
shôgatsu kotoba mina keihaku no sekai kana mizon 1697
(new years words all light-thin (frivolous/shallow) world !/?/ 'tis)

a world where   *the new year*   *new year's day*
all words are frivolous   *a world where all our*   *a world where all we say*
the new year   *words are light*   *feels shallow*

on new year's
our world of words
immaterial

the new year   the new year
do our words today   a world where empty
end in play?   words rule

new year words
on this day all we say
is for display

the new year   new year speech
in this world all words   a world where heavy
are superficial   words are taboo

new year's day
a world when words
lack substance

new year's day   new year's day
a world where no word   when saying something
is good enough   says nothing

the new year
when we can see through
our own words

The problem is it is hard to tell if the *ku*, by a poet whose name (probably adopted for this *ku* alone) means "pre-existence," describes words actually exchanged as greetings on the New Year, in which case it belongs in this chapter, or describes the split nature of the world we now live in, as opposed to the mythical one where words and deeds were one in a literal sense we can only grasp indirectly (in dreams) today. The connotation of the double-character word "light-thin" (*keihaku*) is almost always bad, but, I cannot help wondering whether it might not allow a positive nuance in this magical time. Could the poet be extolling the freedom of pre-existence, when, lacking body, words fly? In my blossom-viewing book, I defended the apparent banality of skeletons in costume as an *epiphany* experienced with a shudder while sitting below leafless cherry trees in full-bloom. Here, I imagine myself listening to the greetings of New Year's Day callers, or, to my own voice, and suddenly feeling how shallow – ghostly – the words were, while dropping into a deeper reality. [The first 3 readings were near the head of a chapter; later I came back to do more.]

The New Year, a separate season coming at the head of Spring before Japan felt obliged to conform to the Occidental calendar to survive, was larger than Christmas, Easter, Thanksgiving, Independence Day, the Arrival of Spring and your birthday combined, as it was *all* of these things and more: a re-creation of the world, a time tunnel or an enchanted spell in dreamtime. Such abstraction is ineffable. I had to alternate chapters with *ku* expressing New Year generalities with concrete subjects (mice, rice-cake, etc) to avoid an overdose of sublimity.

~~~~~~

むらさきを諸事に補ひ初霞 支考
murasaki o shoji ni oginai hatsugasumi shikô 1731
(purple[obj] all-things-on/to/with supply/complement first-mist/haze)

all things
blessed by purple
first haze

purple enough
to ennoble our world
the first haze

all things are
repaired with purple
the first haze

the first haze
today all things get
to wear purple

In Japan, as in many parts of the world, purple was a hard color to dye and restricted to nobility, or depending on the shade of purple, the highest ranks of nobility (Hence, the English proverb *"An ape will be an ape, by kind as they say, / Though that you clad him in purple array."*). My purple haze feeling is more along the lines of Jimmy Hendrix's electrifying guitar performance, but here the idea would seem to be that the patina of purple graces all with nobility or even divinity, for the Imperial line was a link to the Age of the Gods and, in a sense, therefore, immortal. Since Shikô was a convoluted character and the verb *oginai* suggests the officially supplying apparel (something done at the end of the year), it is possible he meant this in a light vein as per my creative last reading.

~~~~~~

ぬけて出る夜着よりすぐに花の春 成美
nuketederu yogi yori sugu ni hananoharu seibi 1748-1816
(slipping-out-nightdress-from immediately flower/y/beautiful/festive spring)

popping out
of my nightrobe, right
into the spring

just outside
the pajama cocoons
flowery spring

slipping out
of her night-dress
spring blooms

splendid spring
as soon as we shed
our nightdress

141

It is fun to imagine pj*s* on the *tatami* (straw-mat flooring), empty legs resembling a snake skin; but you should imagine a robe and, unless this *ku* can be dated to the year after the Year of the Snake, the better metaphor would be an abandoned *cocoon*. The poet, or all of us (the third reading is unlikely), immediately don/s his/our "flower/floral," which is to say, celebratory, garb and leave/s the nightwear as is. This scenario would be impossible in the Occident where the departure of the Old Year and arrival of the New Year is celebrated at midnight alone and there is no New Year's morning to speak of (unless we include the year's first hang-over!) To properly feel [Issa's employer] Seibi's poem, you should recall waking up on your birthday, Christmas and Easter [slight change in the last line].

古歌に曰く千歳そ見ゆる鏡餅　梅翁
koka ni iwaku chitose zo miyuru kagamimochi　sôin 1604-82
(old-song-in, to wit, thousand-years see-can mirror-mochi)

rock of ages

as sung of old
eons can indeed be seen
mirror-mochi

This *ku* is only a lead in for what is introduced next, so I skip the text. Let me just explain that *mochi* is a smooth cake of pounded sweet-rice, and mirror mochi was generally two fat discus-shaped cakes with the smaller sun on top of the larger moon. They often were topped with an orange or bigerade. The "old-song" mentioned in the above *ku* probably refers to the following *waka* by Minamoto Nakamasa 源仲正　夫木集巻三十二雑部十四 1310:

千代までも影をならべてあひみむといはふ鏡の用ゐざらめや
chiyo made mo kage o narabete aimimu to iwau kagami no mochii-zarameya
(1000-realms-until form/s[obj] lined up, eachother see[+] celebrate mirror-*mochi*=using-not so?)

soul conference

and is not this
mirror of mochii round
we toast with wine

worth keeping for it keeps us
in touch with men of all time?

shall we not
celebrate our mirrors
of pounded rice

that bring us face to face
with men of all ages (& mice)?

The grammar at the tail of the poem escapes me, but how cleverly verbed the *mochii*, an old pronunciation of *mochi*, often written with the character for doing or business (用), is! This knowledge I owe to Yamamoto Kenkichi's explanation in Kodansha's large *saijiki*. He also points out something I knew – round *mochi* can stand for the soul – and something I did not – that in Kansai (Osaka, Nara and Kyôto), disc-like mirrors are rare, for they have *balls* of *mochi* which, eaten, bring vitality and rebirth. Some say the shape is modeled on the heart. Most importantly, he claims *mochi* is not called a mirror because of its shape but because, as a reification of our soul, it reflects us and came to celebrate/toast a person's thousand realms of life (*sono hito no senyo o kotohogu*), *i.e.* longevity I think it wrong to phrase it in not-this-but-that terms. The round shape may have come more from the idea of the soul than the standard mirror shape, but the mirror connects with *clarity* (ironic considering the opacity of the *mochi*) and that, as we can tell from old *waka* mentioning pristine water together with everlasting memories, was important for what I call *time travel*. I also doubt the idea is *just* the longevity of a person (*sono hito*). It may be a single soul – Japanese have several types of souls and one is permanent, or recyclable if you prefer – but, I think we have a sequence of bodies, or *persona*, united here.

opaque looking glass

let's celebrate	and why not
our mochi mirrors,	put to use our mirrors
line them all up	of pounded rice
to bring back the faces	we now toast to reflect
of a thousand generations	a thousand generations?

The last two chapters of *The Fifth Season* treated the material rite of picking young greens and the subsequent chopping and eating of them. The theme is one of the oldest treated by haiku, and I went back to the beginning.

the proposal

pretty basket, pretty maid!
picking greens of tender blade!
pretty scoop, in pretty hands!
guess ye who before thee stands!

confess thy clan, confess thy name!
i'll tell mine first, just do the same!
they call me lord of this whole land
for man and god know my command!

but you, alone, i deign to ask
what i could, by right, demand!

This is a very loose sense-translation of the very first "song" of the 4,516 poem *Manyôshû*, Japan's oldest anthology of poetry. A more direct rendering would be: *Basket! Pretty basket holder! Scoop, too! Pretty scoop holder! On this hill, child [=young woman 1] picking greens! Tell [me] your family! Tell [me] your name! All of the country of Yamato, all of it is my reign, and I, on my part announce my family and name!* There is some debate in Japan about the meaning of the last part, but I incorporated it into this translation and added the title and last two lines because asking a girl's name is said to have been tantamount to a proposal of marriage, and the politeness of that proposal – if the last line is correct (granted the middle part seems a bit pushy) – seems out of character for the brusque and, according to some historians, cruel, Emperor Yûryaku (5c). . .

The maiden addressed by the Emperor is . . . not necessarily a farm girl. Chances are she is noble (nobles married, or at least were promised for marriage young) engaged in the ancient ritual of picking the first greens of the year=spring. This event is thought to have included wooing in the form of song-exchanges. The term used for picking greens in the ancient poem, *na-tsumasu*, is, excluding the conjugation of the verb, identical to the later *na-tsumu*. Since *na* was a homophone for "name" and *tsumu* or "pluck," was slang for "intercourse," nominally speaking, the ritual activity could not help but be erotically charged. The poem is also intriguing because the Chinese characters used as phonetic letters for the "pretty-scoop-holder" (Japanese did not yet have its own letters) literally mean "do you want a beautiful/handsome mate?"

I do not have other translations of this song in my book for it is not a book *of* composite or multiple translation, and all the translations I have seen are boring as hell. As my library and I are separated, I only have one to offer for comparison's sake. It is from Steven Carter's *Traditional Japanese Poetry*, the best such anthology I know. With apologies to the translator, I will deparse it to save space: *O maiden / ■ with a basket, / a pretty basket, / with a scoop, / a pretty scoop, /maiden picking greens / ■ on this hillside: / I want to ask about your house; I want to be told your name. / In the sky-filling land of Yamato, / it is I / ■ who rule everyone, it is I / ■ who rule everywhere, / and so I think you will tell me / ■ where you live, / what you are called.* (my italics ■ = two letter space). Carter's translation follows the original more closely than mine which shifts some things around and gives the reading between the lines as the last two lines. (If you should wish to compare my paraverse and Carter's translation to others, some more information: 1) house=family=clan and 2) "sky-filling" is but one of several possible meanings of a phrase (*soramitsu*) attached to Yamato, 3) basket holes had a female connotation and the scoop was bamboo=tubular=phallic, so the idea might be (this is my guess) that she has the boy-girl set there, so why not complete the set in real life, too? and 4) The original has a rhythm unlike that found in the other five or six thousand song/poems in the *Manyô-shû*. 5) The purely Chinese-character transcription includes a hint about the marital intent.)

土手の馬くはんを無下に菜摘哉　其角
dote no uma kuwan o muge ni natsumi kana kikaku -1707
(levee's horses' eat-not[or would?][+emph. contrad.] directly green-plucking!/'tis)

~~what the horses
would not eat on the bank
green-plucking~~

~~green-plucking
i snatch one up from under
my nag's nose~~

~~going straight
for what the horses leave
green-plucking~~

Though horses would eat, why must man rob this bank of all its green! ♪

Here, I paraversed to buy time, hoping to choose one reading, eventually. But the poem came up again in relation to a poem in *Mad In Translation* (pg 432) and I realized that, caught up by the fact those greens – that were ritually chopped (called "beating") before being cooked – seem so puny as to be hardly worth the attention of a horse, I failed to catch the drastic tone of *muge ni* (not "directly" but "indiscriminately") and went for the less likely negative reading of *kuwan*.

天地のゆるむひまより初若菜　松宇
ametsuchi no yurumu hima yori hatsu-wakana shôu - 1827
(heaven-earth's loosening freedom/play/space-from first-young-green/s)

*the first greens
between winter and spring
heaven and earth*

*heaven and earth
relaxing, gave birth:
young greens*

*from the play
between sky and earth
the first plants*

*from space born
when heaven and earth let go
first young greens*

*from the rest
of heaven and earth space
for young green*

*from freedom
given of heaven and earth:
the first plants*

*when heaven and earth give
the first young greens
fill the gaps*

*born of heaven
earth and man at leisure
first-young-greens*

*the first greens
when heaven and earth
give a little*

The original *ku* is faultless. English cannot match the verb *yurumu*, used when ice in a stream begins to slip, a tight knot loosens, or we let our guard down after going on vacation; likewise for the noun *hima*, meaning *play, give, freedom, leisure, time-off* and simply having nothing one has to do. There may also be an allusion to a *Kokinshû* (905) *waka*, where the frothy waves breaking through the cracks in the ice made by the warm valley breeze are called "spring's first blossoms." (谷風にとくる…春のはつ花). As many readings as a body has holes, yet not one is half as good as the original.

雪礫返す間もなし若菜摘　千代
yukitsubute kaesu ma mo nashi wakanatsumi chiyo 1701-75
(snowball return space[interval/time] even not, young green plucking)

young-play?

my snowball's
only response: "we're busy
plucking greens!"

young green

just too busy
to return fire: the pluckers
eat snowballs

plucking greens,
"i've no time to return
your snowball!"

145

The last reading makes the *ku* a spontaneous response, perhaps shouted aloud to the culprit, the second interpretation seems the most likely [so vague it cannot be wrong, either]. Still, my heart lies in the first reading, for I want to think our playful nun is the one throwing the snowballs.

手の跡を雪のうけとる若菜かな 千代
te no ato o yuki no uketoru wakana kana chiyo -1775
(hand-print/s snow receive-takes [a receipt] young-green 'tis)

the snow accepts
our handprints when we
take young greens

voucher

the snow takes	your snow took
our handprints for	my hand-print for each
the young green	young green

Thinking of so-called primitives who drop gems or coins into the holes of plants they dig up as payment, I first read barter into this: You take my handprint, I take your produce. But the combination of the hand-print, a common signature for goods bought on credit, and the verb *uketoru*, meaning to receive something in a formal, if not legal way, suggests a modern economy. The last reading supposes Chiyo plucked on private property. Regardless, I believe the *ku* a good example of the light humor in which she excelled. Bashô realized in his last years that *karumi*, or a light touch, was harder to master than an elegant or austere one, and a respectable pursuit in poetry. Had he lived longer, Bashô might have pointed out the positive role of logic in composing such *ku*.

Take note of the *suppositions*. I don't make them for the hell of it (though I do indeed like thinking them through and enjoying multiple narratives for single poems). They are *needed* if we are to choose the pronouns without which English translations are as good as dead. And if we make those choices for life, we must either explain or publish more than one translation if we are not to lose the rich bouquet of possibilities inherent to the original.

♪ **Hogging the Greens** (also translated as seven herbs) Actually, I am *still* not sure if I get Kikaku's haiku. I feel fairly safe with "would eat" (as opposed to would not eat) but not confident. I would need to know the poet better to ascertain whether he was complaining on horses' behalf about humans out gathering the new growth of Spring or celebrating in a warped *haikai* way the crowds of people out plucking in good weather . . . Maybe I should put up a cluster of all those possibilities and call it a composite *guess*.

XV
Sun Flower Seeds & Bare Trees
◎ <u>how to make one poem feed a dozen</u> ◎

why not try
a limb-viewing party
naked trees

winter trees
let's invite the poets
limb-viewing

imagine a tree
dropping its leaves to show
diana still there

men and trees
naked above and below
blossom-viewing

leafless trees
call the limbs female
the bark male

winter trees
i would view them with
a pathologist

men and trees
one covers up, one strips
every winter

men and trees
whose character is more
obvious bare?

warts and all
with winter trees it is no
figure of speech

not many
recognize them now
leafless trees

we could play
a game: pin the leaf
on the tree

every winter
there are trees that go
incognito

I am paraversing one haiku by Harriet Kimbro coupled with drawings by Chuzo Tamotzu from *Tamotzu in Haiku* (1977: Santa Fe), a book a friend gave me: *"Shape of winter tree / intrigues me . . . its bumps, its trunk, / its own character."* The missing article is telling: it keeps the five syllables mandatory to one school of Usanian haiku, but makes no difference with respect to what counts, the *beat*. With "the," and "a," or, possibly, "that," line one would still be an excessively long 3-beats, but at least it would have sounded *natural*, as haiku do in Japanese.

that winter tree
draws me: its trunk, its bumps
its character

that winter tree
its trunk, its bumps – do i
feel character?

A tree *can* have something that moves us, where we suddenly feel it has come through a lot over time. That is, we feel it has character, we acknowledge its presence 貫禄. This realization may happen when we touch the tree and probably is more likely when a tree is leafless. This is not necessarily because more is revealed. As Josephine Johnson puts it: *"Is late Autumn more honest than midsummer? . . . Is the naked and leafless tree any more the true tree than the whole tree?"* (*The Inland Island*) Still some trees – and some species of trees – do exhibit individual forms we clearly recognize as such and bark is closer to skin, more mammal than leaves, so we may be more touched by it, even though we glorify the leaves as we do our hair.

again this winter
i wish for a tree-viewer's
book of bare trees

my winter wish
a guide book w/ nothing
but bare trees

Coming from Florida, I was as excited with all the naked trees as I was with snow. I bought a camera for no other reason than photographing those trees. Books do give us basic types such as ovoid, umbrellate, weeping, etc., but I have long wanted more. Another of Kimbro's *ku,* next to Tamotzu's drawing of half a dozen birds eating a sun-flower, was so godawfully plain (*So many birds seek / breakfast in the sunflower / they seem inside it*) that I, fortunate the birds outside my window were not the nondescript ones of the drawing, found myself over-reacting:

danaë's skirt
fills up with tit-mice
my sun-flower

Danae. Here, too, I cannot help quoting Josephine Johnson's *Inland Island.* And, strangely, the passage is right before the one we saw above:

> Silver gnats dance, but they look like go-go dancers to me, mechanical, trapped in an insane pattern. A shower of gold leaves falls in the sunlight. I think of Danaë's rain of gold. Jupiter was all those cold tickling coins on her stomach . . . Soon all the trees will be bare. Is late Autumn . . .

So much of Johnson's prose *is* poetry that I felt no urge to haiku or otherwise paraverse it *in English.* Instead, I scribbled about ten *ku* per page *in Japanese.* I will back-translate two and add one that reflects the fact I am sipping wine.

fall sunlight
a shower of leaves tickle
danaë's belly

trees with leaves
and without, which
is more honest?

bare trees
who says in nudity
is veritas?

Getting back to those birds eating sunflower seeds, we have two Tamotsu drawings. The first shows a bird on another sunflower's bent stem reaching up to pull a seed from a showerhead-like sunflower and is accompanied by *"You are a smart one! / The sunflower bends low, you / reach it from beneath."* I like the affection for the bird in the first line of the *ku*, and gave it a fitting title: *No Bird Brain*. But, the feeding behavior depicted is a no-brainer. I *had to* paraverse:

icarus never
had it so easy, a bird
eating sunflower

when sunflower
turns narcissus, a bird
eats his face

from below
a bird pecks the face
of a sunflower

The *haiku* describing the second, showing several birds working one flower, is even less poetic than most nature-writing prose: *"Now three of you come . . . / how can the sunflower head / feed you all at once?"* Naturally, that made me scribble paraverse after paraverse into the margin.

how many birds
can fit on a sunflower?
how many seeds?

the sunflower
eclipsed by a flock
of song-birds

my sunflower
swarmed by birds: call it
a total eclipse

one sunflower
ten birds, a hundred petals
a thousand seeds

lucky buntings
sunflower seeds thick as
ticks on a hound

Though the drawings are close-ups, they are too sketchy to reveal the species. You may make the buntings, blue birds, blackbirds or vireos, but not cardinal. crow, sparrow or wren, for the birds are medium-size and not tufted. While, we are discussing drawings, let me point out that there are many ways to combine them with haiku. 1) Make a drawing *for* a haiku; 2) Write a haiku *for* a drawing; 3) Write a haiku with a drawing. The little book *Tamotzu in Haiku* belongs to the second variety and such tend to produce poor haiku whether or not the drawings are good. These drawings are so and so and many of the poems worse – I guess my friend only gave it to me because there are some cats in it and she knew I was as big on felinity as haiku. But, as you can see, that did not prevent it from bearing progeny. If anything, it probably helped. And that, I think is food for thought. If I had a newspaper column for poetry, I think I might use bad poems to bait good ones. (♪My apologies to the poet: others may feel differently. My paraverses might be too clever for their own good. I seek wit, but that is me.)

XVI

Mining *"The Mountains of California"*
◎ for haiku John Muir might have written ◎

(As mentioned in ch. 12, one reader found this chapter "a bit long." I considered shortening it, but will leave it as is until I receive better distillations from my readers.) John Muir, the man most responsible for saving large tracts of wilderness as park in the USA, unashamedly *loved* Nature. In chapter 10 (*Wind-storm in the Forests*) of his 1894 book, *The Mountains of California,* he describes climbing up and lashing himself to a spruce to experience a winter storm *as a tree* might. The chapter starts –

> THE mountain winds, like the dew and rain, sunshine and snow, are measured and bestowed with love on the forests to develop their strength and beauty. However restricted the scope of other forest influences, that of the winds is universal. The snow bends and trims the upper forests every winter, the lightning strikes a single tree here and there, while avalanches mow down thousands at a swoop as a gardener trims out a bed of flowers. But the winds go to every tree, fingering every leaf and branch and furrowed bole; not one is forgotten; the Mountain Pine towering with outstretched arms on the rugged buttresses of the icy peaks, the lowliest and most retiring tenant of the dells; they seek and find them all, caressing them tenderly, bending them in lusty exercise, stimulating their growth, plucking off a leaf or limb as required, or removing an entire tree or grove, now whispering and cooing through the branches like a sleepy child, now roaring like the ocean; the winds blessing the forests, the forests the winds, with ineffable beauty and harmony as the sure result.

some may break
but trees owe the wind
their good looks

the new year's off
to a lusty start: just hear
the trees moaning

for every tree
there is a wind, there
are many

< natural fitness >

< for erasmus darwin >

wind shape-up
a personal trainer
for every tree

also a wonder
the way of the wind
with a tree

Perhaps this was a poor choice for this exercise. How can one distill the panapoly of diverse detail in John Muir's description of the way of the wind with the trees? All I could do was try to capture concepts and moods. The last is the only *ku* I am totally satisfied with. I doubt Muir read Erasmus Darwin's *Loves of Plants*, but, if he did, he would have loved his erotic view of nature, and good doctor Darwin, who visited caves and held that all all (life) came from the cockle shell (or was it conch?), would have chuckled to see my Biblic allusion.

*whispering, cooing
howling: another winter
w/ the wind & trees*

*winter gales
make a tree's character
and test it*

*no kamasutra
needed for the wind
and the trees*

*muir's wind
cooing, carressing, and
plucking limbs*

*the trees, actors
weather, producer, & wind?
choreographer*

*good breaks
and bad, what don't trees
owe the wind?*

When I first read Muir, immediately after reading the scintillating prose of Annie Dillard's *A Tinker at Pilgrim's Creek,* I was not impressed; but, on rereading, I am. I have read entire books on the wind, learned (and soon forgot) countless fascinating names for it, marvelled at the practical yet magical compass add-on, the wind-rose, reviewed its relation to the God of Judeo-Christian-Muslimity and reread Aesop on its relative power vis-a-vis the other elements, but I'll be damned if anyone has expressed the importance of the wind to our landscape half as well as Muir did in that single paragraph. If the "measured and bestowed with love on the forests" stopped you, *please* go back and try again.

*no tree knows
the wind: all trees know
their winds*

*blessed winds
not one tree remains
a wall-flower*

*not one tree
that has not known
many winds*

*and how will
we live without wind
up in space?*

To decry our personification of "the wind" is patently absurd, for no abstraction can be *a* man. Muir, who wrote of blood coursing through the veins of boulders did indeed personify things. Thus, he writes of "winds,"

> After one has seen pines six feet in diameter bending like grasses before a mountain gale, and ever and anon some giant falling with a crash that shakes the hills, it seems astonishing that any, save the lowest thickset trees, could ever have found a period sufficiently stormless to establish themselves; or, once established, that they should not, sooner or later, have been blown down. But when the storm is over, and we behold the same forests tranquil again, towering fresh and unscathed in erect majesty, and consider what centuries of storms have fallen upon them since they were first planted, – hail, to break the tender seedlings; lightning, to scorch and shatter; snow, *winds*, and avalanches, to crush and overwhelm, – while the manifest result of all this wild storm-culture is the glorious perfection we behold; then faith in Nature's forestry is established, and

we cease to deplore the violence of her most destructive gales, or of any other storm-implement whatsoever. [my *italics*]

wind, hail, lightning, snow
tools that turn the woods into
a beauty you know

roughly treated
by storms: vernal beauty
owes the beast

forest sublime
a product of centuries
of storm-culture

the wind this,
the wind that: the natural
history of a tree

natural beauty
this forest long-tormented
by wild storms

who can hate
the winds that only break
what they create?

not the silence
of a graveyard: the woods
after a storm

I doubt all my *ku* are worth Muir's single coinage: *"storm-culture!"* Muir's description of the post-storm tranquility, "towering fresh and unscathed in erect majesty," is the weakest part of his essay, which focuses on more dynamic matters, but my background in haiku makes me wonder: Do woods after a storm seem as they seem because the howling wind still echoes within us? Or, are they genuinely peaceful, like spent lovers? A page later, Muir continues:

There is always something deeply exciting, not only in the sounds of winds in the woods, which exert more or less influence over every mind, but in their varied waterlike flow as manifested by the movements of the trees, especially those of the conifers. By no other trees are they rendered so extensively and impressively visible, not even by the lordly tropic palms or tree-ferns responsive to the gentlest breeze. The waving of a forest of the giant Sequoias is indescribably impressive and sublime, but the pines seem to me the best interpreters of winds. They are mighty waving goldenrods, ever in tune, singing and writing wind-music all their long century lives. Little, however, of this noble tree-waving and tree-music will you see or hear in the strictly alpine portion of the forests. The burly Juniper, whose girth sometimes more than equals its height, is about as rigid as the rocks on which it grows. The slender lash-like sprays of the Dwarf Pine stream out in wavering ripples, but the tallest and slenderest are far too unyielding to wave even in the heaviest gales. They only shake in quick, short vibrations. The Hemlock Spruce, however, and the Mountain Pine, and some of the tallest thickets of the Two-leaved species bow in storms with considerable scope and gracefulness. But it is only in the lower and middle zones that the meeting of winds and woods is to be seen in all its grandeur.

sequoia sway
but only pines know how
to play the wind

sequoia impress
but only pines show us
the wind's will

                              the pines, said he
                        are the best interpreters
                              of the wind

which the fiddle   *mountain pines*
which the bow? wind and   *where winds visit for all*
    mountain pine   *the old ballads*

                                wind-instrument
                        and singer-song-writer
                              century-old pine

climb too high   *the mezzanine*
and even the conifers can   *where to see wind & tree*
     barely dance   *in harmony*

                                 give me a book
                         showing the dance moves
                                  of all the trees

One of the most beautiful and exhilarating storms I ever enjoyed in the Sierra occurred in December, 1874, when I happened to be exploring one of the tributary valleys of the Yuba River. The sky and the ground and the trees had been thoroughly rain-washed and were dry again. The day was intensely pure, one of those incomparable bits of California winter, warm and balmy and full of white sparkling sunshine, redolent of all the purest influences of the spring, and at the same time enlivened with one of the most bracing wind-storms conceivable. Instead of camping out, as I usually do, I then chanced to be stopping at the house of a friend. But when the storm began to sound, I lost no time in pushing out into the woods to enjoy it. For on such occasions Nature has always something rare to show us, and the danger to life and limb is hardly greater than one would experience crouching deprecatingly beneath a roof.

                          山嵐逢いたいと云い山登り
                      yama-oroshi aitai to ii yama-nobori

                                  leaving town
                     to share a storm with friends:
                                mountain trees

Japanese call a gale a "mountain-descender." I erased a haiku going *"you slide down / and i'll climb up / sweet winter gale."* One tasteful *ku* suffices.

It was still early morning when I found myself fairly adrift. Delicious sunshine came pouring over the hills, lighting the tops of the pines, and setting free a steam of summery fragrance that contrasted strangely with the wild tones of the storm. The air was mottled with pine-tassels and bright green plumes, that went flashing past in the sunlight like birds pursued. But there was not the slightest dustiness, nothing less pure than leaves, and ripe pollen, and flecks of withered bracken and moss. I heard trees falling for hours at the rate of one every two or three minutes; some uprooted, partly on account of the loose, water-soaked condition of the ground; others broken straight across, where some weakness caused by fire had determined the spot. The gestures of the various trees made a delightful study. Young Sugar Pines, light and feathery as squirrel-tails, were bowing almost to the ground; while the grand old patriarchs, whose massive boles had been tried in a hundred storms, waved solemnly above them, their long, arching branches streaming fluently on the gale, and every needle thrilling and ringing and shedding off keen lances of light like a diamond. (I cut 300 words of detail and a stupendously bad line: "Nature was holding high festival, and every fiber of the most rigid giants thrilled with glad excitement.")

flecks of green
and brown fly by like birds
a clean gale

during the gale
trees fell but nothing's amiss
nothing's a mess

old trees sway
above the bobbing heads
of young trees

a winter gale
how clean the debris flying
through the woods!

a winter gale
summer scent is slapped on
the mountain

I jumped the gun with the "give me a book" paraverse on the previous page, for I, too, have long thought "the gestures of trees" would make "a delightful study." I have watched in awe as a young avocado with a huge head and thin trunk heroically battled a hurricane on Key Biscayne. Boxing terms, such as *bobbing and weaving* came to mind, though I realized *aikidô* might be the more appropriate comparison. On a path I took daily for years in Japan, I admired the undulating swing of slow-*S* stemmed wild chrysanthemum; and how it hurt to be too poor to own a video camera when the meter-high Tallahassee Grass I grew inside and kept by the window a couple years ago, bounded back and forth with a geometrically amazing syncopated jiggle. I wanted to share it with the world as much as I wanted to share the tactical genius of my warring gecko. Someone with a better hand for drawing and a more exact eye than mine, should compile a whole dictionary of plant movement! Back to Muir. This time, I'll give the *ku* first:

distinct voices

a winter gale
each tree w/ its own song
its own dance

storm effects
each singing its own song
california trees

trees in a storm
some mountains polyphonic
some plain-chant

I drifted on through the midst of this passionate music and motion, across many a glen, from ridge to ridge; often halting in the lee of a rock for shelter, or to gaze and listen. Even when the grand anthem had swelled to its highest pitch, I could distinctly hear the varying tones of individual trees,—Spruce, and Fir, and Pine, and leafless Oak,—and even the infinitely gentle rustle of the withered grasses at my feet. Each was expressing itself in its own way,—singing its own song, and making its own peculiar gestures,—manifesting a richness of variety to be found in no other forest I have yet seen. The coniferous woods of Canada, and the Carolinas, and Florida, are made up of trees that resemble one another about as nearly as blades of grass, and grow close together in much the same way. Coniferous trees, in general, seldom possess individual character, such as is manifest among Oaks and Elms. But the California forests are made up of a greater number of distinct species than any other in the world. And in them we find, not only a marked differentiation into special groups, but also a marked individuality in almost every tree, giving rise to storm effects indescribably glorious.

There are biologists who specialize in the sounds of various bugs or birds, but I am willing to bet few if any have paid serious attention to the sound of trees unless they read Muir. And we have flower gardens designed to tell the time or supply a seasonal parade of scent, but has anyone designed one with the soundscape primarily in mind? A blind millionaire musician, perhaps? I could essay this for pages but it is time to see what makes Muir Nature's first man:

Toward midday, after a long, tingling scramble through copses of hazel and ceanothus, I gained the summit of the highest ridge in the neighborhood; and then it occurred to me that it would be a fine thing to climb one of the trees to obtain a wider outlook and get my ear close to the Æolian music of its topmost needles. But under the circumstances the choice of a tree was a serious matter. One whose instep was not very strong seemed in danger of being blown down, or of being struck by others in case they should fall; another was branchless to a considerable height above the ground, and at the same time too large to be grasped with arms and legs in climbing; while others were not favorably situated for clear views. After cautiously casting about, I made choice of the tallest of a group of Douglas Spruces that were growing close together like a tuft of grass, no one of which seemed likely to fall unless all the rest fell with it. Though comparatively young, they were about 100 feet high, and their lithe, brushy tops were rocking and swirling in wild ecstasy. Being accustomed to climb trees in making botanical studies, I experienced no difficulty in reaching the top of this one, and never before did I enjoy so noble an exhilaration of motion. The slender tops fairly flapped and swished in the passionate torrent, bending and swirling backward and forward, round and round, tracing indescribable combinations of vertical and horizontal curves, while I clung with muscles firm braced, like a bobo-link on a reed.

a winter storm
i climb up a spruce to sit
in the orchestra

dancing trees
do they feel something
like ecstasy?

riding a spruce
how wildly we doodled
in that gale!

in the gale
i did not ride that tree
for science

Only a good Chinese-style painter could properly depict Muir clinging to his tree.

In its widest sweeps my tree-top described an arc of from twenty to thirty degrees, but I felt sure of its elastic temper, having seen others of the same species still more severely tried – bent almost to the ground indeed, in heavy snows – without breaking a fiber. I was therefore safe, and free to take the wind into my pulses and enjoy the excited forest from my superb outlook. The view from here must be extremely beautiful in any weather. Now my eye roved over the piny hills and dales as over fields of waving grain, and felt *the light running in ripples and broad swelling undulations across the valleys from ridge to ridge, as the shining foliage was stirred by corresponding waves of air. Oftentimes these waves of reflected light would break up suddenly into a kind of beaten foam, and again, after chasing one another in regular order, they would seem to bend forward in concentric curves, and disappear on some hillside, like sea-waves on a shelving shore.* The quantity of light reflected from the bent needles was so great as to make whole groves appear as if covered with snow, while the black shadows beneath the trees greatly enhanced the effect of the silvery splendor. [*my italics*]

a mountain gale
trees wave us back eons
to the ocean

storm mountain
my tree-top lookout above
the raging sea

winter gale
tree-top waves meet
waves of air

riding a spruce
in the gale: how far was i
from capsizing?

pine in a gale
waves of light chasing
waves of light

Where Muir writes best, I do worst, partly because good writing is always harder to play with, for we measure our work against the original but, mostly, because Muir, who lays on platitudes for things that do not require careful description (eg. the swaying treetop as "so noble an exhilaration of motion"), ironically, does much better when he wrestles with something difficult to describe. If you carefully read the lines I italicized, you must, like me, find my "tree-top waves meet waves of air" or "waves of light chasing waves of light" totally inadequate. Something longer than a haiku is clearly needed. Coincidentally, I, too, have exciting memories of a Winter gale. If Muir looked down, I viewed the surface of a sea of bamboo from *below*. lying flat on my back, looking up. As Muir was safe with his spruce, I was safe knowing that I was in the only woods where one need not fear for a falling limb in a gale. As true for any wave, amplitudes combine or cancel, and I was treated to a fantastic dance of the gaps in the cover. With many hills and a flitty wind, the "surface" effect was close to that found above a deep pool within a coral reef reaching almost to the surface, with channels, spill-overs, treacherous currents, maelstroms and choppiness far too complex for a short description. *How much like an ocean was it? So much so I later drew the bamboo grove with fish swimming through it.* Enough digression:

Excepting only the shadows there was nothing somber in all this wild sea of pines. On the contrary, notwithstanding this was the winter season, the colors were remarkably beautiful. The shafts of the pine and libocedrus were brown and purple, and most of the foliage was well tinged with yellow . . .

a winter gale
the petticoats of the trees
still colorful

not black & white
as you might think, a gale
in a sea of pine

Despite pine being ever-green, we tend to see them against the snow from below (gazing up from town on the surrounding mountains), so the beauty we see is generally stark. *Ibsen*. But seen from the lit side, *above* . . .

> The sounds of the storm corresponded gloriously with this wild exuberance of light and motion. The profound bass of the naked branches and boles booming like waterfalls; the quick, tense vibrations of the pine-needles, now rising to a shrill, whistling hiss, now falling to a silky murmur; the rustling of laurel groves in the dells, and the keen metallic click of leaf on leaf – ~~all this was heard in easy analysis when the attention was calmly bent.~~

> *sounds of every*
> *tone and type born within*
> *a winter storm*

> *sierra pine gale*
> *more jubilee than a high &*
> *lonesome sound*

> *limb bass, needle hiss*
> *rustling groves & leaves that click*
> *mountain symphony*

Light, motion, sound. Muir could have produced stunning nature documentaries.

> The varied gestures of the multitude were seen to fine advantage, so that one could recognize the different species at a distance of several miles by this means alone, as well as by their forms and colors, and the way they reflected the light. All seemed strong and comfortable, as if really enjoying the storm, while responding to its most enthusiastic greetings. We hear much nowadays concerning the universal struggle for existence, but no struggle in the common meaning of the word was manifest here; no recognition of danger by any tree; no deprecation; but rather an invincible gladness as remote from exultation as from fear.

> *invincible gladness*

> *recognizing trees*
> *by their dance clear across*
> *the mountain*

> *plants enjoying*
> *a winter gale: no struggle*
> *just existence*

> *it's how they dance*
> *various tribes of trees spotted*
> *three miles away*

> I kept my lofty perch for hours, frequently closing my eyes to enjoy the music by itself, or to feast quietly on the delicious fragrance that was streaming past. The fragrance of the woods was less marked than that produced during warm rain, when so many balsamic buds and leaves are steeped like tea; but, from the chafing of resiny branches against each other, and the incessant attrition of myriads of needles, the gale was spiced to a very tonic degree. And besides the fragrance from these local sources there were traces of scents brought from afar. For this wind came first from the sea, rubbing against its fresh, briny waves, then distilled through the redwoods, threading rich ferny gulches, and spreading itself in broad undulating currents over many a flower-enameled ridge of the coast mountains, then across the golden plains, up the purple foot-hills, and into these piny woods with the varied incense gathered by the way.

♪ *stormy weather* ♪
closing my eyes the better
to hear the trees

stormy branches   *mountain storm*
fiddling out melodies   *double tree polyphony*
scent of rosin   *sound & scent*

mountain storm
sight, sound and scent: trees
are three-track

sailing a tree   *mountain storm*
through a gale, do i   *the sight sound & scent*
smell the sea?   *of tree music*

Without a coat of rosin (fancy for hard resin, or pine sap), no bow, horse-hair or artificial – I have used monofilm and even metal rods! – rubbed over a string (metal/horse-hair/silk/gut/steel) will sound out. That is why I changed the second reading's "with a scent" to "scent of rosin." The same rosin, wrapped in Mexican toilet paper, put into a woman's stocking, tapped over a copper plate, heated, allowed to fix and given a bath of acid, can create aquatint for natural shading in an etching, but *back to Muir* (who, like me, would have loved Retsina!).

Winds are advertisements of all they touch, however much or little we may be able to read them; telling their wanderings even by their scents alone. Mariners detect the flowery perfume of land-winds far at sea, and sea-winds carry the fragrance of dulse and tangle far inland, where it is quickly recognized, though mingled with the scents of a thousand land-flowers. As an illustration of this, I may tell here that I breathed sea-air on the Firth of Forth, in Scotland, while a boy; then was taken to Wisconsin, where I remained nineteen years; then, without in all this time having breathed one breath of the sea, I walked quietly, alone, from the middle of the Mississippi Valley to the Gulf of Mexico, on a botanical excursion, and while in Florida, far from the coast, my attention wholly bent on the splendid tropical vegetation about me, I suddenly recognized a sea-breeze, as it came sifting through the palmettos and blooming vine-tangles, which at once awakened and set free a thousand dormant associations, and made me a boy again in Scotland~~, as if all the intervening years had been annihilated~~.

mountain storm
blown back to my childhood
the scent of the sea

Is the wind a collector? Or is it more of a palimpset upon which one scent is imprinted only to be subsequently replaced by another? Regardless, it brings us far more olfactory information than we can perceive, much less "read." Were Muir a dog (like Quoodle, Chesterton's poodle who lamented "goodness knows the noselessness of man!") just back from visiting China, maybe, he could have recognized some Gobi desert mixed in with the Pacific. But until James Lovelock, best known for his Gaia hypothesis, son of a man who scooped wasps up out of water ("they too have a right to enjoy life"), and independent inventor, gave us the Electron Capture Detector in 1956, Muir's beak of a nose was the best we could do.

Most people like to look at mountain rivers, and bear them in mind; but few care to look at the winds, though far more beautiful and sublime, and though they become at times about as visible as flowing water. When the north winds in winter are making upward sweeps over the curving summits of the High Sierra, the fact is sometimes published with flying snow-banners a mile long. Those portions of the winds thus embodied can scarce be wholly invisible, even to the darkest imagination. And when we look around over an agitated forest, we may see something of the wind that stirs it, by its effects upon the trees. Yonder it descends in a rush of water-like ripples, and sweeps over the bending pines from hill to hill. Nearer, we see detached plumes and leaves, now speeding by on level currents, now whirling in eddies, or, escaping over the edges of the whirls, soaring aloft on grand, upswelling domes of air, or tossing on flame-like crests. Smooth, deep currents, cascades, falls, and swirling eddies, sing around every tree and leaf, and over all the varied topography of the region with telling changes of form, like mountain rivers conforming to the features of their channels.

seen from above
the wind clear as a stream
upon the trees

they, too, stream
merrily merrily merrily
mountain winds

who says that pigs
alone can see the wind?
snow banners

my mountain view
whatever a river can do
the wind does it, too

In *The Song of the Sky,* pilot Guy Murchie describes the ocean of air in language and drawings both clear and enchantingly beautiful, an extraordinary feat; but no one has, to my knowledge, observed its interface with the land as well as Muir. Again, my distillations cannot capture the complex windscape. I can only pull allusions from a hat to express Muir's delight with the hitherto invisible element. And, now the chapter comes to something better than a climax, an epiphany.

After tracing the Sierra streams from their fountains to the plains, marking where they bloom white in falls, glide in crystal plumes, surge gray and foam-filled in boulder-choked gorges, and slip through the woods in long, tranquil reaches – after thus learning their language and forms in detail, we may at length hear them chanting all together in one grand anthem, and comprehend them all in clear inner vision, covering the range like lace. But even this spectacle is far less sublime and not a whit more substantial than what we may behold of these storm-streams of air in the mountain woods.

learn to read
the brooks, then translate
mountain storms

a green chorus
rings clear as any stream
stormy woods

We all travel the milky way together, trees and men; but it never occurred to me until this storm-day, while swinging in the wind, that trees are travelers, in the ordinary sense. They make many journeys, not extensive ones, it is true; but our own little journeys, away and back again, are only little more than tree-wavings – many of them not so much.

riding the gale

     how many hours
    for a tree top to go
     a hundred miles

we all travel   *not as lumber*
the milky way together   *men and trees traveling*
trees and men   *the milky way*

     sitting in a tree
    i see: trees are travelers
     like you and me

trees in a storm   *sitting up a tree*
some go a hundred miles   *riding out a storm: how far*
some just ten   *have we gone?*

     i dismount
    after riding one spruce
     a hundred miles

moving ten feet   *a winter storm*
or twenty at a time   *my tree moves miles*
trees in a storm   *ten feet at a time*

     tree tops moving
   go nowhere? so, when have you
     gone somewhere?

Please, someone. Investigate the tip of a tall evergreen and give us statistics: 1) how far it moves in the course of a powerful storm; 2) its mean movement per day/season/year; 3) the top *absolute speed* reached by a tip (without breaking) 4) the top *maintained speed* during a storm (over the course of an hour, a day, etc.). The "not as lumber" alludes to a line – *Dead, we become the lumber of the world* – from the *Fragments of Seneca,* translated by the great dirty wit and rhymster without parallel, the earl of Rochester. Traveling the Milky Way is not identical to merely whirling around a globe, but I would guess that Muir knew the poem in question, while 99% of my readers do not. As far as *going somewhere*, how right Muir is! The extent of *my* travels this week have been over and back across a railroad track for mail and newspaper (with little in either for me) and back and forth to the leaky old barn and from there to the old stable dragging tarpfuls of hay – call me *a human tractor* – for the cows (*Ah, the irony of it!* We – for, reader, the time comes out of my editing what *you* now read – are being taxed by my sister's "tax cows." How much further I could travel by sitting still before the bird feeder, just beyond the computer into which I feed these words, and surfing on the world-wide web)! And, most people who travel around the world, I dare say, go no further! Back to Muir, who is moving into his epilogue:

> When the storm began to abate, I dismounted and sauntered down through the calming woods. The storm-tones died away, and, turning toward the east, I beheld the countless hosts of the forests hushed and tranquil, towering above one another on the slopes of the hills like a devout audience. The setting sun filled them with amber light, and seemed to say, while they listened, "My peace I give unto you."

after the gale
trees glow in beatific light
and turn in

after the gale
trees to the east go to sleep
illuminated

I tried and failed to come up with a single *ku* that distilled this scene so as to improve it. Even adding the idea of the coming night failed. I prefer the original.

As I gazed on the impressive scene, all the so-called ruin of the storm was forgotten, and never before did these noble woods appear so fresh, so joyous, so immortal.

after the storm
even the fallen are still
green evergreen

afternote: *An Appreciation of John Muir*

This chapter is already long, but the story of my first *use* of John Muir might amuse some readers. In the late 1970's, I wrote a series of books taking issue with the antithetical stereotype Japanese/Occidental. One commonly encountered belief was that Occidentals, unlike Japanese, only engaged nature as their antagonist and one of my prime counter-examples of someone clearly Occidental yet one with nature was John Muir. While my book was written in Japanese, I felt it better to leave the translation of literature I quoted to a native-speaker with a better style than mine. Her first draft of Muir was not very good. When I pressed her to improve it, I found out why. She found Muir maudlin, artificial and representative of everything bad about the way the West related to nature. In particular, I recall she was almost nauseated by the blood Muir had coursing through the veins of boulders, his "dear friends," revisited on a mountain and, I suppose his overuse of "noble" and other adjectives that irk me, too. To appease the translator, I added long paragraphs explaining why style did *not* neccesarily make the man, detailing the time Muir spent in the woods and how he walked the spine of the mountains as no man ever had, how he rode down a hillside on a rock in a landslide, lashed himself to that tree, jumped up to celebrate an earthquake – mother nature rocking him on her knee, as he put it – when the whites and the natives were equally afraid and horrified it was supernatural punishment, and his saintly attitude, as represented by his encounter with a rattlesnake that was not only live and let live but appreciative of the rattlesnake's place in *our* world.

But, before I could teach my translator, John Muir and nature-poet John Clare (whose naive "I love this, I love that" style also rankles us) had to teach *me* not to judge content on its style. It was not an easy lesson to learn, for our top literary magazines are pure style (Do our wealthy publishers and smart editors lack the broad reading experience required to evaluate content?). Reading such, one comes to assume that if anyone has something worth saying, it will be well written, when nothing could be further from the truth. And the result is that truely original content is so rare most readers no longer even know they miss it (I *do*. And, that is why I no longer read literary magazines). As we have seen, Muir was no stranger to purple prose, but how many more tasteful writers could match his insight? Look at this passage (#16) from his 1870 *Mountain Thoughts:*

> Nothing is more wonderful than to find smooth harmony in this lofty cragged region where at first sight all seems so rough. From any of the high standpoints a thousand peaks, pinnacles, spires are seen thrust into the sky and so sheer and bare as to be inaccessible to wild sheep, accessible only to the eagle. *Any one by itself harsh, rugged, crumbling, yet in connection with others seems like a line of writing along the sky; it melts into melody, one leading into another, keeping rhythm in time.* (*Italics mine.*collected by Linnie Marsh Wolfe and published in John of the Mountains (1938))

"Smooth harmony" is an obvious oxymoron, but look at that last line! Elsewhere – near that earthquake he celebrated – Muir details the way the fallen boulders and other so-called debris improve the appearance of the foot of a cliff in the manner of the flaired pedestals found in some classical columns. *I* would not have praised Nature like that, for I am no fan of Classic architecture, but Muir's judgment that the fallen debris beautifies the natural vista is as sure as the hooves of the rams he shared the peaks with. And, when he writes (#2) –

The sun shines not on us but in us. The rivers flow not past, but through us, thrilling, tingling, vibrating every fiber and cell of the substance of our bodies, making them glide and sing. The trees wave and the flowers bloom in our bodies as well as our souls, and every bird song, wind song, and; tremendous storm song of the rocks in the heart of the mountains is our song, our very own, and sings our love.

– there is only one possible word to add, and that is: *Amen*.

~~~~~~

EXTRA. I just found my favorite passage from Muir's *Yosemite.* If you have not yet read it, be prepared for a treat! Before introducing it, I will sum up the rest of the essay.

When an earthquake shook the Yosemite, at "half past two o'clock of a moonlit morning in March" 1873, John Muir scrambled from his cabin,

> both glad and frightened, shouting, 'A noble earthquake! A noble earthquake!' . . .The shocks were so violent and varied, and succeeded one another so closely, that I had to balance myself carefully in walking as if on the deck of a ship among waves . . . (*Yosemite*)

Muir gives a beautiful page long description of the "rock storm" he was treated to. Then, he ran up the valley to climb upon the newly fallen rocks, "slowly settling into their places, chafing, grating against one another, groaning and whispering." Then he ran about the Valley and found the other whites and indians quaking. No one else was pleased that "kind Mother Earth is trotting us on her knee to amuse us and make us good." There are pages on the aftershocks and the reaction of the animals. (worried robins, nonplused owls.) He even appreciated the rearrangement of his beloved Valley, noting that "rough places were made smooth and smooth places were made rough" by the earthquake. His conclusion belongs among our greatest essays on the aesthetic.

> But, on the whole , by what at first sight seemed pure confounded confusion and ruin, the landscapes were enriched; for gradually every talus was covered with groves and gardens, and made a finely proportioned and ornamental base for the cliffs. In this work of beauty, every boulder is prepared and measured and put in its place more thoughtfully than are the stones of temples. If for a moment you

are inclined to regard these taluses as mere draggled, chaotic damps, climb to the top of one of them, and run down without any haggling, puttering hesitation, boldly jumping from boulder to boulder with even speed. You will find your feet playing a tune, and quickly discover the music and poetry of these magnificent rock piles a fine lesson; and all Nature's wildness tells the same story the shocks and outbursts of earthquakes, volcanoes, geysers, roaring, thundering waves and floods, the silent uprush of saps in plants, storms of every sort each and all are the orderly beauty making love beats of Nature's heart. (*Ibid*)

Describing Muir's discovery from memory, I had forgotten that he first felt the melody of the fallen rocks by running down them! If anyone does a movie of this John of the Mountains a good stuntman will be needed!

John Wilmot, Earl of Rochester's translation of *A Fragment of Seneca* mentioned in the text. I wish I had more translations just to demonstrate his unmatched genius.

After Death nothing is, and nothing, death,
The utmost limit of a gasp of breath.
Let the ambitious zealot lay aside
His hopes of heaven, whose faith is but his pride;
Let slavish souls lay by their fear
Nor be concerned which way nor where
After this life they shall be hurled.
Dead, we become the lumber of the world,
And to that mass of matter shall be swept
Where things destroyed with things unborn are kept.
Devouring time swallows us whole.
Impartial death confounds body and soul.
For Hell and the foul fiend that rules
God's everlasting fiery jails
(Devised by rogues, dreaded by fools),
With his grim, grisly dog that keeps the door,
Are senseless stories, idle tales,
Dreams, whimseys, and no more.

♪ My beautiful late-19c reproduction, with all of John Wilmot's in/famous but hard-to-find obscene poems, sits side-by-side with my other most treasure, Isaac Walton's *The Compleate Angler*, full of something I once made, *etchings*, on the bookcase of a publisher in Japan awaiting my escape from the pauperdom. You would think a google of "lumber of the world" would show *dozens* of hits for this translation, well-known among those who know. That I found but one (at druidic.org) suggests the internet is still not doing nearly enough to provide us with quality literature. Of course, it may be hidden within closed data banks, but to those without access, such places are already lumber. If you would keep great work (and small) above ground, where its fruit may be enjoyed by all, please help out Googlebooks, Guttenberg, Luminarium, The Virginia Text Initiative, Wiki and other open sites. If you have clout get J-Stor to at least offer a reasonable annual fee for would-be users not in a well-endowed university or rich prep-school. When we run across a fifty year old article, we should be allowed to see it rather than salivate, cuss and hit the return key, or beg someone with access to break the regulations and send us a copy! When it comes to literature, call me a Marxist: *Literature belongs to those who can read it!*

XVII
Tinker Bell & Marot's L'embonpoint
or, the metamorphosis of *plump* in translation

About 1990, I reread Peter Barrie's *Peter Pan*. I have *two* recollections *why*. 1) After reading an essay about flying dreams by Lafcadio Hearn, I asked my English students about the same and one adult (a high-school teacher) told me about hers, which picked up night after night where it left off, like a soap opera, and, better yet, related her husband's jealous reaction when she told him about it: *Can't you be serious even when you sleep! Sleep seriously, will you! (majime ni ne-nasai)*. When another student added that she flew prone but only a foot or two over the ground, so it felt degrading rather than liberating, I felt I had the start for another book (I had dozens in various stages of development; now, scores). Vaguely recalling that the magical realism, or plausible fiction in Peter Pan was similar to that I enjoyed in *my* dreams where I logically proved I could fly by flapping my arms under certain weather conditions, I bought the book to see how *they* managed to fly. 2) The other story seems more plausible. Somewhere, I came across words to the effect that Tinker Belle (the fairy) was too tiny to hold more than one emotion at a time, which I had to check out because some Japanese claimed the same about Occidentals, whom they felt lived in a black & white world of *love* or *hate* but no mixed emotions whatsoever, and I wanted to mention Tinkerbelle in an article taking issue with such stereotypes, and that meant checking the source. Most memories would choose one or the other story and settle the matter, but not mine. Things remain in parallel forever. Be that as it may, the first thing that surprised me when I read the book for the first time since childhood (when I must have read an abridged version) was that *I had to go to the dictionary for a word on the very first page of a children's book!*

> It was a girl called Tinker Bell, exquisitely gowned in a skeleton leaf, cut low and square, through which her figure could be seen to the best advantage. She was slightly inclined to *embonpoint*. (1903)

Embonpoint. After noting it meant healthily or *pleasantly plump* – call it literally well-rounded – I could not help recalling the sassy-looking fairy on the *Playboy* Magazine joke page. Then, shortly later, I read an article from *The Observer* carried by *The Japan Times*. I was *astounded* to find Peter Barrie, Peter Pan and Tinker Belle blamed for *anexoria!* Obviously, the English or Scott reporter had not read his countryman's book, or, if he had, did not stop to look up the big French word. Of course, the reporter was not *all* wrong. Tinkerbelle *on stage*, or rather flying over it, was usually a wee wisp of a thing. But that is hardly Barrie's fault. The blame lies with the acting companies or stage unions or whoever budgets for the people who pull down on the guy-wires. With most Englishmen, like all those guys on Montie Python, thin as poles, one would need two on each side to keep a buxom Tinker-belle in the air. Or, to put it another way, if the world had only taken better care of poor, involuntarily thin men,

165

which is to say fattened us (i.e. your author included) up, so we could provide more ballast, little girls would not have seen thin Tinkerbelles flying through the air and grown up to starve themselves. Either everybody is healthy, or no one.

Si tu dures / Trop malade / Coulere fade / Tu prendras, / Et pedras / L'embonpoint.

French is not one of my better languages, so the first time I opened *Le Ton beau de Marot*, I failed to read all 28 lines of *A une Damoyselle malade,* or *Ma Mignonne* (the 16c French poem Hofstadter & friends practiced their variations on), though each aabbccddeeffgghhiijjkkllmmaa rhymed-line was but three syllables-long. I only read it after finishing the rest of this book, and was wondering how to give *Le Ton beau* the space it deserved (more than the *100 Frogs, 100 Poets* or *19 Weis*), when, there, 4 lines from the end, *Embonpoint!* I only give lines 20-25, above, for *we* will not play with the whole poem which means *something* like this:

> *Honey, do rise from bed, a living hell,*
>   *Be not dead, but, quickly, become well!*
> *Gain meat, eat – become fat and happy;*
>   *When we meet, Clement wants you sappy!*
> *Grant good health to Honey, Dieu, I pray,*
>   *Let her eat cake, pound cake, si Vous plez!*

We will skip all details (and macaronics + other "improvements" in my reading) but one: the original "Dear" is *mignonne*, according to OED from the Old High Greek *minna* (love) or Celtic *min-* (small). I know, from familiarity with its cognate in 16c Portuguese, it meant *baby* and *child*. As the former means *lover* in many tongues, I took a romantic reading. *Le Ton beau* has over 70 complete translations of the poem (a "minuscule opus" to Hofstadter, but *long* for a haiku guy like me), many in two versions. That is *a lot*. In order not to spread myself too thin, I concentrate on how *L'embonpoint* is Englished. We shall use Hofstadter's numbers with the translations, so readers with his book can refer to them in their entirety. We will skip #1a, a meta-poem listing the formal properties of the original, #1b, the original French, and #2a, #3a, #4a and #5a, all prose translation/explanations of almost everything but *embonpoint*.

> 2b . . . *If thou stayest / Too sick, / Pale shade / Thou wilt acquire, / And wilt lose / Thy plump form* . . .   D. Hofstadter

> 3b . . . */ And wilt lose / Thy round shape* . . .   D. Hofstadter

> 4b . . . */ And [you (familiar)]will waste/lose / The plumpness/ stoutness/portliness/(i.e., well-fed look)*. . . .   D. Hofstadter

Hofstadter's first take is perfect for *plump* is *pretty* (and euphonious) for all who feel it is; and *round,* in the second, philosophically good. In the Sinosphere, as in Greece before muscle-worship, rotundity was *ideal*. A literally round baby, god/dess or written character incarnated *harmony, happiness* and *good fortune*. The *stout* and *portly* reading included in the literally meaningful 4b dutifully rounds off the connotative bases, but is not sweet enough, given the context.

> 5b . . . *Just get strong . . . You'll get ghostly pale and start looking like skin and bones . . .*   D. Hofstadter

Page 5a mostly continues the explanation that came before, but also addresses translation itself. Coming up with the imaginative reading, eg., "skin and bones," is attributed to the way prose translation freed up the translator "from the constraints of word-for-word fidelity." *Whatever works.* In my case, poetry is more likely to set me free, or rather guide me in odd directions, for the form of a poem, whether identical or different from the original, can make even the nonsensical *seem* fitting (the choice being not reason *or* rhyme but the reason *of* rhyme). We also see a choice to avoid something late-20c Usanians or, at least most highly educated whites, failed to appreciate: *plump-as-desireable* by reversal: *bone-skinny-as-undesireable.*

Page 6a explains Hofstadter's transition to freer variation mentioned in 5a. 6b examples it, keeping the *"Just get strong"* from 5b, and playing with the food, taking Marot's jam and making it: *"Buttered bread / While in bed / makes a mess / so unless . . ."* and substituting "Douglas" for "Clement." *This* is what I call *paraversing.* But, *embonpoint?* Nowhere to be seen. Likewise, with 7b, the wild *Cutie Pie* version (each variation has a name as well as a number), which includes this memorable rhyme: *""Quick!," says Clem, / "Flush your phlegm!""*

> 8b . . . *If you stay / Ill this way Pale and drawn, / You'll put on / But then cede / Pounds you need." . . .* Robert French

> 9b . . . *If you're still / Wan and ill / You will cede / Pounds you need." . . .* Robert French

The "elegance and suavity" of the 8b translation (not the above lines, but the whole thing) done quickly and garnished with *ham* to match the *jam,* by a professional translator made Hofstadter "depressed about" his own efforts, until he noticed French was two lines too long and then, "one day" found "that it contained a mistranslation (oh, joy!) on lines 24-25." Needless to say, *there was no gaining and losing weight* in the original. It is just ambiguous enough to allow such a reading, but logic makes it implausible. Kudos to Hofstadter for confessing a sort of glee few authors will admit and French for permitting the publication of his mistranslation. Honesty is as hard to come by in writers as it is in politicians, and I appreciate every such admission. 9b kills the two lines with one correction. Then, after a chapter for Marot's *Ode to Good Tits*, where I learned that Germans use the same word for a wart and a nipple, new blood. A woman, who worked with French at the "Fluid Analogies Research Group" (!) contributed a paraverse that flows as sweetly as *Julia's Clothes* (I wish I could quote more!):

> 10b . . . *Courage, Dam / Up thy tears. / Stay thy fears, / Lest thou pale / And thus fail / Swift to mend. . . .* Melanie Mitchell

The archaic style "To My Sweet" boldly called the *mignonne* "sweet" and, best of all coined a new term of endearment: "My sweet-tooth." *Embonpoint* is not even hinted at; but, with French making it seem weight was purely a matter of health rather than charm, can we blame Mitchell for switching to *tears* and psychosomatic medicine? Then, a formal surprise: (11a) two collaborators independently pointed out to Hofstadter that the semantic and rhymed couplets were a line off. Since we naturally tend to rhyme so as to tie together a thought, composing such a poem takes concentration, like stagger-singing *Row Row Row Your Boat*. Mitchell rose to the occasion with her next, *"My Dear Sue:"*

> 11b . . . *If you pine / And still ail, / Skin so pail, / Will be Sue's. / You will lose / Your plump self. / God, good health / Give to you, / My dear Sue* .   Melanie Mitchell

Hurrah, *plump* is back! There is much more fun in the poem, but we are far from done, so I will quote no more, though you may note I could not resist finishing the poem. When you think about it "Sue" not only matches "you" but evokes "sweet" so naturally the adjective would be wasted. Hardly "arbitrary" this! We will skip the author's 12b, inspired by Mitchell's psychologically weighted 10b but addressed to a child, *"Sweet and milde"* and blessed with a beautiful rhyme of *"God had smiled / On thee child,"* following a novelty not found in the original: a *dream*. There is no *embonpoint*, but who cares! Hofstadter is clearly coming round to the joy of paraversing, as opposed to mere multiple translations. Then, again, there is also delight in hitting a nail square on its round head:

> 13b. . . *Thou wilt lose / Thy round thigh . / God grant thy / Health complete, / O my sweet*.   William Cavnar

The beauty of *embonpoint* is more than thigh, breast and cheek, above and below. Fleshiness conceals ankle bones, collar-bones, shoulder bones, and backbones, too. It speaks of a cushion in a hard world. But, who is complaining, when we even have that *O* giving the whole picture! Cavner did this version by tastefully tweaking Hofstadter's responsible but stiff 3b and the latter finds it "all in all, beyond doubt, the best translation" in the book. I am not sure I concur, but if all's well that ends well, *"O my sweet"* ties Mitchell's *"My dear Sue."*

> 14b. . . *If you stay / Home all day, / Sick in bed, / You'll lose weight. / What a fate! / Sitting home* . . .   David Moser

You do not notice from the above alone, but Moser (who Hofstadter first introduced to Chinese and is now a well-known translator), does something new. He boldly recrafts the greater flow of the narrative (see discussion on pg.__). The above lines, near the end in the original, are near the middle in his version, which ends *"I'm sincere, / On my knees: / Get well, please! / You're the one, / Honey bun!"* While the idioms also seem to distance his reading from the original, I feel it, like Pound with the *Shi-ching*, remains at heart closer to the spirit of the original than most of the more timid translations. In his next, 15b, Moser *hints* at plump beauty with "All cooped up / buttercup?" near the start and talks up food but still fails to clearly take on *embonpoint*. Odd, I thought, for one versed in Chinese. . .

> 16b. . . . *All shut in, / You'll get thin, / . . . This I pray: / Lord above, / Give my love, / Back her form, / Soft and warm. / Make her skin / Pink again, /Smooth and plump / Sugar lump . . .* David Moser

At last, the body I was waiting for, the pink expressing the original wan in reverse and the form-warm rhyme fine even if large rumps tend to be cool. Hofstadter appreciated Moser's "modern American English – line 3 is "Sick-bed blues" and I find the added "above" for the "love" rhyme, masterful? Only the "sugar lump" rubs me the wrong way, for I have not seen smooth and plump ones, though I suppose they *might* exist. It would be so much easier in Japanese, where there is a food item just the shape, texture, color and flavor one wants here: *botan-mochi*, or peony-*mochi*. *Mochi*, which is steamed and pounded highly glutenous "sweet-rice" cake(?) dusted a thin layer of starch-powder is synonymous with smooth skin, while the ball-shaped *botan(peony)mochi* was a nickname for the *kamuro*, adorable little round-faced girls who served courtesans much as pages served knights.

> 17b. . . *Wan and pale / As in jail / In your bed, / Thin, ill-fed. / . . . / If you stay / Sick all day, / Your allure / Won't endure* . . David Moser
>
> 18b. . . *Eat food! / Indulge, / And bulge, / Anew, /Sweet Sue!* D.M

Moser had a great string of rhymes in the hard-to-label 2-syllable 42-line version 17b. Who can argue with *"Flee your room! / Leave that tomb!"* Still, I wanted a positive *plump* and was happy to see it in 18b, though the word "bulge" is ugly, which is why I would have left Mostadter's 19b, *Sweetmeat Sue*, with its *"Eat stewed food! / Win! Indulge! / Stand and bulge: / A new you, / Sweetmeat Sue,"* in the canning factory (likewise for 20b). The Joycean pun "Meat-sweet Sue" starts-off 21b well, but *win-indulge-stand-bulge* is so bad I find myself wondering if it is a subconscious agenda to undermine the beauty of *embonpoint* by conflating it with middle-age weight-gain or, worse, the only weight most (?) Usanians feel good about, hard muscle. (Here Hofstadter inserts a chapter on Chinese => English translation, where I find myself on the opposite side of the fence, defending Geremie Barme for the dirty language (*"arse-licking," "screw 'em," "a load of crap," "a hayseed"* etc.) he used for translating *Chinese Lives*, that Hofstadter felt stripped "Mr. Average of his Chineseness," where I feel, to the contrary, that it helps correct the inanely polite Oriental stereotype and reflects the rough language Chinese do indeed use – and Japanese do not (More? See pgs 134-5 of my *Orientalism & Occidentalism*).

> 22b. . . *Pray / stay / in / thin, / slim, / trim, / love / dove.* Robert French

This, first of the batch of paraverses called "Bold Ventures," reduced the poem's lines from three syllables to one monosyllable word – and, likewise, pared down the body, about which Hofstadter rationalized "One might justify Bob's transmogrification of Marot's thought by pointing out that whereas back in the sixteenth century, buxom ripeness was all the rage . . . , our century is obsessed by svelte sleekness," thus, making it "a proper transtemporation" of desire of the poet; though, he continued, chances are French did it without thinking, because he associated looking good with thinness. But, Hofstadter re-itterates, even a reflexively executed reversal "could still be claimed to be one of many valid manners of effecting cross-cultural translation." He is right in that *unless a translator is willing to explain and publishers willing to allow notes*, detail (*fat/thin*) is sometimes best reversed in order that the deeper level of significance (*attractive/unattractive*) does *not* reverse in the mind of the unaware reader. Changing the skin, consciously or not, can help communicate original intent by preserving the meat (as meat can be sacrificed to save the bones).

> 23b . . . *If thou endurest / In this malady, / A faded color, / Wilt apprehend, / Along with perdition / Of thy bounteous points.* . . .
> Melanie Mitchell

How delightful! More Melanie (Not knowing her, I should not use her first name, but I cannot help myself!)! *"Alley-oop!"* indeed! I wish I could quote all of *My Minion*, for her paraverse, an attempt to use an English word cognate with a French word in each line – is itself *"a manger of confectionary!"* And, look, *just look* what *embonpoint* has turned into! Melanie set me to thinking about that "point." OED has *embonpoint* defined as *plump* or *well-nourished* in either the complimentary or euphemistic (bad) sense, originally meaning "in good condition." That puzzles me. The *bon* is "good" (and root for bounty). OK. But "point?" "Point" comes from "punctus" or "sharp." Could that mean that the boy and muscle-loving ancients of the Occident equated good and sharp, i.e. hard bodies, and that later, in France, when a softer corpulance came to be appreciated, the term reversed? If so, then Robert French accidently took us back to where it started! And, here, I was ready to stop, until I saw the next paraverse, *Dear, Your Bard*, a masterpiece of paraverse by the (then) director of the Folger Shakespeare Library, which ends like this:

> 24b . . . *You'll be moot / If you stay / Sickly gray – / Your plump ass / Like dry grass, / And bony. / So honey, / God heal you. / Then we'll screw.* O.B. Hardison

Midway into the poem, the term of endearment *sweet bon-bon* tells us what the translator likes. *C'est bon!* The Hardistadter variation, which is to say Hofstadter revamp, also 24b, turns that dry/plump gr/ass into a *" . . hey / Nonny-no"* (*Nonny-no* once meant something punfully no-thing, lyrically enjoyed on a plush bed of grass) which is chased down with a way to rhyme that would have astounded even Ogden Nash, *"Heal you, He'll; / Screw then, we'll!"*

> 25b . . . *Eat fruit / stay cute* . . . Hugh Kenner
> 25b . . *eat an apple pie / Or something sweet as you are* .. M. Kandel

Both of these paraverses were short and had no room for embonpointedness.

> 26b . . . *Go pig out, / Ope wide your mouth /. . Unless you're hale, / You'll turn pale, / Lose oo-la-la / That wiggles your tail/* . . .
> *Mon petit chou.* Nancy Hofstadter

If you combine the food, *oo-lal-la*, the wiggle, and the little cabbage (*petit chou*), *Hi Toots!* gives *embonpoint* its due in many ways, some new. Reading his mother's dynamic *Mon petit chou*, Hofstadter asks:

> "Now if you can get away with one line in the original language, how far could you conceivably go . . . ? . . . The logical conclusion of such a tendency, would of course be a translation that was *completely* in French. But such an ambition, even if "logical", would be totally absurd."

Not, *really. Of course* we can remake poems in the language in which they are written. It is just more difficult to paraverse that way than to translate because of what might be called *compunction*. We are unsure we should be doing it. Aesthetically speaking, however, the fun is in the mixed language.

> 33b . . . *But, dear, you / Will stay plump / 'Round your rump* D.H.
> 37b . . . *She who stays / Sick for days / Grows too thin, / And her skin / Glows no more.* . . . DH
> 38b . . . *for days / Gets pale skin / And grows thin / . . / o, to gain / Health complete, / My pet – eat!* D.H.
> 39b . . . *Sure hope God / Cures your bod, /* . . . D.H.
> 40b . . . *In my book. / a good look- / ker ain't spin- / dily 'n' thin.* D.H.
> 41b . . . *Crammed with cream, / Bright you'll gleam! / Jewels are prized / More when sized / More.)* . . . D.H.

42b gilds her with 18-24 Carrot cakes, but what interests me is the progression from *plump* to *glow* and, eventually, a *gleam* and a *Little Gem* series of which 41b is one. Plump can be soft and comfy (as Darwin sitting on the hard wooden chairs of the Beagle thought of it), but here we end up with the Desmond Morris view of rumps and breasts, ideally round and taut, or so it seems to me.

> 43b . . . *To gain brawn, / Champs chomp on /* . . . *Box that pox, / Goldilocks!* DH
> 44b . . . *Your old skirts, / Now a bit / Loose, will fit. / Cheeks aflush, / You will crush / Luster's lack.* DH
> 45b . . . *'Twill put hair / On your chest /* . . . *Bless, you, son – / My wee one.* DH

A pox boxer? *Yeech!* But, using loose clothing to show the need to gain weight is fine, and the gender change to a *boy* – why not? Translating from Japanese, which rarely uses pronouns, to English, a translator is constantly having to – or, *able to*, if you enjoy *fiat* – sex his or her protagonists.

> 45b . . . *Losin' weight / makes your great / figure flat. / Don't do that!* . . (45b2 . . *God, not that! / Fat's divine, Darlin' mine!*)

45b is another inverse way to favor *embonpoint*, though the curvaceousness associated with a great figure in Usanian culture assumes a waist too thin for the term. Pardon an aside, but the idea of "a figure" or the proportions that accompany such a concept did not even exist in the Sinosphere, where human bodies were not deified. The second 45b dropped the final wish for getting well to add the fine *"Fat's divine!"* to go with the Clement-inspired darling, Clementine. Whether Hofstadter knew it or not, it is also literally true in the sense that people are always free to lose weight, but to gain it, one must be *blessed* with good digestion and absorption; if you are not, no amount of will-power or food can put a single pound on you. Or, to turn that around, to suffer from involuntary thinness is to be abandoned by God, so to speak.

> 55b *Salut, ma vieille! . . .* F. Recanati
> 55b2 *Old gal, God bless! . . . Thou lovely frail, / You'll soon grow thin. / Food must go in . . .* F. Recanati / D. Hofstadter

At first, Hofstadter writes, the idea of Englishing a French variation did not interest him as it defeated the purpose of translating *from Marot*. I am glad he loosened up and allowed it, for French is Greek to me and it is refreshing to see this Parisian linguist solve the *embonpoint* problem by wishing it for someone of an age where many must fight to keep their flesh. And, good translation, too! Let me add that I am afraid translations of same-language translations from old work into English is far from rare. I have seen ancient Japanese poems in English which bore far more resemblance to modern Japanese translations than to the original, in meaning and style. In all too many cases, the modern Japanese translation had no wit; and the English, sadly, copied it!

> 60b *. . . Too long your mouth has lain in sad repose; / It hungers for the honey'd sweets of youth. / For if you seek life's chapter thus to close, / A wilted frame will be your path to truth. ...* Anthony Guneratne

To put 60b next to 55b, I must skip some *metaverse* variations, Hofstadter's 56b *Mignonnette* (pretty pet), which includes *"As Clem wrote,"* 58b, which *"Like Marot"* paints the poem *". . . Bright- / 'ning up white / Canvas zones, / Like to bones / Adding flesh,"* and English computer scientist John Galton's amusing complaint, 57b, *Mademoiselle,* with its *"I'm too dense / To make sense / of old French"* and criticism of the original's structure. Guneratne, a Sri Lankan who had lived and studied in Italy, uses the inverse *embonpoint* (don't get thin) idea we are used to while replacing flesh with spirit. I recall reading a fine book about anorexia and female saints, who did, indeed, take that path. If the original French contains the kernel of the allusion, Guneratne's sonnet is a great sense-translation, and, if it was not there, it is a great paraverse. Only lack of permission (if I wrote those I'd quote for permission, I would have no time to write, so, as a rule, I don't) prevents me from quoting all of it! We shall skip 61b, *Yo There Dog*, the artificial rap version for the closest it comes to *embonpoint* is a basketball hoop – I hope that the next edition of *Le Ton beau* has better *real* Black English variations and maybe a Hawaiin Nikei (Japanese)English one as well.

> 62b *. . . Health to you! / Rise and moo! / . . . On your rump / feel Sue's thump . . . / Chew your cud / lest your milk / Lose its silk / (Too low-fat / for a cat) / And your bright /black and white / Fade to gray –* Susan Wonder

Hofstadter spliced together this delightful variation titled *Gentle Cow* – wondrous for turning inverse embonpoint into concern for lack of fat in milk and making its dull/shinyness corollary witty *for the first time in all translations* with her black/white/gray idea – from "two cow-based poems" he received from SW! I hope quoting 12 of 28 lines (again, you want to see them all!) will not land me in jail, which is where 63b, taking what had been metaphor in the original and all other variations literally, go. 64b is not for me. Let us see the next, *My Nice*:

> 65b . . . *If you hard / Too sick, / Insipid couleur / You will take, / And lose / The embonpoint / . . .*   Systran

DH notes that it is understandable that Systran missed antiquated French words, but why, then, was *couleur* left as is? I wonder if the software included the word *as English*, where said color came to mean "roseate" (interesting contrasted to *blanc* (white), which lost its color to became *blank*), but did not "know" a good complexion could only be lost, or, to put it another way, pink cannot take on sallowness/gray but only turn into it. Systran made one mistake made by DH early on and another we saw with RF's 8b. Such mistakes bring to mind a Grook by Danish mathematician Piet Hein about a new-fangled *thinking elevator* that not only can think, but is clearly *"thinking wrong."* Yes, *that* should endear it to us. But let us leave further discussion of machine-translation and examples to DH, who is more at home in that brave new world than I am.

> 68b . . . *If you stubborn / Too sick, / Color dull / You take, / And lose / Full and developed body / . . .*   Zhang Jiaying

Zhang, a friend of David Moser, just arrived in the States, knew almost no English or French and did "My Treasure" *by dictionary*. DH found the result within the range of machine-translations, the only difference being 3 hours of labor versus 10 seconds of work, if work it could be called, on the part of the machine. The one noteable difference is the treatment of *embonpoint!* Either Zhang intended to choose "full" *or* "developed" and forgot to eliminate one, or she lost herself in thought when she read the word's definition. *What thought?* Perhaps, the hyper-trophied sexual characteristics of many Caucasian women in comparison to the relatively neotonous and, therefor, unisex Mongolian. In the 19c, white Europeans found "our" more specialized bodies evidence that we were more highly evolved, or modern, than the East where women still lacked wide hips and large breasts and men with wide shoulders and large you-know-whats were rare. In the Far East, people are *still* very conscious of such racial differences. A third possibility is that Zhang thought a plump line would better fit the meaning of the word.

> 70b . . . *Listen to / Jams by Fats – / Or if that's / Not your mood / Chow down food.*   DH
> 71b . . . *Regain strength / And fight gloom. / Soon you'll bloom, Have no fear, Carol dear.*   DH

I like the idea of using paraverses of existent poems for personalized greeting cards. DH's mother, who likes Fats Waller, had a quintuple cardiac bypass (sounds like the express-way on the Northside of Miami!) and "Soon you'll bloom" is so perfect for DH's wife, Carole, who had "a serious abdominal operation performed in order to allow her to have a safe second pregnancy" that I did not miss the absent *embonpoint* at all.

> 72b ... *Flu consumes / Scrawny birds; / Heed my words / And take care* ...   Carol Hofstadter

Carol Hofstadter's *Chickadee* had the last word, and it is such a kind one that we cannot help but feel *her* sweet character: Within years she would die, and *Le Ton beau de Marot,* which is in part a journey of growth from the brilliant but, to me (with decades of experience translating and correcting translations), restrictive formality of a man versed in hard science to the equally brilliant play of a poet, tempered but not too tightly armored by his intellect, would surely have given her great delight. Half of good translation is logistics, the linguistic horsepower and word-smithing skills to carry precious cargo across a linguistic divide. The other half is attitude. A translator must not only *carry* but *care* – care for the meaning, care for the style, care for the poet, care for the audience – and, most importantly, take care to mind the sixth sense that science has yet to explain and no machine can ape. This is especially important with exotic tongues, where there is more creation than carrying. I have never met a good translator who was not a good person (The only possible exception I can think of is a *well-known* translator, who definitely *knows* more than others in his field; but, his *translation*, itself, is terribly short on style, so it is questionable whether he really is a *good* translator).

a note on the proper length for haiku, with an
Apology to Hofstadter

Since my first book in English, *Rise, Ye Sea Slugs!* had multiple translations of haiku, a fair amount of natural history, and many notes of the sort guaranteed to bring joy to a hyperlogical soul, I thought DH would enjoy it. After all, I had read some of his books and knew two of his Japanese translators. Hearing my sister was in contact with him, I sent her a copy to forward rather than googling down a contact. Some time later, my sister called, furious at me for "attacking" Hofstadter in my criticism of his rigid s*yllable-ism* in a footnote to page 31. The next thing I knew, even my mother got into it, lecturing me on attacking people. Since I never heard from Hofstadter, I assume he, too, took umbrage at it. In retrospect, it is perfectly fair, but too *ad hominen*, considering something I did not realize at the time. Since I cannot apologize for something the reader has not seen, here it is, slightly edited, but with every possibly offensive word, intact.

Beats, Not Syllables! Reading Hofstadter's *Le Ton beau de Marot* (1997), I see a word may not be sufficient even for the wise. *Look.* I agree that sticking to form is a stimulus to the imagination and, myself, love rhyme (and have published essays in defense of rhyme) for that reason. But you are mistaken if you think haiku always forms "a symmetric 5-7-5 pattern." Your example, Bashô's *furuike ya / kawazu tobi-komu / mizu no oto,* – the most famous haiku ever written, not "what he [Sato] *says* must be the most famous haiku ever written" (my italics) – is, in fact, a good example of an asymmetrical 5-12 split, for the *ya* cuts the first part (the old pond) from the rest. The verb *tobikomu* (jump-in) bringing the middle seven to an end modifies, i.e., links to the *mizu-no-oto* (water-sound) that follows. The poem has 8 beats,[2] one more than usual in the first part, which gives the old pond a strong presence. (the *"ya"* is not too strong, though, so we might say 7 beats plus a hint of one more). Many old haiku had 6 syllabets[3] in the first or last part, so 8 beats were not uncommon. But no Japanese has ever come close to the plodding 13 or 14 beats (!) of Hofstadter's *"We won't hiccough back, / won't spring through time toward the past. / It's phony, it's dead."* ("Once Upon a Time Alone")[4]

A phonetic atrocity such as this belies the subtitle of Hofstadter's book, *In Praise of the Music of Language!* Content aside, the "formal constraint" of a haiku is, first and foremost, *to sound right*. [note: the notes to the note, below, are items explained elsewhere or new]

~~~~~~~~~~~~~~~~~~~~~~~~~~~~~~~~

1. One article, I recall was in IBM's elegant Japanese magazine ∞, and pointed out that hard-science scientists enjoyed and supported rhyme because they understood it was only natural.
2. Japanese do not think of beats and some deny there is any stress in Japanese, but I can sense it.
3. *Syllabets* is my term for the letters of a syllabary and, by extension, their uniformly short sound. I hope it will catch on, for it is a more transparent word than *mora*.
4. I just noticed DH's middle 7 is *8* unless "toward" is pronounced "t'ward." When Japanese haiku *are* long it is usually not in the middle of the poem.

~~~~~~~~~~~~~~~~~~~~~~~~~~~~~~~~

Obviously, the note needs a rewrite. The second-person is too abrupt and clashes with the third-person used later. Had my sister and mother read DH's chapter on haiku, they might have noticed that he can be rather sharp-tongued himself, and, if they had read my books (impossible, for all previous to *Rise, Ye Sea Slugs!* were in Japanese), they would also have known that I only put top-rate people on the chopping board. I recall when the chief editor at Kousakusha (a publishing house where I worked) read a draft chapter of one of my books and told me, "That's worthless (*tsumaranai*), arguing with someone like _____ (I forget the name)." "Alright, I countered, "*you* tell me someone *better*. I prefer to mention no one at all and engage in pure arguement, but doing so leaves me open to charges that I am setting up a straw-man or beating a dead horse." She gave me the names of two far more prestigious scholars. So, I read *their* books, found they, too, were furthering stereotypes I did not care for, and tore *them* apart. Doubtless, it helped my book get good reviews. If I seem too personal with DH, it is because I had spent enough time with his books to feel I knew him and because there is so much I *like* in those books that I was dissappointed with his poor understanding of *haiku,* a form of poetry I care deeply about. My words were not meant to be sticks and stones swung or thrown to be mean, but a whack on the back with a stick by a Zen priest – *intended to awaken him (and others with similar misconceptions)*. And, if you still think it uncalled for, please look at how I chew out Issa, perhaps my favorite poet, and about 180 years dead, in the section of the preface to *The 5th Season* warning about excessive Bashôism. Same thing. Hofstadter can be ferocious in his defense of formalities, I can can be the same in my defence of aestheics, something I consider essential to haiku.

Yet, I *was* unfair to DH, in a way I only came to realize a year or two *after* publishing *Rise, Ye Sea Slugs!* At the time I wrote the footnote, I assumed all who really studied Japanese poetry no longer translated with seventeen (*haiku* or *senryû*) or thirty-one (*tanka* or *waka*) English syllables. After all, the best-known translator of haiku, Blyth, realized *beat* was the way to go about a decade before his death in 1961, and the Haiku Society of America, trying to rationalize what all bilinguals picked up on automatically, had debated the nature of the Japanese *mora* (the linguist's term for a short uniform syllable) and what to call it for almost a decade. The only 17-syllable haiku I was coming across were either old or by people who knew nothing about haiku other than it was supposed to be 17 syllables! That was where *I was wrong*. Because my own interest was in *old* Japanese haiku, in the original Japanese, to boot, I did not read broadly enough in English to discover that a die-hard school of syllable-counters was still out there. I doubt most translators identified themselves in that way, and it seems to have been (or, still is) centered more around *waka* (5-7-5-7-7) than haiku, owing to the considerable influence of the brilliant yet, imho, aesthetically limited, Helen Craig McCullough; but, as it happened, the best books still exhibiting what I would call syllable-ism were published by Stanford, a university where Hofstadter spent time. So, in retrospect, Hofstadter (who knows little Japanese) was set up. He followed the practice of of some of the highest ranked academic specialists, and it is *they*, rather than Hofstadter who deserved my "attack," if that's what you would call it.

Meanwhile, not long ago, I got a newsletter that sent me to hacketthaiku.com, where I saw Blyth's first letter to young James W. Hackett, whose haiku Blyth would soon put at the end of his classic *History of Haiku* as an example of a nonJapanese who could outdo the Japanese at their own art. After a word of high praise for Hackett's sense or spirit, he had but one piece of advice: *stop the 5-7-5 stuff*.

> The only thing to do, it seems to me, is something revolutionary for you, – either to forget the 5,7,5 in English, or do what the Japanese does, pad out the verse with meaningless syllables.

The *reason* is interesting and, I would hope, says something important about the nature of haiku: The less made explicit, the more still within it. Blyth also opined that "if we count the syllables instead of words, as in Japanese, we would get, I suppose,

> Za o ru do po n do (7)
> A fu ro gu ja n pu su i n (10)
> Za sa u n do o vu za u wo ta (11)

(If you could not catch the above, use Latin/Spanish pronunciation of the vowels). By "syllable" here, Blyth means what I would call a *syllabet*, for he is talking about syllables *in the Japanese sense of them*. He correctly feels, which is to say *knows*, that English syllables are often far too long to be syllabets. Blyth hyperbolizes, for English speakers do not pronounce their own words in the expanded manner Japanese, who put a vowel after most consonants do. We pronounce "frog" faster than a Japanese would "fu-ro-gu." But Blyth exaggerates on the side of truth. The average length of recited haiku with seventeen (Japanese) syllabets and seventeen (English) syllables has been carefully timed by a number of people and fully support his general conclusion. English is far too long. Going by syllables not only sounds wrong but, by allowing too much information and semantic wiggle room, makes haiku in English too easy. In retrospect, the way I should have framed it would have been to more carefully explain the parameters to the benighted scholars and misguided D.H.. If *beat,* the natural restraint for English found in every nursery rhyme, which Blyth and I recommend counting, is too irregular for your taste, would you be willing to accept a minimum and maximum time span for the poem? Is that not about as formal, even scientific as one can get?

And, finally, while I cared no more for the content of the haiku in *Le Ton Beau* than the style (it takes time to learn how seasons are used in haiku) there were two ideas for playing with haiku I found delightful. 1) Noting that haiku was unrhymed – it has more vowel-rhyme than most people realize, but it is not formally required – DH came up with *haiku that did not themselves rhyme, but rhymed instead, line by line, with the haiku paired with them.* There are formats the names of which I forget where what seems to be unrhymed poetry rhymes with another *stanza,* and I have tried arranging haiku in pairs and larger clusters for what might be called *semantic* rhyme, but this idea of rhyming *poem to poem* is, as far as I know, a brand new *meme!* I will surely try it myself. The second was his transformation of James Kirkup's transformation of Bashô's Old Pond, a staircased *"pond / frog / plop!"* into *"swamp / tadpole / plunk."* Such conceptual play can enhance haiku.

Between *Form/Medium/Hofstadter* & *Content/Message/Sato*

Hofstadter topped off a three-part criticism of Sato, *"The Utter Irrelevance of Five-Seven-Five"* & *"Liquid Beast Immersion"* with *"Messagism as Literary Machismo."* He quotes Sato, who, noting that for most translators, "our best effort is embarrassingly inferior to the original," ends up finding "salvation only in Nabakov's dictum," namely, "The clumsiest literal translation is a thousand times more useful than the prettiest paraphrase." After commenting "Had Sato's hope been to set that bee a-buzzing in my bonnet, he could hardly have picked a better (or worse) person to quote," Hofstadter gave an example of a pukingly boring and, after the first three words, literally figuratively wrong direct translation of a classic French *pi-ku* where the number of letters in each word of the original tell Π, which he claimed was neither an exceptional nor extreme example of direct translation. It *is* exceptional, but Hofstadter is right about it not being extreme. Most literal translations are indeed *awful.* And who could argue for Hofstsadter's conclusion that "art must be rendered as art or it is no longer art" and that Message and Medium must be wedded to be pronounced a Poem?

Yet, Hofstadter does a disservice to Sato and Nabokov by not explaining where they come from. Hofstadter, if you recall, gave literal translations of Marot's poem with multiple connotations for the words near the start of *Le Ton Beau de*

Marot. He has managed to do justice to both parties in the "marriage." But, with the only accepted way of presenting translations in English being to give no more information than the occasional note, usually hidden at the end of the book, other translators have not been able to have it both ways. With languages as removed from English as Russian (semi-exotic) and Japanese (about as exotic as one can get) so much of the message is lost even in literal translation, that I cannot help feeling sympathetic toward Nabokov and Sato. You must try to understand how frustrating it is for someone who is fluent to see a stylized translation which leaves out things you feel at the heart of the original while adding details, that is not only published but copied with tiny variations done for no other reason than to justify putting the "translator's" name on it by many who are not even fluent enough in the original language to do their own translation. If a real translator (someone who really knows the original language) does a good job of literal translation – and, as we saw with Bashô's Old Pond, even Sato had to choose one of two facets of the original, thereby proving that a full literal translation may be grammatically impossible even where the vocabulary is not a problem – the majority of readers, including subsequent would-be translators, have what they need to rewrite the poem any way they want to. With message in hand, they can themselves create an artistic medium for it, spice it with wit. The reverse, however, is not true. What matters is how a translator perceives his main role. I can well imagine how many times Nabokov and Sato must have put their hands to their foreheads and groaned to see people poeticizing fundamentally wrong or inadequate messages. If I am not mistaken, Hofstadter did not get far enough with his Chinese to feel for Nabokov's and Sato's position. And, I am not sure if the two fully understand where their own position comes from – or, at least, I have not seen it adequately explained. (Let me add that when I wrote Sato about *Rise, Ye Sea Slugs!* because I thought he might be interested in what I was doing, he replied "What exactly do you *want* of me?" I was so put-off by his attitude – and I have subsequently heard worse from several friends (all male: women find him kind) – that I have not tried again. So, I do not defend him out of affection, but because it is clear he knows far more than most of his critics.)

To my mind, the impossibility of consistently good – forget about great – translations is not a problem but a fact, and nothing to be upset about. It only goes to show the world of language and experience is too wondrously diverse to be captured the same way twice. The problem is that unless literal translations and substantial notes accompany the art translation, i.e. re-created poetry, this fact will never be grasped by those who are not bilingual. My books of translated haiku and *senryû* are all experiments in how to do just this, and multiple translation – though I may do it for the fun of it – is a tool to help fill in the content while re-creating the art. What I cannot know is how sucessful my methods are. For that, I need feedback from thoughtful readers, including, I hope, Douglas Hofstadter.

---

p.s. *A Sweet Note.* The "ton beau de Marot," explains the book jacket, means "The sweet tone of Marot" but puns on "tonbeau," or "tomb" – that explains the cover showing the latter. I must confess to missing that pun but remembering the book title the first time I heard it. *Tonbô*, in Japanese is a *dragonfly*.

xviii

Octopussy & The W~~o~~man Without a Hole

Waiting for the reviews of this recent book, published under two titles (*Octopussy, Dry Kidney & Blue Spots* and *The Woman Without a Hole*) is scary, for it is my first book of translations of poetry some would call smut, some trivial and some, I hope, literature. If a learned critic, not appreciating the value of the book for semiotics (reading Japanese erotic prints), historical sexology (Japanese sexologists often cite dirty *senryû*), the literature of humor, metaphor (all my books of translation are studies of metaphor, though none have noted it), etc., were to make out my work to be a prime case of *materium superabat opus,* I would not know whether to cry sadly for wasting my time or happily to find my translating technique appreciated even when the material to which it was applied is not. I will example this chapter sparsely because this book already has more bawdy content than I planned to include (and wait for the next chapter!).

千ずりをかきおふせたが支配人 葉四
senzuri o kaki-ofuseta no ga shihainin
(1000-rubs stroking-bore-the control-man)

delayed gratification

the clerk who beat
his rivals by beating off
alone? – the boss.

the masturbator
is the one who became
the master later

he who made do
with jacking off is now
the company boss

Senzuri, a "thousand-rubs." The quantity often means "many" in Japanese. Idiom is idiom, but that doesn't stop the stereotypical hick-samurai, the *asagiura* from taking it literally: *"'bout fifty jerks is plenty to get us'uns off"* (五十摺りぐらいで身供罷りすむ 葉 18 *gojû-zuri gurai de midomo makari-sumu*). That *ku* is a witty re-do of *"About fifty / and a thousand-strokes / is done"*(五十ほどかくと千ずりしまいなり」万安四 *gojû hodo kaku to senzuri shimai nari*). Samurai, even hicks, were supposed to do their business with dispatch (eating & pooping in a minute so as to be ready for an attack), but the secret for success at anything big is not *that.* It is *delayed gratification.* The boss, above, had the discipline to take care of himself for years – or decades – in order to work up the ranks until he was made manager, passing over others who let things get out of hand by wasting their, and the company's time and money on prostitutes or marriages they could not afford.

当テがきもちがわず主の聟に成り 葉別三
ategaki mo chigawazu   nushi no muko ni nari
(aimed-stroking errs-not: boss's groom becomes)

*All that jacking off did not fly wide
the boss's daughter is now his bride!*

Here, I have given you the first page entire, minus only the title *Different Strokes*, and subtitle, *Masturbation as a Public Good*. The next page explains the idea of "aimed-stroking" as opposed to just stroking and the practice of male marrying-in. The *"muko"* can also be translated as "son-in-law" in cases like the last *ku*. I should have included that in the gloss but the aesthetics kept the word out – remember, this translator was also the editor and the designer. As the page had no more room, I was happy to have justification for doing it as a two-liner: the original *ku* has its clearest pause dead center. The same thing happens in haiku and is one reason 5-7-5 three-line fundamentalism is misguided. Had I more time to think, I might have come up with a second reading where the protagonist becomes his boss's groom. For if the parents are already dead, that would be the case. But note, even when there is a single translation, where license is present, there are two, for there is always the ghost, the literal reading against which it may be read. I will not say all translation is paraversing, but with exotic tongues most is.

相イ方の無イはかゝとでほねを折 末摘 1-10
aikata no nai wa kakato de hone o oru ねかひ社すれ／＼
(partner-not-as-for heel-with bone[acc] break [i.e.bust one's balls])

*being alone
she breaks the bone
of her heel*

~~*lacking a man
with balls to bust, she blisters
her own heels*~~

*partnerless ones
must bust the balls
of their heels*

One cannot tickle oneself, but, as explained elsewhere in the book, attaching a dildo to the heel would estrange it and make it much more effective. The center reading is redacted because the lack of a "(female) partner" in the 'harem' is the original meaning. But note how the mistaken second reading contributed to the metaphor in the third reading. Starting work before you know what you are doing is a good idea, so long as you come back for a good long second look.

牛の果テ又世に出て色おとこ 万宝十三
ushi no hate mata yo ni idete iro otoko million
(cow's/ox's end, again world-in/to appearing color-man)

*the ox dies &
is reborn from his horn
as a playboy*

*the end of an ox
and its rebirth on earth
as a lady's man*

*moving on to
greener pastures, an ox
serves a lady*

dead, an ox rises
to heaven in the right hand
of a chambermaid

A "color-man" is a one who self-consciously lives for sex and practices it with many women. The "horn" added to the first reading might allow the poem to be quoted out of context and still be understood, yet betrays the original in that senryu are supposed to be riddles. The third is as riddlesome as the original though the metaphor is distinctly English and the last might tell you I once memorized some Christian mythology for catechism. With senryu, I feel freer to play than haiku, for the medium is more of the message and that medium is humor and not just form. In this case, I had to keep light on my feet for there were two possible readings and I was unsure which was correct. I still am unsure. Probably, we are talking about an ox horn dildo being the rebirth of the slaughtered ox. But we could also be talking about lady's men being reincarnations of dildos, for dildo were sometimes just called oxes (a synedoche for the horn). Without bothering good Japanese readers, I did not want to make a final judgement, but as you can see, that was no problem for the translation.

～～～～～～～～～～～～～～～～～～～～～～～～～～～～

I hesitate to introduce this next *ku*, as my faithful readers will find it again when I finally publish a potpourri of salacious marine senryu, *Mullets In Maids [& the Fisherman in the Ray]*. But this crab *ku* is so ridiculous, I cannot help wanting to share it, repeatedly!

蟹のチン摺りうろたへてツイ羅切 葉
kani no senzuri urotaete tsui rasetsu 別八

    crab consoles   *crab beats off*
himself & in his dither   *and in his excitement*
      cuts it off   *loses his meat*

a crab's masturbation
can end in castration!

★ A great illustration by a top cartoonist of just such a crab, who, taught to masturbate, injures himself, will be found in the aforementioned *Mullets*, if and when it is published.

The original has two slight breaks before and after *urotaete,* a verb meaning *to be worked up,* or excited. That is to say the syllabets break 7-5-7. That does not matter in the original, presented in a single line, but would look ugly in three lines, for it would destroy the rounded-off object-like quality. It is one reason why the two-liner seems as authentic as any, if we forget the unmentioned excitement. So, now the crab has gotten into two books before the one I translated it for is done! That book will include an exhaustive haikuing of *shellfish* by a little known female poet, Greek marine poetry and much more, but no blowfish because that goes into yet another book-to-be, *Swellfish Soup*.

～～～～～～～～～～～～～～～～～～～～～～～～～～～～

Summer Parlours
夏座敷ご存知か

五 5

鼻の落度
Losing Nose

~~~~~~

たかの名におはなおちよハきつい事 摘
taka no na ni ohana ochiyo wa kitsui koto 1-24
(hawks[street-walkers]' names-as hon.-flower=nose
hon.1000-eras[=drop-will]-as-for tough thing)

a bad joke

> street-walker names 　　　　　　　　　flowery names
> like sherri or rose: try to enjoy them 　for old whores say your nose
> 　　without your nose! 　　　　　　　　　　is next to blow!

　　It's easy enough to translate the "[night-]hawks," as street-walkers, but name puns are indeed *kitsui*, tough! I could not re-create the Japanese, which takes two common street-walker names meaning "flower" and "thousand-ages" and puts them together to get a homophonic phrase meaning *your honorable nose falls off*, which is to say, you contract the disease the Portuguese brought from Africa or the Americas, or Africa, probably via Europe to Japan, syphilis.

　　Here, I decided that I might as well give you the full chapter-head as it was more easily split than the poem with it's exceptionally long gloss (the brackets of which I have jiggled a bit). This is like Hofstadter's French Π-ku, where the pun is the larger part of the message (pg 177). I was too happy with the first translation and did not try hard enough or I might have come up with this:

> *Floras & Roses!*
> *w/ old whores, the first to blow*
> *will be our noses*

　　I am sure that there are many more translations in my dirty *senryû* book and, for that matter, all of my books, that could be improved or added to, and chances are I will not find time to get back to them. You are welcome to send in your translations when you feel I missed the best, which is to say most obvious possibility. The *noseless* chapter followed the masturbation one because it helped show why the latter was a wiser move than risking illness by buying sex.

~~~~~~

たうがらし喰へば若衆も怖くなり む八
tôgarashi kueba wakashu mo kowaku nari 1755
(chili eat/ate-if/when young-crowd even scary become)

<div style="display:flex">

even catamites
are scary after eating
chili peppers

after chili
even a pretty youth
can hurt you

</div>

chili pepper
after eating them beware
gay power

This senryu followed a translation of haiku and senryu about competitive hot-chili eating in the honkytonks of the time, of which the best is Issa's haiku: *"Called a man / as his tears roll down / chili peppers."* One reason for so many translations was incertainity over which was the best term to use for *wakashu,* literally "young crowd." The other reason was explained in my original:

> At first, I was *sure* this meant that the senryu writer, A) having experienced a burn coming out as well as in, considered what would happen *if* . . . . or, B) that one appeal of *wakashu,* their effeminacy, would be belied by this macho act as a man would lose his confidence of being in charge. But, considering the way *wakashu* were said to come on strongly in some towns, it could also be read C) "if you eat chili, even the *wakashu* will shy away (from you)." Unfortunately, I have not received a comment from a senryu specialist about this. One Japanese respondent (learned, but out of his field) voted for A).

~~~~~~

御寵愛足が八本ないばかり 安四礼 1
gochôai ashi ga happon nai bakari (又秘蔵は)
(favorite/adored legs-the eight not only 女陰万考に)

his favorite
you can almost see
her eight legs

his mistress
begs but one thing
eight legs

Concubine #1

from the way
he begs, we know
what she hides:
eight legs

"Lacks only ~" means *as good as has. Ergo* she is an octopus. That works in English, as per the second reading ("begs" could be "lacks" or "wants," but I wanted the rhyme), but the rhetoric is, or was, more common in Japan.

The *octopus* – short for an octopus pot with an octopus inside that can grab a probing hand – is a prehensile vagina and/or its owner, hence the word "octopussy," no relation to Fleming's. It comes from a chapter on *Ideal Members*.

~~~~~~

For our final sample, the lead-off *ku* for one of the two oddest chapters in the book (the other being the *Blue Spot*), *The Sound of Piss*, subtitled *From Wee Tinkle to Woeful Torrent*.

娘シイ年増のはじゅウ?乳母のはザア
musume shii toshima no wa juu uba no wa zaa 一五六
(daughter/maiden shii, years-increase-as-for juu, wetnurse-as-for zaa)

daughters go *shi~i*　　　　　　　　　　a maiden *tinkles*
experienced women *ju~u*　　　　　mother *showers*, wet-nurse
and wet-nurses *za~a*　　　　　　　　　just *pours* down!

This is very late *Willow ku* (bk 156) is poetry if *Old McDonald Had a Farm* is. Yet you can bet it made its author and editor happy, for chances are no *senryû* (or haiku) before it contained more than *two* piss noises in 17 syllabets. Such is the nature of competitive short-form literature. Moreover, onomatopoeia *itself* takes on the nature of a word game in Japanese where one may find whole dictionaries devoted to matching sounds both physical and psychological with their proper subject (or, is it object?). Perhaps the closest English equivalent would be the collective nouns of venery (as in *hunting*) assembled after Sir Arthur Conan Doyle, who did it in a novel (where a young man was quizzed as to the proper terms for various groups of game), and thoroughly but not exhaustively supplemented by James Lipton (*An Exaltation of Larks, or the venereal game:* 1968). It turned into a parlour game. Old McDonald aside, English keeps the lion's share of its extraordinarily good sound sense (it suffices to consider *stop* and *shrimp*) under wraps – I call it *built-in* as opposed to apparent mimesis – so such games combining aspects of matching, collecting and guessing, do not work.

<div style="text-align:center">

an
Edo
observation:
girls go *tinkle,*
their mamas *shower,*
but wet-nurses can *power*
a hydro-electric plant !!!

</div>

I feel the same way about obvious anachronism as I do about obvious anthropomorphism: why not? The reader can see what you've done. I only mind when a translation is incorrect and not obviously so. Multiple translations allow play by taking care of business with one translation and giving the translator a free hand with others. The middle term "years-increase" mean a woman in her twenties and thirties, a bit old for remaining single. English has no perfect equivalent, for it is between a young and middle-aged woman. Wet murses were often women with many children of their own and famously loose/large.

XIX
Pangur Ban Finds Lesbia
from white cat & jack to calipygosity and back

While I had done multiple translations of poems and created them from prose before, the possibilities of paraversing as a social game must have come to me before late-1990 or early-1991, for that is when I asked Jack Stamm, "a minor beat poet" (his words), copywriter, blues harpman, translator of international childrens haiku, who favored the same Hank Williams (Sr) songs I did (we met in a country bar in Tokyo when I sang a medley of other songs I parodied – *"I'm Caulking the Floor Over You," "All Of You, Why Can't I Have All of You?"* etc. – with only the base guitarist in a break), to contribute a paraverse of an old Irish poem about the cohabitation of the monk poet and *Pangur Ban*, a white cat (from the original and an utterly prosaic translation) after which, I would show him mine. He delighted me with a masterpiece in *days*. I am sure of the date because Jack died in 1991. I wanted the poem here but could not find it. Then, I recalled that after hearing my country music parodies and reading my versions of a dozen or two *tanka* (31-syllabet poems) from Tawara Machi's *Salad Anniversary* (which he had translated), Jack asked whether I wrote any poems *of my own* about something I cared for, so I sent him some of my hymns to calipygosity –

Venus Calipygous
(one hymn to her)

Slave to your beauty
I ought to bow my head;
But here I stand
Erect instead.

On top of the World
(or is it below?)

She makes me
Feel like Atlas, and then some,
Holding two globes
To his one!

Tut! Tut!

God apparently forgot
To cut the pages
Of her butt!

(The last referred to the all-too-common *asslessness* of the Japanese,
– the crack often starts so low down the back that it cannot be located!)

– I peeked into my *Rump Rhyme* dummy book in case my misplaced *Pangur Ban* paraverses were sandwiched between the pages. There I found the above and his response, prefaced with a date, 3/5/91: *Bibbity Bobbity / Gluteus Maximus – / surely a wondrous thing / has come to pass. / At last a poet who hymns / callypigosity . . . / Rump in rhymed couplets, yet! / Ain't it a gas?* and followed by one word, "tra-la-la," then, a sentence for my edification: "This 8-liner calls itself a 'double-dactyl.'" *Pangur Ban* was nowhere to be seen. But, as it happened, luck was with me: I opened the pages where I had pasted a pair of the most amusing translations I had ever seen: *Martial XI.99*, Englished by Robert Wind and Joseph S. Salemi, which I clipped out of *Maledicta X*, a one-man journal I subscribed to for a year or two in the late 1980's or early 1990's.

> *De cathedra quotiens surgis – iam saepe notavi –*
> *pedicant miserae, Lesbia, te tunicae.*
> *quas cum conatra es dextra, conata sinistra*
> *vellere, cum lacrimus eximis et gemitu:*
> *sic constringuntar magni Symplegade culi*
> *et nimias intrant Cyaneasque natis.*
> *Emendare cupis vitium deforme? docebo:*
> *Lesbia, nec surgas censeo nec sedeas.*

TO LARGE LESBIA

I've noticed often when you rise
Your undies give obscene surprise.
Right hand, left, push, pull – no use –
Tears, groans – ah! They're loose.
How tight they're squeezed between those nates,
Gigantic gates to dark estates!
How might we end this ugly bit?
You mustn't stand. You mustn't sit.

(trans. Robert Wind)

~~~~~~

(trans. Joseph S. Salemi)

When you rise up from a chair, Lesbia
(I've seen it happen frequently)
You get buttfucked by your skirt.
The damned thing catches in the narrow crack
Between those massive buns of yours,
Those ship-crunching Pillars of Hercules.
You pull with your left hand, you pull with your right,
Wincing and grunting till it comes loose.
An unladylike faux pas, to say the least.
Want a tip on etiquette, Lesbia?
Don't get up, and don't sit down.

Wind, manages to rhyme yet keeps it short as the original, by not mentioning the Symplegades, the giant gnashing rocks Jason and the Argonauts had to pass between, or the Cyaneas = *blue rocks*, another name for the same, except in his notes. Salemi, despite not rhyming, is three lines over, partly for explaining the rocks and partly for ornamentation such as "an unladylike *faux pas*." On the other hand, his "buttfucked" is proper, for *pedicant* means "to bugger." To get an idea how *good* both of these translations are, compare them to the standard, or at least for years the most available version, an English Translation by Walter C. A. Ker in the Loeb Classical Library edition of *Martial's Epigrams* (1968):

> *Whenever you get up from your chair – I have often noticed it ere now*
> *– your unhappy garments, Lesbia, become sodomites.*
> *when you attempt with your right hand, attempt with your left,*
> *to pluck them away, you wrench them out with tears and groans;*
> *they are so gripped b y the straits of your mighty rump,*
> *and enter buttocks difficult and Cyanean.*
> *Do you wish to cure this ugly defect? I will instruct you:*
> *Lesbia, I advise you neither to get up nor to sit down.*

De cathedra quotiens surgis – iam saepe notavi – / pedicant miserae, Lesbia, te tunicae. quas cum conatra es dextra, conata sinistra / vellere, cum lacrimus eximis et gemitu: sic constringuntar magni Symplegade culi / et nimias intrant Cyaneasque natis. Emendare cupis vitium deforme? docebo: / Lesbia, nec surgas censeo nec sedeas.

The Loeb edition offers what is supposed to be a literal translation – useful for reading the original – but, as a read, it seems to demonstrate how poetry may be lost in translation: by not re-creating it. Likewise for this next version by D.R. Shackleton Bailey, found on a webpage lamenting the absence of the "self-inflicted kind" of wedgie in the Wiki article on the same:

> Whenever you get up from your chair (I have noticed it again and again), your unfortunate tunic sodomizes you, Lesbia. You try and try to pluck it with your left hand and your right, till you extract it with tears and groans. So firmly is it constrained by the twin Symplegades of your arse as it enters your oversized, Cyanean buttocks. Do you want to correct this ugly fault? I'll tell you how. Lesbia, I advise you neither to get up nor sit down.

Compare the prosaic renditions to the rhymed versions. This, for example, from a Swedish or Danish website. I failed to find the translator's or paraverser's name :

> *Whenever you rise from a chair, Lesbia,*
> *your wretched clothes jump,*
> *like buggers, right up your rump-*
> *I've often observed the sight.*
> *You try twitching them to the left or the right*
> *and finally wrench them free with a tearfull shriek,*
> *so deep is the creek they've sailed up, so fierce the squeeze*
> *of those colossal twin Sympeglades.*
> *Would you like a cure this unattractive defect?*
> *Do you want my advice? This is it:*
> *Don't get up – and never sit.*

While not as smooth as the Wind and Salemi translations, I, with my love for Ogden Nash enjoy the rocky ride, not to mention the enjambment right when the tunicae gets jammed and how nicely both the depth and tightness of the glutean vice are accounted for! There is also more going on here than meets the casual eye. Only this eleven-line version holds the parenthetical "I've often ..." until the fourth line – combines two behaviors – *i.e.,* crying/tears and groan/s as "tearful shriek" – and comes up with the *natural* (something hard to be in translation) "this is it" – compare it to Wind's more forced "ugly bit" – to set up the final rhyme on "sit." After pontificating over the efforts of others, I feel obliged to ante up myself.

> *Whenever you rise up from your chair,*
> *Your robes, Lesbia, fuck your derriere.*
>
> *This we've seen time and time again –*
> *Out goes your left hand, then your right*
> *first you pluck, then you pull, until, frustrated to tears,*
> *You leave them up shit creek without a paddle, wedged*
> *between the giant boulder cheeks of your massive bum,*
>
> *Believe me, there's just one thing that can be done:*
> *You must not get up, Lesbia, and you must not sit.*

De cathedra quotiens surgis – iam saepe notavi – / pedicant miserae, Lesbia, te tunicae. quas cum conatra es dextra, conata sinistra / vellere, cum lacrimus eximis et gemitu: sic constringuntar magni Symplegade culi / et nimias intrant Cyaneasque natis. Emendare cupis vitium deforme? docebo: / Lesbia, nec surgas censeo nec sedeas.

Pardon my leaving the tunic trapped like that. Call it compensation for losing the *miserae* earlier. Rightly or wrongly, I took the "creek" (an odd rendering for what might better be called a *strait*) from the last translation to hint at the nature of the crack via an English idiom.. . .

Pangur Ban Found!

As luck would have it, I found Jack and my *Pangur Ban* in a chapter on mousing in my soon-to-be published essay of felinity, *Han-chan, the Cat Who Thought Too Much.* But, how lucky to have lost it, thus finding Lesbia's Wedgie, and the opportunity to add an observation about the nature of most translated poetry in English: it is not translated, but paraverses, *i.e.* variations on translations of poems translated by others. Sometimes it is based on one translation, sometimes on several, but it is debateable whether variations done by people who do not know or are far from fluent in a foreign tongue and must rely on the translations of others is, strictly speaking, translation. Indeed, what seems to be the best-selling Japanese poetry collection in English (at least in the USA) for the past decade – it turns up everywhere – is one such by a poet Laureate who relied on others translations. And I would not be surprised to find the same thing was true for many of the translations from classical tongues over the centuries. I do not mean to denigrate such practice. In fact, I think it a good thing, for most of the few people who become fluent enough in a foreign tongue to translate poetry are not poets. If you would like to play with dirty poetry, Loeb's book of unpoetically but thoroughly translated Epigrams (which are poetically written in the original) is a godsend. If you play with haiku, unless you are a disciplined poet, take care – someone might complain, because many haiku enthusiasts are serious about their genre. No one will be upset about what you do to Martial.

My cat and I have different tastes,
ergo, we go our separate ways,
as far apart as day and night.
His name is Pangur; he is white.

(<= Jack's is on the left and mine below.)

I have my pleasure out of books;
he waits for rodents by their nooks.
He goes his way and I go mine;
both of us think this is just fine.

Pangur Ban, my cat, and I are brothers at heart;
Though our aims differ, there is but One Art.

At home we labor tirelessly:
He hunts his mice, which leaves me free
to rummage in my dusty store
of vintage esoteric lore.

Better than fame how I love to pursue
whatever hides within my books.
He cares not a whisker for what I do;
His interest lies wholly in nooks.

Mayhap he holds a small carouse
following capture of a mouse,
akin to the delight I get
when knowledge tumbles to my net.

Though it's just the two of us together
all by ourselves in this old stone house
We are not bored with inclement weather
for I can read and he can mouse.

Sharp eyed he peers at every wall;
my weaker vision is in thrall
to walls of prose: They fall, I ween,
before my lance of knowledge keen.

Nor do we get on each other's nerves
Lord knows our aims lie poles apart,
Like North and South, when each preserves
a separate end, there is no ground for quarrels.

While Pangur stabs his needle claws
into the mouse beneath his paws,
conundrums yield to my sharp mind.
To monk and feline, God is kind.

White Pangur in the dead of night
Swallows his prize, then hunts anew,
While I, by flickering candle-light
Strive to catch a glimpse of the Truth.

We live in two part harmony:
Each of us lets the other bee.
I have my labors, he hath his.
Our mutual ignorance is bliss.

He directs his bright and perfect eye
at the wall, or rather what is behind it,
As I direct mine, faltering, to what might lie
between the lines, if I could but find it.

And if there be a moral here,
'tis this: Enjoy each passing year,
muster your craft, and love your cat –
– and that, I do believe, is that.

Then he pounces a bit faster
than an inspiration, sinking
Sharp claws into what he would master,
as I, his master, sit still thinking.

My rhyme of the *The Scholar and His Cat* is far more convoluted than Jack Stamm's crisp and professional rendition. It is pretty bad. I should have had the monk and cat reverse their positions for continuity between stanzas. I include it in the hope that my amateur work will encourage hesitant readers to join in with their versions. Indeed, it was the unrhymed and boring direct-translation in a book about old Ireland (read in parallel to reading books about Korea because I felt Ireland was to England as Korea was to Japan) that provoked me to try to create a rhyming verse. Perhaps the biggest difference in our readings is not in the styles (consistant 8 syllable+aabb lines vs. inconsistant 8-12 syllable abab) but the content. His monk is proud of wielding a lance of knowledge and having a sharp mind. Mine is very humble. I suspect the original is closer to his. Jack also told me that he thought he had once read a translation somewhere. Some of the following pre-date our experiment:

Frank O'Connor trans.

Each of us pursues his trade,
I and Pangur my comrade,
His whole fancy on the hunt,
And mine for learning ardent.

Eavan Boland trans.

Myself and Pangur, cat and sage
Go each about our business;
I harass my beloved page,
He his mouse.

James Marchand trans.

I and white Felix,
each of us two (keeps) at his specialty:
his mind is set on hunting,
my mind on my special subject.

Robin Flowers trans.

I and Pangur Ban, my cat,
'Tis a like task we are at;
Hunting mice is his delight,
Hunting words I sit all night.

Seamus Heaney trans.

Pangur Bán and I at work,
Adepts, equals, cat and clerk:
  His whole instinct is to hunt,
  Mine to free the meaning pent.

anon. amanuensis for Aloysius Katz

Aloysius is my name;
Pangur Ban, my archetype,
He who hunted tirelessly,
While his human toiled in ink.

As it turned out, a full chapter on Pangur Ban must await another edition. An internet search revealed more translations, some good, than I had imagined. Given the length of the poem, I would have felt obliged to write for permissions and, given the great and entertaining variation – compare the first stanza of Boland and Heany, both claiming to be from the old Irish – not only need to present the original aabb rhymed verse, but a word-for-word gloss and ample notes. Since I do not know Irish, it would be a big production. Marchland writes "My translation is my own, but it sounds like Murphy. St. Jerome once said: 'Cursed be those who said what we said before we said it.' " And, he adds, "If you want to read some grand _Early Irish Lyrics_ with translation, read the book by that name by Gerard Murphy (Oxford, 1956)." *Voila!* That is the book in which I found the only Pangur Ban I knew, *The Scholar and the Cat*. Jack Stamm had mentioned that he read some translation years earlier and, from the looks, or rather sound of it, I believe it was Robin Flowers' version that Seamus Heaney described as "an idiom at once wily and wilfully faux-naif." Heaney attempted to re-create the original's "packed, donnish/monkish style."

Messe [ocus] Pangur bán,	ní fris 'tarddam ar n-áthius.	hi nglen luch ina gérchrub;
cechtar nathar fria saindán;		hi-tucu cheist n-doraid n-dil,
bíth a menma-sam fri seilgg,	Gnáth-huaraib ar greassaib gal	os mé chene am fáelid.
mu menma céin im saincheirdd	glenaid luch ina lín-sam;	
	os me, du-fuit im lín chéin	Cia beimini amin nach ré
Caraim-se fós, ferr cach clú,	dliged ndoraid cu n-droncéill.	ní derban cách a chéle;
oc mu lebrán léir ingnu;		mait le cechtar nár a dán
ní foirmtech frimm Pangur bán,	Fúachaid-sem fri freaga fál	subaigthiud a óenurán.
caraid cesin a maccdán.	a rosc a nglése comlán;	
	fúachimm chéin fri fégi fis	Hé fesin as choimsid dáu
Ó ru-biam scél cén scis	mu rosc réil, cesu imdis.	in muid du-n-gní cach óenláu;
innar tegdias ar n-oéndis,		do thabairt doraid du glé
táithiunn dichríchide clius	Fáelid-sem cu n-déne dul,	for mumud céin am messe.

My impression from the sound of the original is that it may be not quite as sing-song as Flowers, but less Hopkinesque than Seany. I have no idea if the original has any double entendres such as Boland's "beloved page," but I love it. Now let me give the end of the poem so you may compare it to mine and Jack's and (until the next edition where I would hope to include all of the translations) leave it like that. Boland, who like me, converts to abab (but sometimes lets the a's go), enjambs the stanzas, so I give the last two lines of his previous stanza as well.

Frank O'Connor trans.

Master of the death of mice,
He keeps in daily practice,
I too, making dark things clear,
Am of my trade a master.

Eavan Boland trans.

Both of us, solitaries,
Have each the trade

He loves: Pangur, never idle
Day or night
Hunts mice; I hunt each riddle
From dark to light..

James Marchand trans.
(the last line is too long to fit in one!)

He it is who is master for himself
of the work which he does every day.
I can perform my own task,
directed toward understanding clearly

that which is difficult..

Robin Flowers trans.

Practice every day has made
Pangur perfect in his trade;
I get wisdom day and night
Turning darkness into light.

Seamus Heaney trans.

Day and night, soft purr, soft pad,
Pangur Bán has learned his trade.
Day and night, my own hard work
Solves the cruxes, makes a mark.

anon. amanuensis for Aloysius Katz
(the blog-found whole is four stanzas)

When she paces, muttering,
Hunting for the perfect word,
I roll about upon the rug
And practice being, simply, cat.

Pangur Ban the Cat and Lesbia of the Wedgies must be the oddest combination of poems ever put into a single chapter. But, as you have seen, there is a reason they are together. I wonder if anyone, like me and Jack, finds both interesting.

♪ ***Lesbia's Wedgies In Perspective. In case you have not read Martial, this is not one of his really dirty "epigrams,"*** but it may be one of the two funniest. The other concerns a woman called Galena, or hen, who is overly loquacious from both ends, i.e., she clucks when she fucks. Before you charge misogyny you should read his epigrams for men which tend to be more demeaning for challenging the subject's manhood and more disgusting (eg., accusations of depilated anuses and one split clear to the navel!).

♪ ***Lesbia's Boulders. Beautiful buttocks are always large, but large buttocks are not always beautiful.*** It is not a matter of smooth vs. celluite, either. Beardsley drew women with buttocks as gigantic as the cocks on his men, but they are as round as if drawn with a compass; indeed, I think that is how he must have drawn them. One cannot possibly draw them *smoother;* but, not one is beautiful. They look as hard and cold as marble. To appreciate a woman's behind is to appreciate *softness* and the ever-so-slight jiggle of imperfection that draws one (at least most heterosexual men) to the source of all. That brings us to an interesting question the answer of which must wait for my *Rump Rhymes* Book. Why large nates on a Lesbian? What is the connection?

♪ ***Wedgies to Beat Lesbia in Tokyo?*** I found in my *Rump Rhymes* dummy book one forgotten poem I scribbled next to the ancient epigram. Now I would call it a paraverse:

> *A Brazilian did the Lambada on TV,*
>   *dancing for all of Japan . . . and me.*
> *Again and again, her panties dissappeared*
>   *into that Ass (such a glutinous beast!) . . .*
> *Then, like a Roman tickling his greedy throat*
>   *Her little hand, reaching back, would ever so*
>   *nimbly pull them out,*
> *Though any Pleasure here (for eyes, a feast)*
>   *was less hers than ours.*

The poem should be in the rhythm of the music. It is not. But the metaphor of buttocks *bulemia* is so good in a ridiculous way, I thought it worth printing as an example of a pretty poor paraverse. If you can come up with a better poem using that metaphor and send it to me for the next edition, I can cut it. Here is a new paraverse. Is it as bad?

> *A Brazilian girl did the Lambada on Japanese TV*
>   *her hands as busy as her feet – it was a wondrous thing to see*
> *How her bum bum ate her panties, time after time,*
>   *only for her nimble fingers to pluck them out, again to dine*
>   *like those poor West Coast indians who seldom ate meat*
> *– I read, they tied a string to one piece so many could feast*
>   *by chewing little and lightly, then swallowing it right down,*
> *To fill the belly, pull back up and – Madre de Dios! – pass around.*

"Bum bum" is pronounced *boom boom.* The practice was noted as done by a poor tribe in Southwest California (NW Mexico) and observed by a Catholic priest who was a careful ethnographer. Still, I cannot help wondering if drugs were involved . . .

XX

Multiple Translation Juvenilia
Piss Not on the Moon, or my first paraversing

My seven books written in Japanese were all hand-written on one-letter-per-box graff-style manuscript paper and word-processed by Japanese editors. Don't feel sorry for me, as I enjoyed sharpening the pencils by hand and, well, all of it, while I hated to type. What good luck to start writing in Japanese early enough to be allowed to submit such manuscripts. Today, only old, best-selling authors can get away with it. But, once I saw it could not be avoided, I got a computer and did my best, which is even now, pretty bad, for I am so slow I often lose track of what I was thinking before I can catch up to it. For some reason, I just cannot make myself use the shift-key on the right side and I must keep peeking up and down at the keys and . . . you get the idea. Anyway, I got a computer in 1995 and started by typing thousands of pages on and of Issa's poems, since I bought a collection of all his work and found it fun to translate and write about. I have not spent much time with my Issa since coming back to the USA and discovering that David Lanoue had dedicated his life to his work; But, when I decided to do a book of dirty *senryû* in early 2007, I did so because I knew I had much of the book already written within my Issa, for the notes expanded Issa's body-related haiku with forays into related *senryû* territory. I did not, however, recall just how much paraversing I had done, *how the computer tempted me to make reading after reading after reading,* because I knew I could always edit out the extra translations or move them to another file without losing them or wasting paper, and I was painfully aware of my need to practice my native tongue after years of writing books and articles in Japanese and, besides that, somewhere in the back of my head I entertained the hope of eventually encountering an editor who might help me select and improve what I did so all that abundance would come in handy (never happened). Perhaps, I also felt bad about what was lost in translation and hoped many translations might help find it, but I did not yet rationalize the practice. I just did it. On the whole, it looks ugly as sin to me now, for I did not think to create composite clusters, but just let the readings I now call paraverses string down the page like poop from a goldfish. Some still read well today; some rhyme a bit too well for their own good as haiku, some make me start: Did *I* do *that?* And, of the latter, some shock and dismay me, while others surprise and delight me. Few were really great as translations or as paraverses. Perhaps, the *best* of all were among the exceptionally creative treatment afforded the fart bug, which I have posted on my paraversing web-page and will use to properly end this book. *Definitely,* the *most* paraverses used to translate a single *ku* went to a certain haiku, one of scores Issa made about urination and one of hundreds, if not thousands he wrote on the moon. I found I did scores of translations of that poem spanning two chapters. The following is the lead *ku* for the chapter of my Issa book that was never to be, *To Pee or Not to Pee:*

船頭よ小便無用浪の月　一茶

sendô yo shôben muyô nami no tsuki issa
captain, hey! small-use [pissing] verboten! wave's/s'[water's] moon

hey, captain!
pissing is forbidden
the moon is afloat

Several pages later, we find no less than *two dozen* more versions of the same, that drag on for two and a half pages! But, first, I explained what I should explain here, that the Japanese moon was not "our" moon and used the following *ku*, also by Issa, to example the difference:

許々多久の罪も消へ sic べし秋の月

kokodaku-no tsumi-mo kiyubeshi aki-no tsuki
every bit of sin even vanish-should, fall's moon

all sins
for miles around
absorbed without a sound
the fall moon

Haiku about the Autumn moon compete to praise its extraordinary beauty and brightness, but this is something else again. I will explain shortly. First some more of the paraverses. Notice the titles. Even now, I can recall the elation I felt when I came up with the first one.

buddha's vacuum cleaner

sin everywhere
vanishes into the air
the autumn moon

natural purification	*soul-cleanser*
this autumn night	power enough
all our sins should vanish	to absolve all sins
in the moonlight	the fall moon

communion

all sins large or small
vanishing as i write: how bright
this autumn moon!

It is hard to know where to draw the line. Is changing the "vanish" in the original to "absorb" and "absolve" merely translating for the sense, or is it paraversing?

The "large or small," "as I write" and "how bright" in the last reading, just added, are mine, but only fill out what is implied by the original, while some of the caption-as-explanations are patently outrageous. That is fine. Had they not been obvious, someone might be mislead; but so long as the reader is in on the fun, why not? Here are two snippets from my original commentary, which I referenced for chapter 2 of the senryu book (on menstruation metaphor) – to further explain this *ku* and the *Hey, Captain ku* translations, which will resume below*:*

> . . . most important, at least for understanding Japanese poetry, [the moon] stood for purity and truth. This association holds true for both Shinto — despite the ancient "way of the gods" reverence of the Sun — and the relative newcomer Buddhism. For in Shinto the moon stands for the mirror that reflects best when perfectly clean, and in Buddhism it embodies the round perfection of the light of the Law. This revered Otsuki-sama has no crazy or dark associations whatsoever.
>
> Where our moon brings out the witches and the werewolves, the Japanese moon sends them packing!

for law's sake!

captain, command
no pissing from the boat!
tonight, the full moon is afloat

are you blind?   *it's verbotin*

captain! stop pissing   captain, command
from the boat! – can't you see   that none piss now the moon
the moon's afloat?   is on the waves!

holy mackeral!

captain, can't you
hold your piss tonight
there! on the waves
moonlight!

Note, four lines on the last and the vanishing sin *ku* on the last page. Since I was not yet arranging my readings in clusters, uniformity was unnecessary.

cap'in, please,
don't piss and cloud
the beautiful harvest moon!

In haiku, a moon worth such concern implies the big moon of mid-fall. A simple "the" or "this" might be more suitable than "the beautiful," but the adjective goes so well with the moon that each time I cut it, I ended up putting it right back.

for shame! for shame!

*capt'n
only a goon
would pee
on the moon*

Issa's *ku* can be read as a rebuke, where the captain has just done the nefarious act.

don't even think of it!

*captain, I say, no pissing is allowed!
the full moon floats without a cloud*

This was followed by *"Captain, you had better stop, you goon! / Your pee will swamp the crescent moon!"* but, that is just too far from the original, for a crescent "moon-boat" is always specified. It did, however, lead to an idea: *Cap'n, if you dare / make water on the moon / your boat will spring a leak /and sink but soon!* This might be rewritten:

poetic justice	*superstition?*
captain, your boat will sink, and soon, if you take a leak on the moon	the moon's afloat if you don't want your boat to rot capt'n, piss not!

divine revenge

Cap'n, you'd better stow your tool!
he who pisses on the moon becomes a fool!

If one reason is possible, so are two, three or . . . four:

captain, forebear!

though your bladder should burst –
he who pees on the moon is cursed

I also remembered a boat has two sides and qualified the poem:

POETS AT SEA	HOLD YOUR WATER!
the moon is afloat! no pissing, cap'n, least of all on this side of the boat	cap'n, take note: the moon is just off your side of the boat.

The second is snappy, but is it OK to have the main point as the title? Come to think of it – this was not in the Issa pages – two sides means one has a choice:

the moon at sea
so, do i pee on its face
or my shadow?

the moon at sea
i can piss on it, or i
can piss on me!

Rhyme suggested rhetoric that otherwise might have been overlooked.

the open sea

cap'n, save your piss
for a man can hardly miss
the autumn moon

if you must

then cap'n, when
you piss take care you miss
the full moon

rule of thumb

when the full moon
is far too large to miss:
captain, don't piss!

the poet at sea

captain, tonight,
no whizzing's allowed!
the beautiful moonlight.
will turn to cloud!

moon-viewers

cap'n, forgive me
if i fuss, but if you
pee now you're not
one of us!

the buddhist moon

captain, pissing is out of question!
moonlight has turned the sea into heaven
~~~~~~~~~~~~~~~~~~~~~~~~~~~~~~

i want mine straight

captain, don't you dare make water in the sea
and dilute the moonlight's purity!

For "the poet at sea" I thought of piss+moonlight as water+anise absynthe. The next, a softly fashioned couplet, relying completely on the title, which in capital letters seems all the more officially verboten, is my favorite.

NO PISSING TONIGHT

Stop, captain!
You're going to ruin
the watery residence
of the Moon!

Or, *was* my favorite for a long time. Now, I am not sure, but there is something appealing in the *ruin+moon* rhyme.

incompatibility

captain, no leaking into the sea!
piss and moonlight do not agree.

ownership

captain, you had better hold your pee
'tis the moon that rightly owns the sea!

cap'n, close your fuckin' fly!
the moon is floatin' by.

Not knowing how many people are aboard, we have two possible readings. One assumes the Captain himself is the guilty party. This is likely, for the word used for "captain" (*sendô* rather than *senchô*) favors a small ferry or pleasure craft operated by one man, and few, if any passengers. Since Issa had a student/friend with the pen-name of Gessen (moon-boat), who had a boat business, and they spent much time together (about 30 nights sleeping over at each other's houses), I think there is a good chance they were the only ones on the boat, in which case Issa would have had to be a party to the crime, for to safely *kapsaitim wara* ("to urinate" in Papua New Guinea), without literally capsizing, cooperation would be necessary. * So, could Issa's *ku* have been made to expiate his guilt at having helped to pollute the moon? *I joke*. Issa, for all his religion, was a very down-to-earth guy, and it wouldn't be surprising if he, too, gleefully peed upon the moon, then composed the poem and had a good laugh with the captain! I forgot to search out a paraverse best representing this view. Let's make one:

tonight, all pissing
is verboten: captain, we
cannot miss the moon

The less likely interpretation assumes a party aboard, with the Captain given responsibility to forbid pissing *or the release of urine*. At this point, my manuscript has two full pages on the piss-pots used by maids sightseeing on boats. We see how buying one was part of the preparation and expense of going and how unpleasant it was to have to carry them off. If this were in Kyôto, where there was a shortage of urine (for fertilizer), I bet there would have been people waiting by the dock to buy the precious stuff but, in Edo, that seems not to have been the case. A *senryû*: *After the pots / are emptied into the river / the boat docks* (*hôroku-o kawa-e hogasu to fune-ga tsuki*). The draw for the last senryû – which is to say one of the expressions used by the *senryû* judges to solicit verses from hundreds or thousands of participants in the contests by which the books were compiled – was *"[they are] dead-tired"* (*kutabire-ni-keri*). As Issa was still a dirt-poor poet without a place of his own, when he wrote the "Captain!" poem, it is at least possible that he was traveling third-class, in the company of such maids. In that case, we must add a few more readings yet:

a poet's request

a load of tired maids
but the moon is on the waves
cap'n, stay the pots,
stop the maids!

home-bound

moon to starboard
captain, are you blind!
don't let the maids leave
their piss behind!

captain, no piss!
keep it on the boat tonight
the moon's afloat

As I wrote in that manuscript, *we'll never know for sure what Issa meant*, and this is

> "*Fine.* If we knew, I would have no excuse for my wild translations! I sometimes make it a practice not to investigate poems until I've already had my play with them. But I do like to know, *eventually.*"

I still agree with this and make an effort to start translating *before* I am sure what is what. This removes me 180 degrees from the way Gibbon *read*. When he hit upon something he recognized as a subject in a book, he would suspend his perusal until he had read up on that subject in other books, which he likewise read only until he hit upon another subject, which took him to yet another book, which . . . I also wrote something I had long forgotten.

> " *Pissing Forbidden!*" is *the* poem which, more than any other, so closely resembled the material in Oldenburg's *HAIKU: TONGUE IN CHEEK* that it incited me to begin this project."

The book mentioned, small but nonetheless of the tasteful coffee table variety, had spoof haiku about drunkenness and elimination with some simple black and white brush paintings. The author did not seem to know that equally "dirty" but better *ku* already existed. By "project," I meant collecting Issa's earthiest work and comparing it with *senryû* to prove that haiku did not have to be precious.

★ Was paraversing born of lack of skill and indecision, or excess imagination?

♪ ***Balance at Sea.*** Our family had a little red dingy called The Bloody Auk. That was not, however, the name on the transom. The large letters, widely spaced so that two were clearly on the right side of it and two on the left read: "U. P. I. P.". Can the reader think of a more succinct way to express the cooperation essential to safe boating?

xxi

The Fart-cut-bug & Geezer

おれよりははるか上手ぞ屁ひり虫　一茶
ore yori wa haruka jouzu zo hehirimushi issa
me more-than-as-for, far better! fart-cut-bug

Coming from a region noted for gluttony on poor fare, Issa did such a good job of witnessing (?) farts in the winter that the phenomenon should have become a *saijiki* (haiku almanac) theme. Eg., 屁くらべが又始るぞ冬篭 *he-kurabe ga . . .* –

Wintering in – the time to compare farts has now begun!
~~~~~~
Our fart matches have once again begun: winter at home.

His *eau de geezer* also formed a bouquet with plum scent (spring) and he has a horse farting when startled by fireflies (summer), two decades later retaliate by blasting the bugs with a "fart-ball"(*hedama*). Yet Issa's most ambitious fart effort was a baker's dozen of *Fart-cut-bug* (fall) *ku* composed from 1814 to 1821.

屁ひり虫爺がかきねとしられけり
hehirimushi jijigakakine to shirarekeri
fart-cutting-bug geezer's hedge as known+emph,

so it became the geezer's fart-cutting beetle hedge!	fart-cut bugs! so it became known as geezer hedge

This is not the *ku* that will get eight translations in this chapter (one I deliberately left out of the Fart chapter of my dirty *senryû* book to save it for us). It is introduced because it was Issa's *first* fart-cut-bug *ku*, useful for getting most of the explanation out of the way before the real fun begins. We will examine bug and geezer, one at a time, before puting them back together. *Kenkyûsha's Japanese-English Dictionary* defines the *hehiri-mushi* as two bugs,

> 1) The *miideragomimushi* (honorable-temple-garbage-bug /みいでらごみむし), or *"a ground beetle; a carabid; Pheropsophus jessoensis;"*
> 2) Any of the garbage-(gomimushi), walk-about-(osamushi) and turtle-(kamemushi) bugs that release fowl odors: *"a bombardier beetle; a soldier bug; a pentatomid."*

Looking up the "any of" examples gives us even more names, including *stink-bug* and *shield-bug*. Yaba Katsuyuki, in his Issa Dictionary (一茶大辞典), gives the above *ku* the theme name 「放屁虫」 *hôhi-mushi,* or "release/blast-fart bugs." That suggests Yaba has determined the bug in question does not cut the cheeze silently so to speak, but actually lets one rip. It also indirectly brings to mind the historical context. There was an infamous often reproduced picture scroll dating from the Muromachi period (15-16c) called *The Battle of Farts* (放屁合戦 *Hôhi-gassen*) in which bonzes shoot back and forth at one another while shouting out things like "Call me the Windbag!" (referring to the bag carried by the God of the Wind) or "I'm going to shoot down a nun!" Since their "ammunition" was sweet-potato and green chestnuts, we must put this in the Fall. Another *ku* has the bombastic bug crawling *sha-sha* through the grass. While *shasha* means brazen-faced or unperturbed about one's impudent behavior, Issa liked to use psychological mimesis that *also* made *sound* sense, *i.e.,* served as real onomatopoeia, so we can hear the hissing release of gas here as well. Issa was unabashed with depicting body functions (found in 2% of his 20,000 *ku*). By the time he aged enough to be called a geezer, he gamely owed up to having become fartsy, but –

おれよりははるか上手ぞ屁ひり虫　一茶
ore yori wa haruka jouzu zo hehirimushi issa
me more-than-as-for far better! fart-cut-bug

<table>
<tr><td>you beat me
by far, farting beetle so
full of beans!</td><td>at farting i lose
beaten by this beetle
a cut-fart beetle</td></tr>
</table>

Forgive the *beans*. Though Issa once mentions a type of sweet with them in a fart-bug connection once (だんごめせ虫も屁をこく爺が哉（or 家）), Japanese do not equate them with farting, But, *look* at the original: I had to fill it up with *something*. The second reading inobtrusively plays on the English word, *cut-rate*, providing Issa with a good excuse for losing. I just invented both, for it ocurred to me that my older readings – posted for years on my paraversing page with not a single comment from a stranger nor, as far as I know, a link or a steal – were overly elaborate to start with. Here, finally, is one. You be the judge.

To Mister Stink-bug,

You are indeed
true master of the art.

I concede,

An Old Fart

To tell the truth, this is my favorite, though it reads more like a Ben Franklin spoof than a haiku. When I came up with it, I did not know, but the Old Fart is not without substance. The single-volume Kenkyûsha's missed it, but the larger OJD, has a "fart-cutting geezer," *hehiri-jijii*, right before our beetle. This protagonist in a folk-tale is rewarded for being kind to the beasts with the ability to make beautiful music by passing air. In some versions, he swallows a bird. He uses this talent to gain a fortune and is copied by a bad neighbor who ends up with diarrhea when he was supposed to perform for the daimyô.

おれよりははるか上手ぞ屁ひり虫　一茶
ore yori wa haruka jouzu zo hehirimushi issa
me more-than-as-for far better! fart-cut-bug

Cut and Run

I fear i can not hold a Fart
to you, the Master of our Art

Oh, Stink-bug!

The use of the name stink-bug, even if it may not be apropo of the original, is effective here for providing a unit of measurement. Soundwise, the bug may have trouble matching Issa, but stinkwise . . .

i lose, again!

you cut the cheeze
far better than me
o-stink-bug

This is a contest most of us would be happy to lose, though the very idea of contesting said bug suggests *the poet was conscious of having a fart problem.* That puts a whole new twist on the old proverb: *Comparison is odorous.* It is noteworthy that Issa's first fart-cut bug *ku,* the one mentioning the geezer hedge we have seen already, dates to 1814. That was the year he finally got married (within one year of inheriting half of his father's home). His bride was twenty-eight, not young by Japanese standards, but almost half his age. She was a sassy woman who would not have been averse to kidding him about his farts. A couple years later, he wrote *"Going out to toss / farts over the wall / suddenly it's fall."* (垣外へ屁を捨に出る夜寒哉 actually, it's a "night-chill" he encounters – same thing). Damn, all of this is a good story, but we cannot give his bride all the credit (or blame) for making him fart-conscious. The fart bug is probably her invention (meaning, she probably called him a *fart-cut bug,* as that usage is even in the dictionary) but Issa wrote the following masterpiece the year before he married:

十ばかり屁を棄に出る夜永哉
tô bakari he o sute ni deru yonaga kana
ten only farts [+obj] throw-away-for go-out night-long!

out ten times
to throw away ten farts
the night is gaining
on the day

out i go
to throw 'em away;
a long night? i'll say:
ten farts!

growing nights
enough to go out and
dump ten farts

おれよりははるか上手ぞ屁ひり虫　一茶
ore yori wa haruka jouzu zo hehirimushi issa
me more-than-as-for far better! fart-cut-bug

> *out to dump farts*
> *exactly ten times*
> *i know how long*
> *a night can grow*

This reading plays with the traditional bypassed lover's complaint about the long night which we saw in chapter 13. We do not know if he goes out ten times or spends the whole night out, but a windy night can indeed be trying.

How long
　　　　has the night become?
　　　　　　　　　Enough to go out
　　　　　　　　　　　　　Dump ten farts,
　　　　　　　　　　　　　　　　And then some!

Readers familiar with haiku – which often means having set ideas of what it is and is not – must find these translations odd to say the least. I did them as an experiment a decade before my first serious attempt to translate haiku, *Rise, Ye Sea Slugs!* (2003) They are in a 60-pg essay, *Wherever the Fart-God Points: Wind in the Stable, Grass and House,* itself part of about 3000 pages on Issa's haiku and related matters. Today, I do not know what I think of it. Some of the writing and translation can only be called the juvenilia of a man in his forties, yet much is so vigorous even when misguided, that I am happy to cannibalize it, as I did for the *senryû* book and here.

かはい男は芋食て死んだ　屁をひる度に思ひ出す
kawai otoko ga imo kutte shinda // he o hiru tabi ni omoidasu
cute/dear man-as-for yam ate/eating died // fart cut time-when remember

> *Lover-boy choked*
> *on sweet potato tarts!*
> *She still recalls him*
> *whene'er she farts!*

The above, a stanza from a folksong he jotted down in his journal in 1825, *did* get into the *senryû* book (and MMcM's blog). Now, back to the fart-cutting bug:

in praise of the bombardier

my farts
fade before your art
o beetle!

おれよりははるか上手ぞ屁ひり虫　一茶
ore yori wa haruka jouzu zo hehirimushi issa
me more-than-as-for far better! fart-cut-bug

> *thy stink-bug art*
> *makes my fart the work of*
> *a rank amateur*

I just added *thy*, removed a boring title, and came up with the perfect last line: yes, the *rank* – not in the older version – makes it.

> **To a certain beetle**
>
> *You cut them so well*
> *and whenever you please!*
> *If I took the cake*
> *then you take the cheeze!*

At the time I read and wrote my Issa, I still found it hard not to rhyme *ku* that reminded me of light-verse. The "whenever you please" idea is in another of Issa's *hehiri-mushi ku*. I will give it and five more of Issa's fart-bug *ku* before returning to the final two readings of the chapter *ku*.

> Farting away / a brazen bug slishes right / thru the grass (*"Through"*
> Big-ass bug! / Fart after fart slishing / thru the grass *is too damn long,*
> *he o hitte shaa-shaa to shite kusa no mushi.*   *and here's that mimesis*)

> Dusk falls: / Do you fart, bug, instead / of crying? (*So, too, old Issa?*)
> Do you fart / when it grows dark instead / of singing, bug? (*Cry and*
> *yu sareba naku kawari ka yo hehirimushi.*   *sing are both "naku."*)

> Instead of a song / for my window a fart-/cutting bug! (*Issa's reality is*
> *mado ni kite naku kawarika ya hehirimushi.*   *not lyrical.*)

> Stink-bug, / Did you get that mug / from *Hu Mee*? (*Oh, no, not me!*)
> Making another / take the blame, stink-bug / you *do* stink! (*Could it*
> *hehirimushi hito ni nasutta tsuratsuki zo*   *be Issa's self-deprecation?*)

> Cut-fart bugs / I'd say their mugs look / almost human   (*Sympathy*)
> Hey, stink-bug! / That face looks pretty / human to me! (*Is Issa look-*
> *hehirimushi hito ni nasutta tsuratsuki yo*   *-ing in the mirror?*)

> Blown away / by beetle's fart, / the dragonfly / master of martial art!
> *mushi no he ni fuki-tobasaruru tonbo kana*   (*This belongs elsewhere.*)

> Let us make / a dead tree bloom! / Fellow carabid.   (*Issa does not say*
> *kareta ki ni hana o sakase yo hehirimushi*   *"fellow" but he means it.*)

This was after Old Issa and his aging wife lost a son and their beloved daughter. He embodies the folk-tale of the farting geezer with that of the geezer who made a dead-tree bloom in a *ku* simultaneously sad and hopeful.

おれよりははるか上手ぞ屁ひり虫 一茶
ore yori wa haruka jouzu zo hehirimushi issa
me more-than-as-for far better! fart-cut-bug

a flatulent old poet impressed

in fall thou art
a veritable spring of fart
stink-bug!

Very figurative, this. Issa elsewhere puns on Spring fields and farting, because Spring is a homophone for swelling (*haru*), but the original of the *ku* in question has no such idea. In other words, this is a paraverse Issa might have made.

Dear Stink-bug,

I grant you are my master at our woeful art!

Signed, with warm regards,

Issa, an old fart.

Most people who know *something* about haiku might see Issa's cut-fart bug *ku* as a *senryû*. I would strongly demure. *Senryû* did not diverge from what later came to be called *haiku* simply because its focus was on people and humor as usually assumed. Haiku is not lacking in wit or human matters. It can be light as well as heavy. The main difference is that haiku are *genuine and personal*, while classic *senryû* create or deal with stereotypes. To bring out that essential point, I will introduce one typical *senryû*:

he o hiite okashiku mo nai hitorimono
fart-cut even if, funny-not singleman/men

the recluse

what good is breaking wind
when you've no one there
to shoot it with

a sorry sight

looking for all the world
like he would sooner fart than not
a single man

association

a single wino
whenever he cuts the cheeze:
his empty life

boredom

single life
even farts are never
a surprise

> even farts
never get a laugh
living alone

living alone
even our best farts
are wasted

My first two readings gave up the 2-3-2-beat rhythm closest to the original Japanese in order to capture the idiomatic and literal meanings of the original. It goes without saying that the "single wino" in the third reading is is a bit off, though the psychological reverbations of the fart depicted may well lie between the lines, or, rather words of the original. I believe the fourth reading is the best.

◯

yume no ha ka/ga chiru sharakusashi saigo no he   kyôon
dream's leaf/leaves? dropping sake-falling-smell=vanity/cool-odor last fart

A last fart: / are these the leaves / of my dream, vainly falling

◯

In the original, the image of a dream is combined with the cruder image of passing wind. The transition of one to another is made by a play on words: *sharakusashi* means "boastfulness" and "vanity"; the latter part of the word alone, *kusashi,* means "stench."

Joel Hoffman: Japanese Death Poems

Thinking the light verse in this chapter could use a cap, I introduce this *ku* by a dying poet. Hoffman's translation (pardon my deparsing) and explanation are fine as is, but too short to explore the Joycean density of the original. *Sharakusashi* means something that is very *sharaku,* indeed, stinking of it, so to speak. *Sharaku* is more subtle than mere boastfulness and vanity. It is the mindset of the French *flaneur.* That is to say, it is "cool" in the sense of being above it all and viewing all things with studied disinterest. Critically regarded, such an attitude is shallow and affected, but the word is generally as positive as our "cool" (or, *sophisticated*). It is difficult to know what Kyôon meant, but I think he means 1) the fart blows away his last *affectations* (making him death-bed connoisseur Emily Dickinson talking about her *own* rather than another's death) and 2) that he was suddenly aware he was able to observe his end from a disinterested outside point of view, i.e., coolly. The *leaves* probably indicate the time of year, appropriate for haiku, but it was also fitting for a poet because *leaves* 葉 were associated with language 言葉　(lit. *word/thing-leaves*). Think of *words* as you read *"leaves."* It might be sheer coincidence, but *ha* and *ka* (leaves + interrogative), together sound like "grave" (*haka*). Saving the best for last, there is one more reason the *ku* must end on an erructive note. It is what makes the imperfect *ku* a masterpiece: the poet's *nom de plume* means "leaving-sound!"

◯

leaves falling i see
the dream was in my heart, now
to free my last fart

Pardon. Kyôon 去音 was probably not crazy enough to *liberate* a fart. Again,

yume no ha ka/ga chiru sharakusashi saigo no he   kyôon
dream's leaf/leaves? dropping *sake*-falling-smell=vanity/cool-odor last fart

○

leaves fall and i see
the dream was in my heart
now i'm really cool: free
to enjoy my last fart

a dream of leaves
affectations blow away
with my last fart

is life a dream
of colorful leaves, blown
away by a fart?

autumn dreams
colorful leaves, pretentions
of the heart, blasted you are done
blown to kingdom come
by one last fart!

○

My last translation will have almost nothing to do with the original. With it, I'll stop.

○

ぷっ

no longer of
sound body

i do not mind
to leave what is left
of myself behind

– a last fart –

Seasons & Farts. In haiku, various phenomena come to be associated with certain seasons. Once that happens, there is no need to specify the season unless it is a different one. Personally, I feel Winter is right for what Issa implies it is. One cannot open doors or windows without losing heat, so we stew in our farts, or, if we have old dogs, theirs. And, if we choose the cold to breath fresh air, *futon* can keep and release farts like an Amerindian sending smoke signals with a blanket. But, no *saijiki* I know has taken up fartsm as Issa's poem did not become famous even if he did and, I guess, not enough other poets were holed up in small enough quarters to experience the season. However, there are symbolic reasons to make Fall the fart season, too, for it symbolized the futility or emptiness of life turning toward winter while marked by feasting (on foods identified with gas) and drinking. I suppose we could split the fart season into an outdoor (Fall) season and an indoor one (Winter). The fart-cut bug, lengthening nights and night-chill are all clear fall themes. The *senryû* were aseasonal and the death-poem 1749/11/10, in December by our calendar.

2. Out of Place. The *ku* in question was not among the fart-cutting bugs in Issa's collected work, for even though the fart-cutting bug was in it, the *dragonfly* was the subject. The following *ku*, written the same year (1821) featured the former: *A Bombardier! / Dragon- and Butter-flies / blown away!* (*chô tonbo fukitobasaretsu hehiri-mushi*).

Let me add that I do not doubt this is a true observation. At a bluegrass festival on a hill-top near Tokyo, I saw a little green stink-bug crawl over and rob a huge daddy long-legs (with bright-red balls on each joint!) of a potato-chip, so it is easy to imagine a larger fart-squirting(?) beetle could send a dragon-fly packing.

XXII

Ten Thousand Leaves
and all too few translations

小児等 草者勿苅 八穂蓼乎 穂積乃阿曾 脇草乎可礼　万 #3842　8c
warawa domo kusa na kari so yaha-tade ohoseki no aso ga wakisô o kare

*Hey, kiddos! Something is blooming, the meadow can wait!
Mow Sir Aso's underarms . . . before it's too late!*

Reading translations of Japan's oldest anthology of poetry, the *Manyôshû*, usually depresses me. The original is partly to blame. Many poems were chosen more for their author's social position, beautiful sound (if you like *Hiawatha*), or simply because written poetry was so new in Japan that what might bore us today felt fresh; but, timid selection and uninspired translation make it worse. One tires of the same poems conservatively read. I first intended to start this chapter with pages of multiple translations of mowing underarms, mining a red nose for cinnabar and monks with stubble thick enough for a hitching post, but "*Manyôshû's* Mean Little Poems of Little Meaning," a chapter in *Mad In Translation,* took them first, so I ditched all but a token, the single *Axillary Alarm* above. Then, there is *style*. Having read Waley and Pound's translations of the *Shi-ching/jing,* or *Book of Songs* (詩経 poetic-chat/sutra?), the oldest *Chinese* anthology earlier, I had come to expect it.　Let's see a telling example.

YE YOU MAN CAO 野有蔓草、零露漙兮。有美一人、清揚婉兮。邂逅相遇、適我願兮。野有蔓草、零露瀼瀼。有美一人、婉如清揚。邂逅相遇、與子偕臧。
field has vine grass / sets dew copious +emph. / has beauty one person / clear rise lovely +emph. / come upon together meet / fitting my wishes +emph.　// field has vine grass / sets dew flow flow / has beauty one person　/　lovely clear rise　/　accidently each other meet　/　i [&]baby all good?? [???]

(Ezra Pound, left. Arthur Waley, right.)

*Mid the bind-grass on the plain
that the dew makes wet as rain
I met by chance my clear-eyed man,
　　　　then my
　　　　　joy began.*

*Mid the wild grass dank with dew
lay we the full night thru,
　　that clear-eyed man and I
　　　in mutual felicity.*

*Out in the bushlands a creeper grows,
The falling dew lies thick upon it.
There was a man so lovely,
Clear brow well rounded.
By chance I came across him,
And he let me have my will.*

*Out in the bushlands a creeper grow?
The falling dew lies heavy on it.
There was a man so lovely,
Well rounded his clear brow.
By chance I came upon him:
'Oh, Sir, to be with you is good.'*

This, the 20th poem in Pound and, if I recall right, 81st in two Japanese translations, is the 1st song of the first section, *Courtship*, of Waley's *Book of Songs*. Would he contrast it with the male-to-female proposition vector of the first poem/song of the Japanese *Ten Thousand Leaves* (*Manyôshû*)? The Japanese translation by Emperor's Culture Award winner Kaionji, has it *very* different. I present the Romanized Japanese of his translation and my translation

no no tsuru-kusa ni tsuyu shitodo / memoto suzushiku pacchiri to / shittori tayoka de yoi onago / hyokkori to nomichi de au naraba / donna ni yokaro / shippori nurete // no no tsuru-kusa ni tsuyu shitodo / shittori tayoka de yoi onago / memoto suzushiku pacchiri to / nomichi de hyokkori to au naraba / otagai yokaro / shippori nurete

Vines in the meadow dripping dew	*Vines in the meadow dripping dew*
her eyes set wide, bright and cool,	*limpid and lithesome, a lovely girl,*
limpid and lithesome, a lovely girl –	*her eyes set wide, bright and cool –*
How good if we chanced to meet	*How good it would be for you and me*
just like that on a country path	*on a country path to meet and get*
utterly soaked, shippori to!	*utterly soaked, shippori to!*

Please note the above are not paraverses but the two stanzas side-by-side to save space. The original stanzas differ less than in Pound and Waley's translation. Kaionji does not turn the ambiguous Chinese into a past-tense narrative, but fuses supposition and proposition. The best part of the Japanese, adverbs such as *shittori, tayoka, shippori* and *pacchiri to,* with their psychological mimesis, was not translatable. These words are so beautiful, a reader is lost in them. I added "and get" to be sure we got something out of the English, if my *li-li-la* line did not do it. But what caught my attention was the gender: *reversed*. Ditto for another Japanese translation I have read and lost. The proper sex is debatable; the world expert in Chinese characters, a Japanese man eighty-eight at the time and now about one hundred and probably still at work on his monumental studies, wrote me that if *he* had to choose one or the other, it would be the outgoing girl of Pound and Waley for he believed it better fit the Chinese norm for courtship in ancient times. We might also note the bold way the two English translators 1) took the "vine-grass/creepers"(probably standard for plants that can cover a field), added "mid ~ " in one case and made it a powerful singular and symbolic image in the other, where the Japanese translator, for better or worse, simply followed the original; 2) used poetic license to bring-out the central idea, with "mutual felicity" and "let me have my will;" 3) specified "the full night through" only hinted at by the fact that dew lies thickest dusk and dawn.

Putting a quote into the mouth of the protagonist in the last four characters of the Chinese, Waley is still convincing in that whatever he writes seems classic, but Pound combines attention to meaning and sound found nowhere else. His translation is a joy to read, and would be even if the Chinese never existed, while Waley's, as good as it is, requires us to be at least aware of an original to enjoy it. Speaking of which, here is another sort of original, the first translation of the Chinese poem into English, by James Legge (1879/1898):

> *On the moor is the creeping grass,*
> *And how heavily is it loaded with dew!*
> *There was a beautiful man,*
> *Lovely , with clear eyes and fine forehead!*
> *We met together accidentally,*
> *And so my desire was satisfied .*
>
> *On the moor is the creeping grass,*
> *Heavily covered with dew!*
> *There was a beautiful man,*
> *Lovely, with clear eyes and fine forehead!*
> *We met together accidentally,*
> *And he and I were happy together*

With Legge, I would not only need to know there was an original, but want to see it. There is no poetry in the translation, unless the "moor," exotic for Americans, novelty of "creeping grass" "loaded with dew" and a man called "lovely," the awkwardness of "we met together accidentally" and other such stylistic crimes are confused for it. But the translation is a good crib sheet for reading the original. Take the "eyes" and "forehead," neither specified in the original. They had to be ascertained from the adjective/s 清揚 (limpid lofty), impliying the set of the eye and brow area. Japanese has a word for it, *me-moto,* or "eye-base;" English, unfortunately, does not. The closest we approach is "clear-eyed and broad-browed," an expression reminding me of our knights. While the "beauty" (美人) could indeed be male; the character 婉, translated as "lovely," and suggesting *an attractive pliancy* or *gentleness* of character and body seems a female attribute to most of us (modern English, Chinese and Japanese speakers). True, we find very gentle men in many cultures, often in the ruling classes, and the word 美人, literally, "beautiful person" was occassionally used to designate a king or emperor (another reason why Waley might have started with this poem to oppose *Manyôshû's* first poem, where a ruler is involved). Yet, that would not seem to settle the matter. Another story, *"Policy indicated by the odes"* (*The Chinese Classics,* vol.5, reprinted HKUP), ironically, Englished by none other than Legge, may support the man-to-woman reading of the Japanese:

> In summer, in the fourth month, the six ministers of Zheng gave a parting feast to Xuan Zi in the suburbs, when he said to them, "Let me ask all you gentlemen to sing from the odes, and I will thence understand the views of Zheng." . . . . .
>
> Zi Zou then sang the *Ye you man cao* [the above poem], and Xuan Zi said, "Good! young Sir. I have the same desire." . . . .

Xuan Zi was so happy with their selection of Odes, all from the Zheng area (showing local-love, which was proper), that he pronounced Zheng healthy, even flourishing, prognosticated generations of well-being to come, "presented them all with horses, and sang the Wo jiang." The question we must ask is whether *"Good! young Sir. I have the same desire"* means that these men identified with the protagonist, in which case the poem's perspective was either free-gender or male. If it is possible the Japanese reading is correct, maybe we should have a translation that, like the original, does not commit to gender. I tried it below, but the result was so bad, I rewrote and ended up with two more "her" perspectives:

Where creepers fill the field with green
a dewy stream flows through the night;
There I chanced upon my beau,
Clear of brow & eyes so bright,
All a girl could hope to know.

Where creepers fill the field with green
dewy streams flow leaf to leaf;
Lovely man, refreshing dream,
Good it was indeed to do it
before we even knew it!

Where creepers fill the field with green
a dewy stream flows in between;
There I chanced upon my catch
Clear of brow with lucid eyes,
Matchless beauty does surprise.

Where creepers fill the field with green
dewy streams forget no leaf;
My wishes all in one man found
I flew to heaven though I guess
we did it on the ground!

In the process, I forgot the original and paraversed. Here are two more paraverses that comprise a composite translation of ♂ and ♀ readings, to make our (*viva les*) differences explicit.

Girl Meets Boy

A grassy field, a sea of dew
was where I came upon and knew
a handsome man, clear-eyed
broad of brow and, well to tell

He fit my ideal for a mate
& also what I won't relate!

It was a green field, a sea of dew
where i came upon and knew
a handsome man, who moved
so cleanly, he moved me.

Now that is true romance:
to be fulfilled by chance!

Boy Meets Girl

On the grass, in a dewy sea
I came across a beauty
who came across me –
Bright-eyed & bushy-tailed

She was, she really was
Every man's wet-dream!

On the grass, so wet with dew
I came upon my beauty
who came along with me
so lithe and lubricious

She was, she was indeed
delicious as a dream!

The couplet at the end of the second stanza of the first translation may be the only thing that works here. I am afraid, I am only demonstrating why I had better stick to shorter poems! With long ones, I loose my feet and trying to regain them – or cover them up – become downright obscene! Why this should be, I have no idea (Like most paupers, I have never been psychoanalyzed). The couplets after the first stanzas make another point, indirectly. Namely, the sixth line of the original: "fits/fitting/suits/matches-my-wish/request/wants" can mean either the other party *looks like* the poet's ideal mate, or *does* what Waley made explicit with "have my will." Pound artfully avoided a clear choice, hinting at the former meaning with his "*my* clear-eyed man" ("my" meaning her ideal type!) *and* allowing desire to be duly fulfilled. *Damn*, that bad man (Pound) was good!

| A modern Chinese Englishing we might title – *"How I Found My Pretty Bride!"* | A unique 1891 translation by William Jennings – *"Fortuitous Concourse"* |

In the wilds grew creepers,
With dew-drops so heavy and thick.
There was a girl, beautiful and bright,
Her features so delicate and charming.
By chance we met each other,
She embodied my long-cherished wish.

Where creeping plants grew on the wild,
  And heavy dew declined,
There was a fair one all alone,
  Bright-eyed, good-looking, kind.
Chance brought us to each other's side,
And all my wish was gratified.

In the wilds grew creepers,
With dew-drops so full and round.
There was a girl, beautiful and bright,
Her features so charming and delicate.
By chance we met each other,
Together with her life will be happy.

Where creeping plants grew on the wild,
  And thick the dew-drops stood,
There was the fair one all alone,
  Kind, as the looks were good.
Chance let us meet each other there,
Our mutual happiness to share.

These two translations came late to me. The one on the left, by the husband and wife team of Yang Xianyi (楊憲益) and Gladys Yang (aka Dai Naidie 戴乃迭 in the FLP (Foreign Languages Press of Peking) edition of *The Book of Songs* is more or less how a young Chinese friend of mine, an anthropologist living in Japan, read it. Gender-wise, it is like the Japanese translation; tense-wise, like the Jennings; and, style-wise, follows Legge's first, a hundred years earlier in that it is basically prose, a poem only because the lines are parsed. Most notably, however, the added "delicate" makes the questionably female surely so, while there is no hint of sex, unless you take embodiment literally, and the last line suggests monogamy in the making. Is it unfair to point out that Gladys Yang is the daughter of a missionary? William Jennings, whose translation is far more exciting, was himself a retired missionary: "Vicar of Breedon, Berks, Late Colonial Chaplain, Incumbent of St. John's Cathedral, Hongkong." I was delighted to find this translation from his *The Shi King: The Old Poetry Classic of the Chinese a Close Metrical . . .* (1891), proves me wrong about a decent unisex translation being beyond English. It was beyond *me*. "Fair one," which never came to mind, seems to work just fine. Moreover, Jenning's translation of the following poem, #95, is so terse yet lively that I am no longer sure Pound's style was a reaction to the fluffy excesses of Legge. More likely he was inspired by Jennings! The last stanza of poem #95: *When Tain and Wai / Flow deep and clear, / Then men and maids / In crowds appear/ / And maids will ask, &c, &c.*

And that brings me back to my original concern about the *Manyô-shû* in English. While most translations may be technically acceptable, few live on their own, which is to say, *as poetry*. That *depresses* me. I have come to feel, rightly or wrongly, that fun-loving translators are more likely to work with Latin or Chinese, which I may occasionally play with but do not read well enough to fully appreciate, while Japanese, which (at my advanced age) I am pretty much stuck with, either attracts dull translators or makes translators dull or, at least dull translators, for Blyth was anything but dull, only his *translations*, unlike his piquant prose, tended to be so. Could it be that Japan with its aesthetic culture and mixed writing system is so overwhelming that its best students remain timid scholars all their lives and never grow the backbone for bold translation, while China, the fount of most 'things Japanese,' holds so much good, bad and contradictory that it inspires rebellious as well as reverental feelings in its spokesmen? Or, does it, rather, come from colonialistic feelings toward China, which, in the 19c was not yet able to show itself an equal to the West? Must one lack respect to translate freely? I hope not, for I fancy my poetic license as being used for the Japanese poets I most appreciate while such a theory makes me a prejudiced soul, indeed. Or, could it be in the language, itself? Translators from Chinese may find the even lines and abundant rhyme (phonemic and tonal) in Chinese hard to match, but such rules are a formal invitation to play – the *sine qua non* of good translation – and the skeletal language requires poetic license to be re-incarnated in English. The homophonic pun and pivot word-based allusive wit of Japanese poetry, being less formal, tends to be ignored or relegated to footnotes in the back of books (a reader-unfriendly practice that should be banned), the plentiful ellipses call for being filled in rather than fleshed out, while the counting of short relatively uniform phonemes has confounded generations of translators, as it did when English first tried to translate from classical tongues. Or – I hate to ask this, but it must be asked – am I barking up the wrong tree? Could the content be the only problem? If old Japanese poetry was less interesting than old Chinese poetry, boring translations would be natural, would they not? Yet, oddly enough, when *I* translate Japanese poetry it almost always comes out interesting. Part of that is surely the result of my selection, but when I do things others have done, such as Tabibito's drinking songs (in three of my books so far, with most in *Mad In Translation*), they, too, tend to be wittier. That is not a boast but fact, and if knowledgeable critics find the wit lies in me rather than the original, not necessarily good. Who knows, perhaps it was a mistake for me to have tried to translate Japanese poetry, and literature would have been better served had I taken my blasted cleverness elsewhere . . . to Chinese.

Or, is my lament misguided? *There is much I have not read in translation.* When I read the ancient anthologies in Japanese twenty years ago, I had no reason to seek English translations, for I was enjoying them in the original with the assistance of notes written in the same language as the poems; and, now, when I *am* curious, my circumstances (physical isolation and poverty) do not allow it. Maybe there are more great Japanese-English translators out there than I know.

Since writing the last paragraph (a couple years ago), thanks to interlibrary loan I have found some more I share in *Mad In Translation*. Edwin Cranston in the second volume of his grand *waka* anthologies sometimes rises to the occasion and he writes that as he has reached the age where ancient Chinese expected a person to become free of inhibitions he may start translating in a freer vein – all I can say is, by all means, do it! Still, there are, or rather, there *is* one translation of one *Manyô-shû* poem I found in a tattered old paperback bought in 1998 that strikes me as a poem as surely as good translations from Latin are poems:

iwamaro ni ware mono môsu natsuyase ni yoshi to iu mono zo munagi tori-mese
iwamaro[name]-to i thing say: summer-thinning-for good say thing! eel taking-eat!

Making fun of a thin man	*Envoi*
IWAMARO, look!	Ever thinner
Shall I tell you what?	Though you be,
For summer sickness, catch	Better stay alive.
An eel, and let it cook,	When you're after eels for dinner,
Then – down the hatch!	Watch your step. Don't dive.

yasuyasu mo ikeraba aramu o hata ya hata munagi o toru to kawa ni nagaru na
thin[vb]thin[vb] even live-if is-not[+exclam] conversely eel take and river in flow-not

trans. Geoffrey Brownas & Anthony Thwaite: *The Penguin Book of Japanese Verse*

There are other pretty tasteful translations in their Penguin anthology, but this is the only clearly end-rhyming, albeit, enjambed – and, shall we say, delightfully irresponsible? – translation, though it is not without other light-verse. All thirteen of Ôtomo Tabito's poems in praise of *sake* are included – unlike most Usanians, few English are prejudiced about drinking– and though they, too, seem to ask for rhyme (see mine in *Mad In Translation*), none are. Is it possible that the *cruelty* of the Thin Man poems caused the translators to either hand them over to a classics scholar well-versed in Martial's *Epigrams* (See Lesbia's *Wedgies*, pg 185-192) to deal with, or to reach deep down into their own gullets and pull it up from middle-school themselves? (If my memory is correct, one of the translators is a classics scholar). Contentwise, I will not mention what was added in translation (you can ascertain that from the gloss) other than to point out that "dive" was not free. The original idea of a man so slight the current would sweep him away, was lost in translation.   My translation kept it:

Kidding a Thin Man	*On Second Thought*
I tell you, Bones, for summer-wasting,	*But e'er so thin a man may be, life still*
You must go catch and taste of eel.	*Is his best bet! Take care sniggling,*
Swallow it; then, see how you feel!	*Lest the river carry you off wriggling!*

But, who cares! What is correctness in poetry? My translation is lame next to theirs. Though delighted with Brownas and Thwaite, I do hate to lose. Here are two new tries. You can caption them as you like:

Hey, Bones, I'll tell you the secret if you would stay fat
in the summer – you must catch and eat an eel for that.

Though thin is not happy but sad, at least you are alive:
Let the fat sniggle, they float – You will sink: Don't dive!

Hey, Bones, I'll tell you what they say beats the summer blues
Catch a big fat eel then eat it, for weight you will not lose!

~~~~~~

No, no matter how thin, life is life, please keep your seat,
Sniggle not, for any stream will sweep you off your feet!

Any better? Did doing *Mad In Translation* hone my skills? Brownas & Thwaite if you are still with us, what do you think? These *Manyôshû* poems # 3853 # 3854 are sometimes cited in articles about 'the roots of bullying in Japan' for a note in the *Manyô-shû* tells us the thin man was a real person nicknamed Iwamaro, Craggy-guy (the Chinese character is "stone"). In English, "Bones." Since youth, no matter how much he ate, he was bone-thin. This is no laughing concern. The fat were not kidded in the *Manyôshû*, as fat embodied wealth, happiness and good fortune. "Thin" 瘦 is written with the sickness radical 疒 and most people feared thinning in the summer. I was surprised to find the word "summer-thinning" (*natsu-yase*), still used today, well over a thousand years ago, and *astounded* at the longevity of the eel, eaten for the same reason today. Of course, it does the involuntarily thin no good because fat, unabsorbed, literally backfires or floats away (the supposed 'science' of nutrician is practically useless for the Bones of the world). The poet, Ôtomo Yakamochi, a fit man who could roam at night from wife to wife like a tom-cat yet still have energy enough to do his work and write many passionate and clever poems on the side, could not feel the deep sorrow of those who can not get food to stick to their bones. Only the involuntarily thin know what it is like to be foresaken by the world of matter.

~~~~~~

味飯乎 水尓釀成 吾待之 代者曽無<无> 直尓之不有者 # 3810
味飯を水に釀みなしわが待ちし 代はさね<かつて>なし直にしあらねば
umai-hi o mizu ni kaminashi waga machishi kai wa sane-nashi tada ni shi araneba
(tasty-rice[acc] water-with chewed i waited compensation/worth emph.not directly is not-if)

To Think I Could've
Given It to Someone Else
(or even drunken it myself)

what a waste of good saliva,
rice and water chewed for you
while i waited, it turned sour
and *now* you tell me
we are through!

Women in old Japan wove cloth/ing for their lovers and chewed sweet-rice, spitting it into vats to make sake. Why the super-duper *double-title?* At the time I played with these *Manyôshû* poems, I wrote country music parodies by the score. Today, they sit with my books in a warehouse in Japan, where I left them in order not to be distracted from developing more important experiments with instruments to allow people with good ears but unsuited for complex instruments to play music. I did not intend to do anything with these *Manyô-shû* paraverses either and found them after the rest of this book was finished, mixed with material for five variations on Thoreau from his *Journals*, shipped back to me from Japan. Handwritten, they definitely predate my Issa paraverses (and my computer: so much for my computer hypothesis expressed elsewhere). I considered moving them to the front of the book, but left things as they were, reflecting *publishing* priority. As the above poem includes my most *expansive* paraverse ever, it would seem to be good evidence that my paraversing has not slowly seduced me away from the originals, as I imagined, but, if anything, become a bit more faithful to them. Today, I only like the round-looking paraverse above, which I also put into *Mad In Translation*. The following is only meant to show other ways – one longer, one shorter – that paraversing can go.

Nuptial Sake

Good rice and good water
A mother's good daughter
Patiently chews them into good wine.

While faithful, she waited
He dated and mated
Another prettier, but far less kind.

Now sated, frustrated
No longer elated
He crawls back to her in time.

Says she, *"You're to blame*
that I still have my name
But this vinegar, love, is thine!"

I wonder about the last line in this extrapolative paraverse. "Thine" seems artificial. Would *"But this vinegar, love, isn't mine"* be any better?

You Can't Fool Sake
(*in vino veritas,* the test!)

The wine i chewed for us
        of sweet rice & spring water,

Soured on the day you wed
        another mother's daughter.

The idea of the wine ominously turning to vinegar, like the mating and marriages, is all mine. Even the "turn sour" in my first conservative translation is my idea. The original only says that she chewed good rice and water in vain. In the original, even the information about being kept waiting a long time and marrying another is not in the poem. Instead it is provided after the poem.

The Long Wait
all for nothing

I chewed good rice and water to make our wine.

Now it's turned to vinegar . . . this heart of mine.

To me, the original just does not have enough information. The editor probably chose it because there is humor in specifying what was chewed was of good quality. Still, it is one of the *Manyô* poems where I wonder if there might not be a second, dirty reading that enlivened it – or justified its length – in the original to its original readers. For example *kai-wa sane nashi* might mean "my cunt becomes a clit" or "the value is in sleeping (together)" etc., and other things depending upon what connotation, dialect or idiom is chosen. And now, my most ridiculously long paraverse. Please note that at the time I drank very little so, believe it or not, I probably did it sober. It proves paraversing itself intoxicates.

her toes
once tickled
as she tread grapes
to make him wine

~~~~~~~~~~

but fickle men
have a way
of straying
from the
vine

~~

&

~~~~

love turned
to vinegar her heart

~~~~~~~~~~~~~

as sweet meat intended
for fat may end up a fart

~~~~~~~~~~~~~

and, now, she says
"*i am because*
i drink"

~~~~

she is
always
pickled

~~~~

seldom pink.

事之有者 小泊瀬山乃 石城尓母 隠者共尓 莫思吾背
事しあらば小泊瀬山の石城にも隠らばともにな思ひそ我が背
kotoshi araba obase-yama no iwaki ni mo komoraba tomo ni na omoi so waga se
(thing is-if obase mountain's stone-fort[crpt]s in even hide-out-if together don't-long/fret my boy)

A Grave Proposal
(not to be blue)

Honey, don't fret
if worst comes to worst
I know a pleasant place:
High on Mount Ohatsuse
We can always embrace

I was drawn to this poem (Manyô #3806) the instant I saw it, for I knew the "stone-fort" was a mountain-side cave used for a crypt by nobles in pre-Buddhist Japan. *What a thing for a maiden to say!* As one of our poets put it, *"The grave's a fine and private place, but none I think do there embrace."* The explanation was that the boyfriend of the girl who wrote the poem put off proposing because he was afraid to meet her parents. Fed up with his dilly-dallying, she called his bluff: *Was he not ready to die for or with her?* The explanation eased my mind, but the poem probably scared the sh_t out of her cowardly boyfriend.

Mt Obase Awaits	*The Promise*
Whatever happens	*Darling, be brave*
don't worry, be brave!	*Though you should be killed,*
We can always hole up	*I'll join you in the grave:*
in a fortified grave.	*we'll be fulfilled*

I have seen this poem in at least one *Manyôshû* selection in Japanese and suspect it may be fairly well-known. It deserves to be very well-known. After five years of somewhat more responsible haiku and senryu translation, let me try a tighter reading with little extra or missing:

Go Ahead and Ask Them!

Honey, take heart, 'cause you got mine, and it's the bigger of the two;
We'll forever be together, no matter what our parents do.

There's a cozy cave on Mount Obase, so why should we be blue?
A common grave will be divine, for noble me and you!

That is *ridiculous*. I have the first translation in *Mad In Translation* and was going to skip it until I read myself promising to give more versions in *this* book!

A promise is a promise. If I do not keep the promises I made in my last book, my readers will not believe those I make in this book and so, I really had no choice.

in the worst case
we'll hole up in a fort high
up mount obase

just us two, so do not cry
my sweet papoose

This one, on the other hand, is, I dare say, *good*. I guess "high" can replace *stone*, for graves were the only "forts" up there, and "do not cry" is the same as "do not worry" and better fits "papoose," appropriate for the boyfriend here 背 *se,* or "back" is short for 背子 *seko,* or "back-child," *i.e.,* a baby carried piggyback (though always belly to the mother or older sister's back, unlike the Amerindian baby who might be carried facing either front or back). Like the original, the complete situation is not in the poem.

Here, I had ten different paraverses of Manyô #3033 (*naka naka ni nani ka,* ...) a heart erupting like a volcano. But, when I put my Dorothy Parker-style paraverse into *Mad In Translation*, I realized that reading said it all and so . . . *Poof!* Good bye to two pages . . . . And if anyone is interested in *Manyô* #3724, with the woman's rage directed at the road her lover would take to leave, write me for it. We have seen enough for this book. It is hard for me to quit because I put hundreds (or thousands) of hours into reading the 4516 poems and have hundreds, or thousands of them marked for this or that reason, but failed to turn that into a book when I could have – impossible for twenty five years have passed and I have a poor memory. As translating long poems is not my *forte*, I suppose it was no loss for the world, but judging from the recently found handwritten paraverses which forced me to add this chapter, the experience was not a total waste. Without it, I may never have dared to do the multiple readings of haiku and *senryû* that developed into a novel poetic form, composite-translation as a single poem, such as we have seen.

Other Manyô Translations.   **Hirsute armpit.**   Honda did a rhyming translation that I reparse as follows:

O children, trouble not to go to reap the meadow,
since you have plenty here to mow
in Lord Hozumi's armpits

Thin Man & Eel: Boring non-rhyme =*"Iwamaro, I tell you, / Catch and eat eels! / They are good, they say, / For summer loss of flesh."* ////// *"Yet, no matter how lean you are, / It is better to be alive. / So drown not yourself in the river / Trying to catch an eel!"*(NGS).

Wine for Lover: Boring rhyme = *"Alas, I brewed good wine for you to drink, but all / is now in vain, since at my bower you will not call."* (Honda). Boring non-rhyme =*"It did me no good / To ferment the tasty rice, / Brewing with water, / Waiting for you – none at all, / For you're not here to have it."*(Cranston).   But, if you recall, the original is boring.

xxiii

Mad In Translation, or better late than *Ever*

極楽も地獄も活て居るうちぞ 死ての後は何か有べし 空翠 一茶全集3-43
gokuraku mo jigoku mo ikiteiru uchi zo shinde no ato wa nani ga arubeshi kûsûi d.1763
paradise/heaven & hell too living-are during! // dying-after-as-for what? is-ought

Heaven or hell, one thing is true:
You cannot take them with you!

The decision to research and write a book, subtitled "a thousand years of *kyôka*, comic Japanese poetry in the classic *waka* mode," was made with *A Dolphin In the Woods* just a month away from being ready for publication. Now, a year later, *Mad* is out, and here we are. As mad poems, or *kyôka,* are novel and witty, the book produced more wild paraversing than all books combined to date. It all started when I came across a translation I scribbled and forgot in Issa's journal. Why did one Englished *kyôka* Issa copied from the grave-marker of Kûsûi, an Edo (蔵前) *haijin* and sign-maker make up my mind? Because it told me that not only was translation *possible*, but it could *improve* a *kyôka*. Half a dozen other readings are scribbled next to it – *"Heaven & Hell? They are mine while I live! / Death may well promise, but what can it give?"* and *"Even heaven and hell / are fleeting: enjoy them / while your heart is beating."* They are not bad, but only *heaven or hell, one thing is true . . .* thrills me every time I read it, and that, despite the original being more a didactic *carpe diem* than a real chuckle! More precisely, I realizing that the second line of the above reading *made it* mad, and that if I but kept my wits about me I might gain enough in translation to make up for what was lost and, occasionally, go one better. So, I asked an academic friend whether anyone had collected and translated *kyôka.* No one had. And, he egged me on by writing that perhaps only I could do *kyôka* justice. The following three poems are examples of what I think he had in mind. They are untranslatable, but a composite reading can English their essence without boring the reader. All are straight from the short version of *Mad*, namely *Reading Mad In Translation.*

あなうなぎ いづくの山のいもとせをさかれてのちに身をこがすとは 四方赤良
ana unagi izuku no yama no imo to se o sakarete nochi ni mi o kogasu to wa yomo no akara
pitiful=hole(waterhole)-eel, eventually's mountain-potato(a long thin variety)=girlfriend & boyfriend=back(of a body)+acc. // split/separating after body/self+acc. roast/burn-as-for

♪ *The Spitchcock Blues* ♪

Poor country girl
and boy after the fashion
of eels are split,

For roasting on the coals
of their very own passion!

My poor Unagi,
born of wild potato, split
down your back,

How sweet parting hurts
when you're burnt black!

221

Mad poets had to invent truly novel fire metaphor to outdo the flaming hearts of ancient *waka,* with their volcanoes, fireflies and moths. This *kyôka* (万載 1783), one of the three most cited by the most famous *kyôka* poet – Yomo no Akara (later Shokusanjin) succeeds in doing just that. The *Spitchcock Blues* (my title) has probably never been translated. *Why?* Because the reading, like the eel, must be split. At least, this translator could not keep it whole, as in the original, and had to settle for a composite translation. The eel's original form, the "potato," *imo,* is homophonous with "little-sister," or *girlfriend.* The variety mentioned, the *unagi,* a relatively flat "common eel," is split open from the belly for roasting in most of Japan, but in Kantô, which is to say greater Edo (now, Tokyo) it was split *from the back* as required for the pun – a *boyfriend* is a *"back," se,* short for "my baby," *waga seko,* or *papoose,* for that is how they are carried. The roast indirectly boasts "this is how we make mad poems in the new capital city!" Nanpo did not, however, invent the odd metamorphosis. It was part of folklore for hundreds of years and, like most such longheld folk beliefs, supported by many old reports of half-eel-half-potatoes with specific names and places.

大こうのもとはきけど糠みそに打ちつけられてしおしおとなる
taikô no moto wa kikedo   nukamiso ni uchi-tsukerarete shio-shio to naru takuan
daikon(hideyoshi)'s basis-as4 asked-if, nuka-miso-in throw-soak/pickld limp becmes

You ask about making daikon pickles? Thrown into nuka miso, they become soft.
◆ ◆ ◆ ◆ ◆ ◆ ◆ ◆ ◆
You ask about Hideyoshi's situation? Ieyasu pickled him, and he's turned softy.

Takuan, a delightful noble-turned-maverick-monk, made this allegorical report to a friend about Nobunaga's successor: *Taikô* 太閤, "imperial advisor," the title the late-16c unifying shôgun Hideyoshi gave himself. *Daiko* is colloquial for *daikon,* huge radish. The character for *nuka* (*nuka-miso* salted rice bran paste) is 糠; the second for Ieyasu, founder of the succeeding Tokugawa dynasty, was 康. The first name pun requires the mind's ear; the second its eye. ★ *Takuan* is a yellowish *daikon* pickle the monk is sometimes credited with inventing.

太平の眠りを覚ます上喜撰＝蒸気船＝たった四杯＝隻＝で夜も眠れず 無名
taihei no nemuri o samasu jôkisen tatta yon hai de yoru mo nemurezu anon. 1853
indolence/pacific sleep-from wake jôkisen(tea)/steam-ship just 4cups/ships-from night=world sleep-can't

Stolid folk may be roused from their slumber –
Just four packets of Joy Tea to stay up all night.
~~~~~~~~~~~~~~~~~~ + ~~~~~~~~~~~~~~~~~~
The Pacific ocean has awoken from its slumber,
Just 4 steam ships & the world can get no sleep.

This anonymous masterpiece, spicing every textbook account of the Opening of Japan, is the best known *kyôka rakushu* (squib). What an odd time it was! To the prissy officers' disgust and chaplain's outrage, kind Japanese fishermen tossed pornographic picture-books up to the delighted Yankee seamen and traded fish for whatever novelties they might obtain, while the rest of the country was thrown into a tizzy as terrified land and tradition-bound authorities and their charges worked around the clock to throw up ramparts of fake forts on the hills overlooking the river Perry ascended. It would seem only two of the four "black ships" were steam-powered and even those were only partly so to supplement the sails. No matter, the fact the Japanese already had a word for such ships, *jôkisen*, that could be punned into the name-brand tea Jôkisen (up-joy-select), is, in itself, proof that their long isolated nation was ready to engage with the greater world.

うつくしき花のした葉を見るからに くちすいせんと人やいふらん　半井卜養
utsukushiki hana no shitaba o miru kara ni kuchisuisen to hito ya iuran bokuyô　1607-1678
beautiful flower's/s' below-leaves+acc see from, mouth/entrance?-narcissus=kiss-would, so folk say!

> Seeing a beautiful flower's lower leaves, entrance narcissus is what people say.
> +++
> Seeing a beautiful wife in her bloom, I'd kiss her is what other men say!

水仙花をいけて歌よめと有けれは
~ asked for a poem about posing a narcissus ~

> *This beautiful flower has no limbs to hold, but leaves below*
> *to the imagination and Narcissus may be kissed, you know!*

This "facetious fantasy" from *The Untranslatable Lightness of Nakarai Bokuyô* chapter in the 740-page monster (the large version of *Mad In Translation*), has a two-line prosaic gloss but ends up one reading with a good pivot pun on *leaves* that is less convincing than the original pun connecting the name of the flower, the subject itself, with *kissing*. The next translation overcomes a similar challenge more successfully.

眼は鏡口は盥のほどにあく蝦蟇も化生のものとこそ知れ 狂歌百物語
me wa kagami kuchi wa tarai no hodo ni aku gama mo keshô no mono to koso shire
eyes-as-for mirrors mouth-as-for tub-amount open toad too changelng/make-up thing know!

> *Looking-glass eyes, & a mouth that opens like a basin,*
> *A toad's a goblin you can look and wash your face in!*

Precision would require a composite reading to include what Hearn puts inside and outside a parenthesis in his gloss: *"The eye of it, widely open, like a (round) mirror; the mouth of it opening like a wash-basin — by these things you may know that <u>the Toad is a goblin-thing</u> (or, that <u>the Toad is a toilet article</u>)."* I change the pun to a metaphor: The common word for a changeling is *bakemono* 化け物, but here the toad is described by the Sino-japanese *keshô* 化生 for the homophonic double, *make-up* 化粧 (lit. *change-powder*) or toiletry. Note that while Japanese houses had few furnishings by cluttered Occidental standards, the furniture, utensils and other objects had a much busier life of the spirit. Ghost stories where they came to life were well-known. In the most famous one, old utensils thrown out in winter cleaning took blood-thirsty revenge on humans! What better story to teach children the Golden Rule extends to *things!*

223

Composite readings of what cannot be unified in the target language is the most easily justified multiple-translation. The following sort is another matter:

太刀は鞘に治る御代は腹つゝみ うつやうたすやたんほゝの城　友易 有馬下
tachi wa saya ni osameru miyo wa hara tsuzumi utsu ya utazu ya tanpoponoshiro tomoyô
thick-sword-as4 scabbrd-in contrl hon.reign-as4 belly-tomtom beat or beat-nt dndln-frt

> *Beating our tumtums full of meat, swords rusting in their sheaths,*
> *We're off to Fort Dandelion to shoot, or not to shoot, the breeze!*
> ~~~~~~
> *My warrior's pride safely sheathed, this full tum-tum is all I beat –*
> *Dandy times indeed when visiting Ft. Dandelion is dubbed a feat!*

Here the readings are *paraverses*, or alternative translations, as the originals play with dandelion-related associations none of which make any sense in English. Tanpopo-no-shiroyama or Dandelion Fort Mountain 多舞保々能城山 comes from the second *Arima* [sauna vacation spot] book (ed. Kôfû 1678) in a *kyôka* baedeker 地誌所載狂歌少. Dandelion sounds like *drumming* rather than lion-teeth in Japanese, and tummy-drumming is identified with *tanuki*, a racoon-fox that often makes odd noises (a children's song starts *Tan-tan tanuki*) though its *kyôka* usage as a symbol of contentment takes it back to ancient China. Suppose for a moment that you saw only one translation. Whether it was the unique usage of the English idiom "shooting the breeze" or "dandy times" making a visit "a feat," if the translator *and the reader* are sufficiently aware of the fact that the translation was only one of many possibilities – here is where it helps to have a gloss, cramped and ugly as it may be – *even one translation can be read as but one of a constellation of possible translations*.

いにしへのよろひに替る紙子さへ風のいる矢は通さざりけり 蓮生法し 古今夷曲集
inishie no yoroi ni kawaru kamiko sae kaze no iru ya wa tôsazarikeri renshô-hôshi 1666
long-ago/ancient-times' armor-w/ exchanging paperobe even wind shoots arrows-as4 pass-not

> *A paper robe in place of ancient armor, still a man of parts,*
> *can rest, safely protected from the cold wind's chilly darts!*

Unless, that is, one cannot imagine any other translations. Long experience with multiple-translation helped find the rhyme-inducted *"man of parts/darts,"* but, once that was found my desire to try another translation died. Yet, even here, the first part of the second line tempts me. "Can rest" might be "is blessed."

~~~~~~

The *Aren't-we-peaceful!* theme underlying the last two 17c poems became a staple of *haikai* by the 18c, was championed by *senryû* in the mid-18c and lasted until the mid-19c., but it seems to have became identified with late-18c Tenmei *kyôka* such as the next *kyôka*, presented as what might at a glance *look like* a composite translation or paraverses, but is actually something different, a way to present *a take-off*, as it cannot be translated and presented alone, unless the other poem alluded to is well known in the target language.

かくばかり経がたく見ゆる世の中を 羨ましくもすめる月かな　藤原高光 拾遺
kaku bakari hegataku miyuru yo no naka o urayamashiku mo sumeru tsuki kana　takamitsu
this much cross-hard seems/ world+contra+lament. enviously-even clears/lives-can moon!

With the world
this hard a place to be –
How envious to see
Luna's clear untroubled face
looking down on you & me!

To peek down
at a world this happy –
Is that not a trace
of envy that we see tonight
on Luna's pretty face!

this much lucky/happy appears world/society+acc enviously+emph. peek?! moon-form/light
kaku bakari medetaku miyuru yo no naka o urayamashiku ya nozoku tsukikage　shokusanjin 1783
かくばかりめでたくみゆる世の中を うらやましくやのぞく月影　蜀山百集 萬載集

To the left, we have a 10-11c waka where the serene moon serves as a foil for hard times; and to the right, a late-18c kyôka. The originals are *much* closer than the translations. Let me try again, the old *waka* and *kyôka*, respectively:

> *With the world so hard a place to be, how envious to see*
> *Luna with her glowing face a picture of serenity!*

~~~~~~~~~~~~~~~~~~~~~~~~~~~~~~~~~~

> *With the world so happy and care-free, isn't that envy*
> *on Luna's face while she peeks at you and me?*

That brings them closer and, except for the rhyme, would probably satisfy those whose only concern is whether the translations closely follow the originals. But Shokusanjin's well-known *kyôka,* generally understood to be less a riposte than a times-are-changing update, has a barb in it that, judging from annotations and citations, only your translator seems to have noticed. One reading used in the *740-page Monster* incorporates that interpretation of Shokusanjin's intent:

> *i dunno*
>
> *a world that seems*
> *so god-damn happy, why*
> *the moon in the sky*
> *must be peeking at us*
> *out of sheer envy!*

The "i dunno" title and "must be" are meant to be ironic. I believe Shokusanjin jokes about the incessant boasting over how Japan was the most peaceful country and Japanese the most fortunate people in the world. Even his contemporary Issa, with his famous concern for little creatures and outbursts about the bad state of the world, has dozens of chauvinistic *ku*. But he was also religious and viewed the moon as the light of Buddhist law and mercy. Indeed, one of my favorite of his moon *ku* goes even further and seems to turn it into what English used to call a sinne eater (we saw it in chapter 20: *All of our sins / should vanish tonight:/ the fall moon . . .*). So, free spirited as he was, Issa would never have reversed that *waka* as Akara did.   From the Buddhist point of view, it would have seemed not only *outrageous* but *perverse* to have the sacrosant moon that helped raise men above their worldly attachments and even pacify wild animals look on with envy.   But if Shokusanjin meant it sarcastically, *i.e., "it is as if we are so full of ourselves even the moon must look down in envy"* – as I believe to be the case, his poem does not really address the moon itself but the mentality of his fellow Edoites. See, for example, another of his *kyôka* that is far less well known:

祝 戸をあけて ぬれどもさらにいさゝかの かぜさへひかぬ御代ぞめでたき
iwai: to o akete nuredomo sara ni isasaka no kaze sae hikanu mi yo zo medetaki
celebration: door+acc. opened sleep moreover wind/cold even catch-not hon.era+exclam joy/lucky

We open our doors to sleep and, what is more, never catch
The slightest cold in this, the most blessed times e'er told!

The original is captioned "Celebration," the "ever told" is for the rhyme and "times" may also be translated as "reign," but the reading is otherwise very close and its *ad absurdum* claim, proves beyond all doubt that Shokusanjin's envious moon may not be what Hamada Giichiro's annotation naively called it: "reality-positive*"* or "reality-affirmative" (現実肯定的狂歌). Tanaka Yûko, an expert on the social networks of the Edo era called *ren*, citing the same, wrote knowingly

"In waka, the composer envies the moon, but in kyoka, the moon envies us. In waka, this world is difficult and blue, but in kyoka, this world is wonderful. In his kyoka, Nanpo always admires this real world, changes unhappy events into happy ones, and laughs at everything. This is connected with the traditional function of blessing. There were until the Second World War professional entertainers who blessed everything in each house on new year's day. The ren of kyoka produced laughter in all the meetings." 1993 Tanaka Yuko at Nissan Institute, Oxford University (Netted. Translator not named.)

A beautiful tribute to the genre of *kyôka*; but the "always" is wrong. Or, it is wrong *as explained*. Nanpo (Shokusanjin) did indeed appreciate even the chauvanists, but that does not mean he believed life in Japan – for we are talking about Japan, not the world – was a rose garden.   Now, back to our paraversing:

Just look at Luna　　　　　　　　　　*How envious to see*
not a wrinkle in her brow;　　　　*the full moon sail through*
While we suffer　　　　　　　　　　*this world of gloom;*
indignities here below　　　　　　*While we must dog-paddle*
that diva does not know!　　　　*not to sink w/in our tomb!*

In its less obvious way, the old *waka, itself,* was pretty wacky. Envy may be a compliment, but suffering poets usually found Buddha's grace and solace in the serene face of the moon. What if I were to translate it as, say, *"How can ye moon sit so high and pretty in a world where life demands we get down and dirty?"* Can such a mad translation, mostly nothing but a change in style make it a *kyôka?* I think so; but, is it the same poem? *Yes* and *no*. It is a matter of degree.

雁鴨はわれを見捨てて去りにけり　豆腐に羽根のなきぞうれしき　良寛 歌集
karigamo wa ware o misutete sarinikeri　tôfu ni hane no naki zo ureshiki ryôkan 1758-1831
geese ducks-as-for me+acc abandoning leave+fin.　tofu-on wings-not+emph. delighted

    The geese & duck   *Geese & duck*
  abandon me and leave.   *fly & I am out of luck.*

     Thank goodness   *Happily, I see*

that our tôfu, at least   *my tôfu, lacking wings*
does not boast wings!   *cannot abandon me!*

Another case of multiple translations for the hell of it? One reading would suffice and your translator has no favorite, but a reader might have one; or, better yet, sensing that neither reading is perfect, succeed where I failed, in creating a translation good enough to moot all other possibilities. The kernel of the poem by the maverick monk Ryôkan is the *haikai* seasonal motif, the return of the geese to parts West despite cherries in full bloom, choosing, as Teitoku put it in one of his many amusing *ku*, "dumplings over flowers," *i.e.*, food over decoration, the practical over the ideal. Since fowl was eaten – and even monks sometimes indulge – the *tôfu*, or protein, connection is *not* utterly off the wall. But who would have thought to celebrate the winglessness of *tôfu!* True, the finless gefilte fish swims with difficulty (Bader: *Haiku for Jews* 1999), but even it is more aerodynamic than a block of *tôfu*.) This poem shows how little is needed to create fantasy. We imagine a block of tôfu with wings because Ryôkan is delighted that they do *not* have them. If that's not food for thought, what is!

天の川羽衣着たら飛び越えん　げに空事ぞかささぎの橋　貞徳 百首狂歌
amanogawa hagoromo kitara tobikoen ge ni soragoto zo kasasagi no hashi   teitoku 1571-1653
heaven's river feather-robe worn-if flying-cross-would really sky-thing/fiction+emph magpie-bridge

                ◎ Star-crossed Logic ◎

    The Milky Way   *Heaven's River*
is easily crossed, I bet   *Don't they all have wings*
   in a feather robe   *to get across it?*

Magpie bridges in the sky?   *Bird-wing bridges? My, my,*
 How silly can you get!   *That is magpie in the sky!*

The above was Spring. This Fall. Again, two readings where one might do. Teitoku takes a broad mythical idea – the *hagoromo* or feathered robes worn by sky-dwellers, mostly beautiful maidens – to challenge a particular one – the birds were supposed to make a bridge for the Cowherd Star to cross to his Weaver on for one night of love per year on this Seventh Night of the Seventh Month, the first of Fall. The word he uses for *tall-tale*, in the phrase "is really a tall-tale," *soragoto*, literally means "sky-thing." There are so many versions of this tale from China (where, unlike Japan, the Weaver rather than the Herder is the one who crosses the Milky Way) that contradictions abound. When it rained on this night, oar-splash from the herder's *boat* was the common metaphor.

〜〜〜

手にとれは人をさすてふいかくりのえみの内なる刀おそろし 権僧正公朝　後撰夷曲集
te ni toreba hito o sasu to iu igakuri no emi no uchinaru katana osoroshi kôchô pre-1672
hand-in take-if person+acc stab said spike-chestnut's smile-within sword/s scary #483

See Medusa, turn to stone, but chestnuts are best left alone,
For when one cracks a smile, it can pierce you to the bone!

〜〜〜

'He'll be stabbed
who picks up a chestnut
from the ground;

Most dreadful of daggers
within a smile are found!

〜〜〜

The Chestnut has a pleasant smile but beware its tricks,
When you reach for its nuts, you find a beard of pricks!

Here two of the three readings can only be called extreme translation, the maddest of the mad. The middle reading is ordinary, the product of my fully awake mind. With a little time and a bit of help from rhyme, I can usually come up with something like it. The couplets are altogether different. They perculated up when I was able to remain in bed rather than crossing the tracks to get the paper I don't read for someone who was, thank goodness, out of town. I write this because for all my experience paraversing, there are degrees and types of creativity that require circumstance to spring into play. Readers who want to try paraversing but have trouble thinking outside of the box might consider composing while they fall asleep and continuing when they wake. Pardon the *how-to* aside. Priest Kôchô's 17c *kyôka* uses a natural observation – ripe chestnuts crack a smile, but when you try to take the nuts you get poked – to illustrate an aphorism from the 14c *Taihei-ki,* popular tales of the Warring Era: *"In those times, it was typical for men to hone one's sword while one laughed/smiled"* (笑いの内に刀を研ぐは此頃の人の心也　太平記 16). Puns on *within = uchi = striking* and *teeth/tooth=ha=blade/s* are lost in translation. The wild readings regain that wit at the cost of losing the allusion to the aphorism.

〜〜〜

金玉のさだまりかねて火事以後は ちうにぶらつくまらのかりやぞ 月洞軒
kintama no sadamari kanete kaji igo wa chû ni buratsuku mara no kariya zo getsudôkan c.1700
balls' settling cannot house-fire since-as-for space-in dangling cock's glans = rented/temporary house!

Since the Fire, our poor balls, unsettled, never go to bed,
which leaves no pillow for Dick to lay his tired head.

A single reading, but considering the extent of the difference between the original and the translation, it is a paraverse of the original. This mini-ballad is in a chapter titled *From Personal Scoop to Public Squib: Mad Reporting.* By Getsudôkan, the feisty top kyôka-master of his day, it adds the central member to the old saw of balls testifying to the anxiety/tranquility level of leaders before battle or serving as barometers of peace under Tokugawa rule (See *The Woman Without a Hole* for more). The added rhyme for head and "pillow" to boot does not quite make up for the loss of the pun on *kari,* the *glans penis* that puns into the *kariya,* or rented dwelling, hanging precariously out in space over the retracted balls to allegorize the nervous circumstances of the newly homeless victims. Seldom has there been a poem so ugly yet so interesting. It only works in translation because English has a Proper Name for the penis that also stands for everyman (Tom, Dick and Harry) and functions as a sort of metaphorical pun. Another *kyôka* from the same chapter by Nakarai Bokuyô (1607-1678), a physician poet also has just one translation:

べんざいてんへまふでする道にててんかんやみあわをふきけるをみてよみける
benzaiten e môde-suru michi nite tenkanyami awa o fukikeru o mite yomikeru
まふでする道にてあわをふくの神これそまことのべんざいてんかん
môde suru michi nite awa o fuku no kami kore zo makoto no benzaitenkan
pilgrimage-doing-road-on, foam+acc. spew ⇒ fortune/wealth-god/dess
this+emph. true benzaiten(goddess of wealth)⇒epilepsy (& exhibit?)

Read after meeting up with an epileptic, foaming
by the road on a pilgrimage to Benzaiten's shrine

♪ The power of *kyôka,* or how a *Grand Mal* becomes a *Petit Bon!* ♪

On the road to the shrine of the Goddess of Wealth, a sign of plenty:
Foam that overflows a mouth – a charm we have . . . in epilepsy!

Bokuyô morphs *fuku=spewing,* a verb, into its homophone *wealth* and links that to the Goddess whose name, Benzaiten, partially overlaps the disease, *tenkan,* or *epilepsy.* The snapper is where it belongs (at the end of the poem) in the translation, but a partial rhyme does not match a pun that links directly into a symptom. *Some* of the loss in translation is recovered by the title, reflecting my respect for what this kind physician (he even fought for teetotalers savagely attacked by a drinking poet), who knew epilepsy was not a jinx or otherwise bad, and probably stopped to help the sufferer, accomplished with this poem. Such a title is within the broad purview of mad translation or paraversing. And I add the musical notes to indirectly signal that the poem is in good cheer. Still, there is no substitute for the magic of marriage by pun of the Goddess of Prosperity, beauty and the literary arts to a disease that makes others as well as the sufferer uneasy. What an example of private reporting that takes the otherwise un-newsworthy and makes it not only news but good news!

念仏を強ひて申すもいらぬもの　もし極楽を通り過ぎては　桃水和尚
nenbutsu o shiite môsu mo iranu mono moshi gokuraku o tôri-sugitte wa monk tôsui
prayers+acc forcing-say+emph unneeded thing, if paradise+dat pass-by-as-for d.1683

念仏に明け暮れるうつけを嘲笑して
Making light of blockheads who pray day and night.

*With prayers, pushing it too much may prove unwise
I'd take care if I were you not to overshoot Paradise!*

*'Tisn't wise to overdo your prayers, for you might die,
And waking, find you passed it, Paradise, right by!*

*Overdoing your prayers, my friend, is a bad habit
You might miss Paradise, just shoot right past it!*

*Excessive prayer is really asking for it – after you've died,
You could fly right through heaven and out the other side!*

Taken literally, religion is a blast, *a magazine* – in the old meaning of the word – full of ammunition for humor. Popular Buddhism, like Catholicism, stereotypically prospered by providing people with concrete ideas of Paradise and the itinerary taken to get there, then charging them and their surviving family hefty fees for safe-passage. The *kyôka* is not about indulgences per se, but the frame of mind in which they thrive. To be honest, one reason for this multi-translation is my selfish desire to create at least one translation any reader would accept as I like the poem so much that I want my translation to stay with it wherever it might go. This just makes it a bit harder for someone to re-write around me. Only a bit, I am afraid, for I just came up with the last, added translation in half an hour! All it required was substituting the Japanese concept of a paradise one walks to for one up there which happened after fifteen minutes when I tried " ~ is asking for it / in so many *words*" and ended up with blind *birds*.

いかばかりえびを取くふ報ひあらば　終には老の腰やかゞまん　沢庵和尚
ika bakari ebi o tori-kuu mukui araba tsui ni wa oi no koshi ya kagaman takuan
howmany shrimp+acc taking eat punishmnt is-if, end-in age's back bend-would!

~~*The number of Shrimp you eat may be cause for alarm!
You could end up equally bent — that is, if there is karma*~~

~~*If there is Karma, the number of shrimp we do or don't eat
Leaves us straight or bent so low our heads rest on our feet.*~~

~~*If each shrimp we eat comes back to bite us in the end,
To various degrees some day, our old backs will bend.*~~

~~*If we must pay for each shrimp we eat then in the end
Is it any wonder that with age our backs must bend?*~~

This is a case of multiple-translation that failed. Though I could explain that in the Sinosphere every feature of the *ebi=shrimp* (a word including the giant Ise shrimp most call a pincerless *lobster* we call a *crawfish* in Florida) bent with age, yet spry as a fiddle, snappy as jumping beans and pink with good health signifies the ultimate treasure, *longevity*, not one of my readings had an ounce of life in it. Obviously, Takuan (1573-1645) did a double-take on bent as propitious and, as a monk who reflected on the sin of taking life and a logic-loving man, realized how odd it is to benefit by killing and eating rather than protecting something. Finally, after the 740-page monster was published –

> *One can hardly eat a shrimp without causing any hurt;*
> *After years of eating them a crooked back is just desert!*

That has the proper snap! The "just desert" makes all previous translations moot. Here is another poem with *mukui* by Tenmei kyôka master Hamabe no Kurohito (1719-90), where a punning food-association (dessert) for *mukui* (*come-uppance* or *reaping what we sow*) does *not* work:

はゝの七めぐりの忌日になむあみだぶつのもじをかしらにをきてよめる哥の中にあの文字
あとまでも袖の涙のかはかぬは ぬらせし膝のむくひなるらん　濱邊黒人
ato made mo sode no namida no kawakanu wa nuraseshi hiza no mukui naruran
after until (preface says 7 years) even sleeves' tears dry-not-as4 wet lap's karma is!

One of Seven Poems for the Anniversary of My Mother's Death

After seven years	*Why do the tears*
my sleeves are yet to dry, but	*not dry upon my sleeves*
why sob like a sap?	*after all these years?*
It must be karma, for all	*It must be this: Payback*
the times I wet her lap!	*for the times I wet her lap!*

A lachrymal morass of grief transformed into pleasant humor through comic rather than cosmic karma. This is Tenmei kyôka (徳和歌後集 1785) at its best. The long preface explains that each poem started with a letter from the name of the merciful Amitabha Buddha at the start of the Lotus Sutra of the Supreme Law (なむあみだぶつ, *na-mu-a-mi-da-bu-tsu*).

~~~~~~

書物も残らず棒にふる郷の人の紙魚／＼憎き面哉　一茶
shômotsu mo nokorazu bô ni furu^sato no hito no shimijimi nikuki tsura kana issa
print-matter even remain-not pole-on-swing/hometown's folks' keenly:paperfish spiteful faces!

The Poet Betrayed

> *Like silverfish, they don't give a shit for written stuff,*
> *My countrymen, my ass! They live to eat it up!*

231

Written shortly after *haikai*-master Issa (1763-1827) finally returned to his hometown after decades in the big city, this *kyôka* fuses *bô-ni-furu* (letting go to waste) to *furu-sato* (home-town) and turns "intensely" (*shimijimi*) into *"silver-fish-zilverfish"* by repeating the bug's Chinese characters 紙魚 +ditto. The philologist might call it a visual, or orthographically created Tom Swifty! That is to say, the pun would not be guessed by merely hearing the poem. I first imagined Issa's manuscripts were used to heat baths or wipe asses as the greater part of a superb collection of bawdy English ballads once was: *F___ my town of illiterate assholes with bad behavior / To them, a book means but one thing: toilet-paper!* Eventually, I read the notes: Issa entrusted something, more likely to be documents concerning his father's will than what I imagined, to someone and returned to find them damaged and/or missing (害失).

My father's deeds mean squat to my countrymen – talk about pissed
When I look at their faces, all I see are silverfish!

I saw this poem in Issa's journal (文化十年) and nowhere else. Even if he published any of his *kyôka*, which I do not think he did, Issa probably would have kept it under wraps as it puts down the town where he still wanted to live. But the journal reprint has been available for decades, yet I have yet to find a single mention of it. Even one of Japan's most prolific novelists, Tanabe Seiko, despite her attraction for the earthy, failed to find it for her 800-page "faction" novel *Warped Issa* (*hinekureta issa*). As a *kyôka*, it was not in any selection of Issa's collected haiku a busy novelist might have had time to read. I found it before I knew anything about *kyôka*, by chance, because I liked Issa enough – or valued my time little enough – to read his journals from start to finish.

A written deed is worthless to folk whose only wish
is to be remembered as Issa's slithering silverfish!

Pardon the plethora of *paraverses*. They kept coming because, as mentioned above, the *books* I imagined turned to *deeds* and a have-not who is driven to write sometimes needs to blow-off steam that builds of resentment toward the haves who sabatogue ~~their~~ our work. I write "our" because your author-and-translator identifies with Issa who may be considered one of the top three or four classic haiku poets today, but in his time was maybe one of a score of top haikai masters and, not being independently wealthy, lived out his entire life in poverty.

Living with Silverfish!

If they had their way, all books would wipe arses or burn:
The spiteful faces in my hometown, make my stomach churn!

Sorry. It is *books* again! The ascerbic wit that flows from a deftly welded poison pen is cheap medicine for the soul of all whose well-being largely depends upon the consideration of those who enjoy the security we lack. Still, the fact is that by making those *shômotsu* "books," the silverfish come to life and the poem gains broader currency. Another shorter reading:

What Spiteful Faces!

All books must go: that is their wish –
In my hometown, capital to silverfish!

The way Issa rewrote and changed his haiku over the decades suggests he would have been delighted with the paraverses, but if any reader is not, I have a compromise to suggest. Try a paraverse yourself using "papers" rather than *books* or *deeds* for *shômotsu*. If you come up with something good, please let me know!

    *   *   *   *   *   *   *   *

No, *I take that back*. After writing the previous paragraph, I finally found the translation I failed to come up with before publishing the reading-copy-temporary-first-edition of *Mad In Translation!*

Papa's papers, saved for me, the fruit of his hard labor –
Gone! My hometown's motto? "Silverfish thy neighbor!"

Here is how it happened: *paper* rhyme-engendered "rape her" and "her" being the goddess of paper made me think of feminizing the Spanish for papel and that *papela*, not to mention a verb I thought better to avoid sent me elsewhere to the French word for an insect with paper-like wings, the papillion at which point I realized I was getting nowhere and had best stop or the short Mad Reader would never get done, so I took my break to go out to feed the cat and cows (my least unxious chores), and as I was tugging off hay near the core of the round bale – the only time when it is tough-going – a loose rhyme for *paper* came to me, *labor,* followed almost immediately by *neighbor* and shortly – within minutes – the verbing of the *silverfish*, which brings them rhetorically closer to the *shimi* in Issa's original where they are adverbed. Though details of the original content, such as "spiteful faces," are not even hinted at, the quality of the wit has finally been matched and I can finally rest happy, knowing I did justice to Issa's wit and that it was finally unlikely anyone will come up with anything better, unless it be a fine-tuned version of mine, which would be obvious to anyone who read both. I suppose the wisest thing to have done would be to kill all the earlier translations, but, as you can see . . .

♪ ***Nationalism & the Moon Poem.*** There is a whole chapter on nationalism in *Cherry Blossom Epiphany* (2007), for mountains of *sakura* were one thing Japan had that its neighbors lacked. That might be used to support the sincerity (?) of the envious moon poem, but I think the enormous volume of patriotic poems – including chauvinistic *waka* so *bad* they *seem* mad (see ch. 11 of *The Fifth Season:* 2007) makes a facetious or ironic reading reacting to the same *more* likely from someone as rational as Ôta Nanpo / Shokusanjin / Yomo no Akara.

♪ ***Temporary First Edition?*** One is supposed to have reading copies, then first editions, then revisions. I sometimes have one that is revised without changing the isbn # for even the price of that # is too much to waste when you have no money. So long as the name and page count are identical, files may be exchanged. So, if you want a rare book, get my books early. If you want less mistakes wait a while!

XXiv
Crossword to Paraverse
or, why waste your precious words?

凸凹といふ字無筆も感じ入り　柳 樽
dekoboko to iu ji muhitsu mo kanji-iri yanagidaru 92-7 19c
convex-concave/bumpy said letter no-brush even feel=character-entering

common letters

凸 and 凹
even the illiterate
can feel them

Part way through this book, I recalled my first multiple translation. It was in 1980 and occasioned not by a poem but the first words exchanged by the parents of humanity, Izanagi and Izanami. The youth/god wondered aloud what type of body the maiden/goddess had and she replied that a place seemed to be missing. To which, he replied that he, too, seemed imperfect for he had an extra part, and could he use his excess to fill her deficit and mutually found the commonwealth. She gave her assent. My variations were born of astonishment at how poorly the Japanese myth was translated, or, rather how richly it was bowlderized – or, the sentences in question turned into Latin – in the few books I happened across and because of the appealing symmetry of the 凸凹 idea (of course, women have *some*thing, not *no*thing down there, but *still*). I recall sharing a dozen or so versifications with someone I dated at the time and seeing them (on notebook paper) once or twice since I returned to the USA in 1998, only to lose them again by having to move one too many times. And I recall an interesting variation in a mid-nineties broadcast on the blues channel, one of 440-channels on the cable radio service I subscribed to when I still lived in the world (Tokyo). No, it was not Izanagi or Izanami. But it could have been. *Eve* had a part left unsewn, Adam some thread left over. A thread is a mightly thin analogy for a penis, but the song was convincing, as all well-sung rhymes are, and left me in stitches.

izanagi to izanami spoke –

"And how would thy august body be?"
"Fine," she said, *"though i must confess,*
one part is missing from the rest."
"What a coincidence," quoth he, *"i see*
an extra part attached to me!
So let us fill your want with my excess
that we two, as one, are blessed
to bear a nation and a race
with 凸 凹 *at its base!*

I cannot recall exactly what so delighted me about the half a dozen rhyming translations I made. Like the above impromptu reproduction, working in that 凸凹, not found in the original, they were probably not very good or I would have tried to publish them. All I recall for sure is it was so much fun, I thought it odd everyone didn't do it. Then, I got so busy writing books and articles in addition to scouting books and correcting translations that I did no more such play until reading the *Manyô-shû* in the late 1980's, and then, when translating Issa on my computer in 1995, as mentioned in the foreword, where I also pointed out how much more sense it made to paraverse than do crossword puzzles. After Wittgenstein, I repeat myself, for anything worth saying once is worth saying in more than one way. The question is how many puzzle-lovers will enjoy a puzzle with no single right answer, by definition. Yet the feeling of working out a poem or a puzzle is the same – the joy of solution is felt as much for coming up with one of a number of possible acceptable outcomes as for a singular one, and the reward greater for the following reasons:

1) A puzzle accomplished is *done*. There may be some who show-off their finished crosswords, but the usual destination of all word-games is the trash. There is nothing *wrong* with this. The environmental cost of wasting ink and paper is tiny compared to that of most games. But, if the result of your play is an aphorism, poem or poems, you can make not only yourself but others happy, for you have something to keep, collect, send to friends, hang on the wall, or maybe even publish. You will also *feel better* knowing you did not just waste time while your spouse washed the dishes or, heaven forbid, mowed the lawn (motorized lawn-mowers and leaf-blowers should be *outlawed*), but *created something* valuable enough to justify your in/action to yourself and others.

2) You will find it easier to wax poetic than you ever dreamed. After college, my interest in poetry waned until I started paraversing. So I cannot help but think it will help others, too. In his beautiful *Defense of Poetry*, Shelly once wrote "A man cannot say, 'I will compose poetry.'" That may be true if poetry means only great *haute culture* works of art *ex nihilo*, but there are two things involved here, *idea* and *detail*. When you paraverse existent work, you already have the first idea and have only to build upon it, or split it into parts and expand upon it. Once you get into the proper frame of mind, you will suffer no more writer's cramp than you would before a crossword puzzle. The only difference is that as you work on those details, you may be surprised to find they sometimes lead to new ideas of your own, while a crossword goes nowhere.

3) Paraversing the work of others, you escape your stylistic habits – look at Hofstadter in *Ton beau de Marot,* tossing off a bag of sand with each attempt until he reaches the stratosphere! – and returning to your own work, improve by paraversing yourself, rather than falling for what you did because you put so much effort into it. I did just that for some of the poems from my other books quoted in this one. And by demonstrating that purism in writing – faith in perfect lines, or even poems or books where you "wouldn't have a word changed" – is misguided, and there is often no single best solution, and even when there is, chances are *your* masterpiece is not it, paraversing keeps us open.

4) Once you realize that your paraverses are fun for others, you will start to realize something millions of haiku writers in Japan know, to be or not to be a poet is not black and white but a matter of degree. You will be able to cure yourself of the the habit (if you have it), all too common among amateur poets, of writing exclusively about your emotional difficulties (or your loves), because you will be sharing an outward-looking poetic space. If you would use poetry to work out your personal problems or share your misery, fine – though I would recommend country weepers: why do it halfway? – but, if you lost yourself in poetry that found friends, those problems might recede.

5) Even if 3) and 4) does not apply to *you*, while paraversing you will find quick improvement in your ability to express yourself, for copying poetic form is enjoyable – Aristotle was right when he wrote in his *Poetics* that, *of all animals, man is the most imitative* (yes, we are the ape of all apes), that we *"receive pleasure from imitation."* Not all paraversing requires the retention of a poem's form or the distillation of prose or a long poem into a specified short form, but having contests which require it will help those of us who participate make more poetic forms our own, and that will free our creativity from falling into a rut.

Paraversing in Public

There have probably been one-time calls for variations on poems by well-known people. Martin Gardner with *The Night Before Christmas* in dialect or local color, Hofstadter with Marot's poem. But, as far as I know, the word-lovers of the world – or the English world, at any rate, have never had *a permanent forum* that encouraged them to exercise their poetic facilities in the same manner a daily crossword helps them to keep their vocabulary on the tip of their tongue. *So what is the problem?* 1) Do editors have less faith than I do in the talent of their own readers? 2) Is there a firmly embedded Crossword Mafia with the power to refuse entrance to competition? 3) Is the very idea of playing with poetry anethma? Are only personal and 100% original poems proper for all but Garrison Keillor? (Why should he alone be given permission to take-off?)

The New Yorker not long ago introduced a contest for readers to suggest good lines for a *cartoon* in every issue. In Japan, magazines and newspapers have done both this and contests for the completion of partly drawn cartoons *for decades*. Why the difference? Is Usanian media less democratic, in the participatory sense, than Japanese media? Are Usanians, on the whole, less creative than Japanese in their writing and drawing and would delegate both to professionals? Before replying, I would need to know the situation in other countries. This is not the sort of thing that can be done small – results good enough to capture the popular imagination require a large number of participants, i.e. a magazine or newspaper with a huge readership. Likewise, I think, for the conditions needed for competitive paraversing. Unfortunately, mass media is mostly run by conservatives (I refer to editing style, not politics), so we who would like to play poetry with others can only pray for the unlikely appearance of editors with both imagination and clout willing to try something new.

Types of Paraversing

In the *Introduction*, I quartered the content as 1) re-creating poems in translation, 2) expanding upon poems translated or not, 3) turning prose to poetry, and 4) multiplying maxims. Categories posted at paraverse dot org in 2003, revised a bit:

1. <u>Reworking a poem</u>. We can often edit others better than themselves. Perhaps that is why we may rise above ourselves to improve another's work. It is hard to draw the line between editing a poem and making a paraverse of it. People might hesitate before redoing a sonnet by Shakespeare, but paraversing poor poems is easy. As a rule, the worse the original, the better the results, for we feel more confident and less apprehensive of doing the original wrong! Magazine or newspaper readers might be encouraged to send in poems needing creative rework and/or reduction by other readers, including the editor of the page and invited masters of the art. In Japan, rewriting in public is common with haiku and there are even popular programs on TV with panelists of different ages and sexes taking a whack at improving them. They tend to be didactic. I would prefer pure entertainment. If we see, we learn. We need not be obviously taught. (*The credit for the joint product?* Most of my experience is with Japanese. When I alter another's *haiku* enough to make it partly mine, I combine characters of our *nom de plume*. For example, after playing with a *ku* by Miyoko, I combined her *mi* with the *gu* (my haigô is Keigu), to create a new name: *Bigu*, i.e., Beautiful-era-child 美代子 and Respectfool 敬愚 begat Beautyfool 美愚. Hence, I attributed Hofstadter's rework of Moser to *Mostadter*, etc..)

2. <u>Making variations on a line</u>. The first line of the *Tao Te Ching* and Dogen's words (if they are his words) of wisdom are but two of countless possibilities. Find hundreds of translated sayings from an obscure tribe by an anthropologist with no sense for style and go to town with it! Turn it into a fine book. Or an old book of sayings translated from a major language. Most are not as witty=snappy as the originals. If I had good internet web-building skills and a broadband connection I would work with thousands of people to playfully compete at such things until we had a product for a great book . . . With famous lines, you *could* search for other versions of the text, since this is easier by internet than it used to be, before doing yours, but, I think it better to *first* do some variations yourself, *then* check. Reading others work may foreclose some possible variations and inspire others. It will be more fun to discover where you have or have not been scooped if you always wait. Then, sfter seeing the others, you can always make more variations.

3. <u>Distilling a poem from a poem</u>. I often see something I like and want to keep in a poem, but have no interest in, or even dislike, the rest. We can do this from minor or amateur poets as the examples from *Braille Me* in the text (pp 125-130). Or we can do it for great poets, such as Wordsworth, not by beating them at their game but by abbreviating work that, today, often seems wordy. His long poems may be boiled down into haiku or couplets. Or, Clare. As pointed out in the text, John Clare's *"I love to see"* repeated *ad nauseum* in some of his poems betrays his genius. Some tasteful distillation (not the patronizing gentrification of editors he fought) could bring him a broader readership. I suppose most poets need editors, or need editors to be readable for certain audiences. Yet, most poets, no, most writers published or would-be, never meet the editors they need. With most publishers today lacking editors, not just dead poets but all of us would benefit by editing one another.

4. <u>Distilling text into poetic prose</u>. The original need not be in a foreign language, need not be a poem, nor even something brief. It can be prose and pages long. You sum it up with a haiku a page, or a chapter, or, take many books and make one haiku (or any short-form poetry, or even an aphorism) for each. Look at the headers for my *Rise, Ye Sea Slugs!* Each sums up a page. Are they not paraverses of a sort? We might think of this as editing games instead of poetry games. Distilling would be good exercise for what Japanese might call "editor-eggs," or budding editors, though I am afraid said species is endangered in a world that rewards wheeler-dealer publicists over word-smiths.

5. <u>Hunting for poems in poems</u> Instead of trying to take *the* essence from a long poem, take up a line or two with good ideas or descriptions as is, and parse it into shorter lines, perhaps doing a bit of rewriting to help them stand alone better.

6. <u>Hunting for poems in prose</u>. This is easier than 5) because the compunction is less. Messing with someone's prose seems a lesser violation than reparsing or rewriting their poetry. My personal preference is finding haiku in nature-writing, as demonstrated with Muir (ch 16). This can be done alone, or in competition with others hunting the same text (Writing many haiku for each paragraph may be excessive. My paraverses themselves could bear selection). Someone once had a column in an English language newspaper in Japan where he condensed prose into haiku. His cross of old pontification and new-science mush turned me off, but if no one else did it before, he may deserve credit for developing the idea of haiku as distillation (I welcome glosses on/of history). For an example of distillation with a purpose neither didactic nor absent (done to do it, "just an exercise"), but to fit a larger narrative – see my haiku formed from a passage in McFerrin's novel, *Namako*, in the *Melancholy Sea Slug* chapter of *Rise, Ye Sea Slugs!*

7. <u>Culling and parsing of prose</u>. This is a more passive version of 3-6. Rather than using our words, we hold the line at selection and minimal arrangement of another's work. Years ago, I saw a fine collection of snippets from the prose letters of Dorothy Wordsworth, the famed Nature poet's sister, that were halfway to haiku already! Culling and parsing of nineteenth century nonfiction writers, with fine perceptions but too wordy for the modern sensibility could do much for correcting the misconception of progress our so-called consciousness and in the arts.

8. <u>Collage</u>. Like the last, but the order of the original words would not be preserved. Sentences and bits of sentences could be moved about and reassembled. Competitors could take specified paragraphs or pages and take whatever they wanted to create a collage. If anyone has done this, I do not know. It would be ideal for a large circulation magazine.

9. <u>Take-offs</u>. This is the one area already well attended to. Martin Gardner has published a fine collection of take-offs on "The Night Before Christmas," including paraverses in the style of this or that poet or work, and what is properly called ethnic adaptions, or dialect. Crossword-like contests for all, need to use shorter poems for the original. Style-mimicry, where poems are written in the style of a famous poet without any parody of content intended, was once a common sport – young Kipling's (or was it Chesterton's? or both?) anti-car verse are a good example – but few of us, myself included, would know where to start today. Actually, I mean for myself, it may be too late. I only have limerick and haiku templates etched deeply enough into

my grey matter to dispense with models. I do know where we should start with our basic education. Teachers (or educational programs) should encourage pre-schoolers and primary school students to re-word nursery rhymes with various meters and rhymes. If we could master only half-a-dozen types, we would eventually enrich not only our poetry but our music. It is absurd that one species we might call the hip-hop chant has almost displaced all other species!).

10. <u>Riposte, Parody or Envoi</u>. Light verse often cries out for reply and poets not infre-quently replied to their own, creating dramatic argument, rather than a balanced but boring compromise. Swift's outrageous comparison of *Clouds* and *Women* and the equally outrageous response from a woman is perhaps the best example. Naturally, the format of the reply should match the original as closely as possible. Country music "answer songs" using the same melody are the best modern examples of this art (the timeless juke-box hit *Honkytonk Angel* – with a reply composed by a different song-writer is only the best known). Parody in the narrow sense of not being any take-off but intended to attack or contradict the original might be called an indirect ripost, while an envoi – or at least my main experience with it in Japanese, the *hanka* – tends to be lightly questioning, summarizing or supporting the original. Mybe we should call it a *tweek*.

11. <u>Filling in</u>. Parts of an old poem – not just the rhymes, for that would be a mere quiz – could be blanked out and competitively re-invented. Or, the first half could be supplied and new caps invented. The same could be done for new poems, left undone to be finished. This would bear some resemblance to the way poems were actually solicited in Edo period (17-19c) Japan. and it proved extremely successful at drawing in participants – even paying submissions and subscriptions – from a broad section of the society (See the introduction continuation at the end of to my double-titled book on senryu). People like to put in their two bits and be recognized for it, provided the form offered is relatively short and easy.

Caveat: If you would paraverse Wordsworth or any great poet, *please take care to read carefully first*. I once found a long sentence of Milton's that had been reduced to a length less patient moderns could read (in the 17th edition (?) of a book called *How to Write More Simply and Effectively* by Dr. Rudolf Fleisch) that was a horrendous mistranslation. I wrote the Dean of Corpus Christi College, Keith Thomas, now a Sir, and author of one of my favorite books, to confirm my suspicion. I would introduce it here but my notes are in a box at my mother's hundreds of miles from my cramped temporary abode (Again, poverty does not always permit me to entertain you properly). I also found that the poet Robert Bly completely misread Pope's intent with *"Lo, the poor indian,"* which also had me checking with the Dean – later, I found Wendell Berry caught it, too, and did Pope justice better than I could have. Since I have no great brainpower and no training in old texts (I must read Chaucer in translation w/ notes), *why was I able to recognize problems these men did not?* Good intuition may help – Japanese reviewers of oneofmy books called it "a bloodhound's nose for mistranslation." But, I believe the main reason is that I treat all I translate (or check) *with respect*. Call it "good faith" if you wish. When I find a line or a passage that lacks logic and/or wit, I assume the problem is *mine* (The late J.I. Crump, speaking of Mongol era Chinese poetry and those who had the gall to proscribe "proper" prosody on it, put it like this: "Now, it is my position that the corpus of *Yüan ch'ü* exists as it is, and if we cannot make sense out of the prosody . . . it is we who are at fault, not they." That attitude is one reason why *his* translations are good). Perhaps it is enough to paraphrase only those you can love. Otherwise, let it be, for reading difficult material depends upon the heart as well as the head. As, I have confessed in my books of translated haiku, when I do wrong (make mistakes), it generally is because I try too hard to find wit where it may not lie in order to do a poet right.

PARAVER*SING*PARAVER*SING*PARAVER*SING*PARAVER*SING*PARAVER*SING*

★ ★ ★ ★ ★

Refinitions for Wittgenstein
who defined nothing once

PARAVER*SING*PARAVER*SING*PARAVER*SING*PARAVER*SING*PARAVER*SING*

Composite Translation Multiple translations of single poems, clustered to create a patent singularity, *convincing* because side-by-side presentation helps us to *feel* the polysemic many as one, a single opus, or object of literary art. With short poems or passages, the result can be *pleasing* for the symmetry, akin to a polyfaceted crystal. While it is easy to demonstrate the necessity for and utility of multiple translation in the case of exotic tongues, it is hard to tell just when it goes over the line and becomes something other than an exceptionally creative translation. That something other, I call a *paraverse*.

Ku Short for poems of 17 syllabets or less. Most commonly refers to a *haiku* but can also refer to a *senryû* or various other short verse (*zappai*). Also, standard-length phrases within Japanese traditional poetry. For example, one might note that it is more common for a first or last *ku* to be a *mora* long than the middle one in a haiku.

Paraverse. When a work, prose or poem, is expressed poetically with change enough to be something different from the original but not unrelated it is a paraverse. Paraverses are not composed *ex nihilo*, that is, out of the mind of the poet, alone. A paraverse is a take-off *ab res extensa,* from something else. Those familiar enough with any form of music or song to experience the joy of improvization, *know* it is by no means inferior to composing from scratch. By starting in the air, you may even soar higher, leaving the original and your self behind, to create the masterpiece only known as it takes form. Deliberately creating these variations is called *paraversing*.

Senryû book. A book with 1300 dirty senryû and two names (the author's little experiment) published shortly before this one. See ch. 18.

Syllabet. A uniformly, or nearly uniformly short syllable (i.e. a *mora*) and the syllabic letter equivalent of an alphabet. Japanese like to point out that English's one-syllable "strike" is five syllables ストライク *su-to-ra-i-ku* in Japanese. Indeed, it would count as such in a haiku. In order not to confuse things, I prefer to use a different term. Hence, syllabet. If a syllabet is not the same thing as an English syllable, neither is it identical to a letter as we know them. For example, look what happens when we try to reverse them. ばら *bara* (rose) backward would be *arab* アラブ in English, but becomes らば *raba* (mule) in Japanese.

Poetry All Wrong?

Write It Yourself!

The above was the first title of the book, before I decided to call it *The* Way is not *A* Way, which was dropped in turn for the present title that I felt more likely to draw my type of reader. *Poetry All Wrong? Write It Yourself!* would attract too many readers who, lacking confidence and reading skills, would find me, with my puny vocabulary, "hard." *The* Way, on the other hand, would only be guaranteed to attract students of Taoism. So I jumped on Horace's Dolphin.

More repetition. But, every time I go back, I go back further. My first steps toward paraversing began when I was in grade school and *loved* Christmas caroling and hymms more than anyone I knew. Partly, it was because singing was the one place I was *free to be different* outside of our house. I could sing *up* when others went *down,* or *vice versa*, and be praised for my "harmony!" And, partly, it was because I got such a kick out of changing the lyrics just enough that some of the other kids caught what I was doing but not the teachers: "Hark, the *hairy* angels sing!" or "Glory to the new born *thing*," and so forth (Or, did *everyone* do that?). In my second childhood, I rewrote dozens of country music hits. The only detail I recall is the *walking* in Ernest Tubbs' "Walking the Floor Over You." I turned it into *caulking*. I am unsure why I did it other than because I enjoyed country novelty songs. But, once I made experimental one-string musical instruments and discovered the joy of musical improvisation, I no longer cared so much for playing with words. Tinnitus permitting, I may yet abandon my computer keyboard for a fretless free-tension string.

Reading paraverses, particularly in composite, is like hearing musical harmony; writing them is like improvising. Like improvisation, it helps to be working with material you know inside out because only if you can chime in or bounce off the blues note almost without thinking can you can wander off track and still sound good or sound all the better – it is why something limited like the blues offers far more room to play to most people than classical music. If you (a musican) must read it, you may be able to play it but not really play *with* it.

Where there is one alternative way, there are usually many, so the act of paraversing quickly triggers one's divergent creativity. The rush is almost spooky.

That thrill is part of it. But it is also my experience that when translating poetry between exotic (rather than cognate) tongues, only multiple translations, each bringing out different aspects of the original can transmit the rich layers of meaning yet not be boring. *Rise, Ye Sea Slugs! Fly-ku! Cherry Blossom Epiphany, The 5ᵗʰ Season, Thw Woman Without a Hole,* and *Mad In Translation* demonstrate this with thousands of examples. Composite translation is not merely a game but a valid way to interpret, or, as the English put it, read.

~~~~~~

When you read my efforts, please bear in mind the fact that what you was done by someone with a mediocre vocabulary and almost no formal training. Seeing the sleek sentences and enormous vocabulary of several of my correspondents, who have clearly attained a level of literacy I will never attain, Quintillian's words "The less we are helped by our language, the better fight we must make in the originality of matter" (trans. Saintsbury), written as a Latin having to write in the shadow of Greek letters, take on a whole different meaning for me.

~~~~~~

I grant you, Aldous, it may not be possible, much less desirable to rewrite *To be or not to be . . .* "in your own words" as teachers request, but most writing, including much of Shakespeare, can not only be equaled, but improved. *Why?* Because few lines are polished to perfection and, usually, there is no single best answer, anyway. In an exotic language, where word-for-word is impossible, *"To be or not to be"* is not quite the same question: but it can and has been written in hundreds of other ways. (Do *any* other languages have a little preposition in front of a so-called infinitive form?) I have seen a dozen in Japanese alone.

~~~~~~

Practically speaking, rewriting another's prose is a waste of time, unless you make a living as an editor, a teacher, a translator (good plots poorly written turn into best-selling novels in the hands of the right translator) or a plagiarist. While not always boring, rewriting is always relentless, tiring work. No one does it for fun. Unless you are a masochist with nothing better to do, or a very sweet person happy just to be doing something of service (translators earn minimum wages for work that is far more specialized than that of most well-rewarded professionals), you go from sentence to sentence dreaming of the last one, your final *parole*.

~~~~~~

Life is brief, too brief for all of us born with eyes too big for our brains and eye-teeth that bite-off more than we can do. As we work toward big things, impossible things, we need our day-to-day "refreshment" (Twain-speak for *coitus*), little things to complete. If you are at all like me, you will find the re-creation of short poems or aphorisms one of the two most delightful activities in the world (the others: musical improvisation, the game go and sex). Addicted, you will forego the crossword puzzle or novel you planned to read – what good is a solved puzzle or a read novel, anyway? – and *paraverse*. You will then get your refreshment *and*, the satisfaction of having something to show for yourself: at best, a work of literature, at worst, a source of amusement for others.

A STITCH IN TIME.

This cartoon by Thomas Hood titled "A Stitch in Time" deserves to be a famous proverbial pun.

No Index?

This is my first book in English without an index. If you would find a person, a thing, an idea, please go to Googlebooks and search for it. Some items may be harder to find that way, but if you are good with concepts, or at guessing my words, most should be easier to find and coming within snippets provide a peek at the context. If you would like to make me an index or indices with people, things, ideas, or whatever, please write. I love making them but unforeseen circumstances did not permit me that luxury this Fall.

AN ILLUMINATED MS.

Thomas Hood, again. An illuminated MS. The quill is on his left. Does that make Hood a lefty?

Reviews & Supplemental Information about books in English by Robin D. Gill

Rise, Ye Sea Slugs! (1,000 *ku* re. sea cucumbers compiled & transl. from Japanese). paraverse 2003. pp 480.

"I wondered, can one really devote 480 pages to haiku on sea slugs? The answer is emphatically 'yes.' Although difficult to read from beginning to end, this book contains great learning and insight, and deserves a wide reading among specialists and non-specialists alike."

"For many of the haiku, Gill gives multiple translations as a way of showing possible interpretations. I know of no other book of English translations of haiku that goes to such lengths to explain translations, which in Gill's hands are accurate, economical, and often elegant."

"For all the eccentricities one might expect (and does find) in a book devoted entirely to Japanese haiku on the sea slug, the author is an accomplished haiku writer, a very talented and engaging critic, capable of reading with an acute understanding of culture and cultural differences."

–Thomas H. Rohlich, Professor of Japanese Language and Literature at Smith College, from *Metamorphoses: the journal of the five college faculty seminar on literary translation* (Vol. 13.1, Spring 2005).

"This single-topic tome may be our best English-language window yet into the labyrinth of Japanese haikai culture. If you have read Yasuda, Blyth, Henderson, Ueda, and Shirane, then read Gill. He will expand your mind. If you have not read those guys yet, then read Gill first. He's more fun."

– William J. Higginson, author of *Haiku World*, in Modern Haiku (volume 35.1 winter-spring 2004).

Re: **_Fly-ku!_** (Translations of fly & fly-swatting ku, + an in-depth study of Issa's famous fly-ku,"Don't swat!") 2005

"An American scholar and poet who writes in an extemporaneous style akin to that of Jack Kerouac; thinks like Herman Hesse, Koyabashi Issa, and Lewis Carroll, all rolled into one."

– Robert D. Wilson, founder of the on-line magazine *Simply Haiku* (2005-summer). Author of *Jack-fruit*.

"Gill strikes us as no less than amazing. Why isn't he teaching at Yale, or the University of California, or Tokyo University? His references include no end of obscure Japanese lore, plus quotes and notes from such artists as Clare, Lovelace, Steinbeck, Dumont, Verdi, Satie, Blyth, Shakespeare, Emily Dickinson."

– Carlos Amantea, author of *The Blob That Ate Oaxaca* R.A.L.P.H. (Review of Art, Literature, Philosophy & History)

Not as much natural history in this wee bk. as in Rise, Ye Sea Slugs!, but a good discussion of the supposed anthropomorphic fallacy & a comparison of translations of "Don't swat/hit/kill" the fly that gives great detail on what makes "precise" translation between exotic tongues impossible.

Re: **_Cherry Blossom Epiphany_** (Three thousand *ku+ka* on blossom-viewing, including many by Sôgi) 2007. pp.740

"It was bad old Ezra Pound, acknowledging his heavy debt to haiku in translation, who affirmed that the first rule of poetry was "Make it new." This is something Gill has done more effectively, as far as remaking haiku in English goes, than anyone else around. . . .

"One of my favorites is on p. 375, where no less than seven translations are proposed, but four of them *"sous rature,"* or _misekechi_ ['erasures shown,' literally]: in old Japanese, words crossed out in a manuscript but left legible enough that the reader can see what was discarded, and imagine why. (Publishers with accountants are not likely to tolerate this kind of haikaiesque mischief. Gill gets away with it only because he is his own publisher.) And (another reason, if needed) in his commentary Gill distances himself from the conventions of pedantry just as effectively as the haikai poets he translates departed from the venerable (and staid and eventually stuffy) traditions of classical linked verse to make something new."

– Lewis Cook, professor of Japanese literature, CUNY (in a blog at one of Gabi Greve's fine haiku *kigo* and Buddhism-related sites, in response to another's questions about my work.

"This book is exceedingly delightful – what word could be more accurate I cannot say! Here is a guide to allow every reader to play with their own translations of these poems – indeed all the important ingredients – are amply included: . . . nothing in this book is cut in stone – it is pure water, ever-flowing – and that is what is so inspiring about it, its generosity and delightful creativity!"   – s.w. at mountainandrivers.org

Re: **The Fifth Season** (2000 *ku* on 20 New Year themes & first book of ten in the IPOOH series 2007, pp.500)

Excluding books on *surimono*, beautiful color-prints accompanied by *kyôka*, published by presses or lines of books dedicated to *art* rather than literature, the New Year, once the Original, or First Season, of the *five* seasons of haiku, has been neglected in favor of the other four by Occidental translators. *The Fifth Season* finally gives this supernatural or cosmological season – one that combines aspects of the Solstice, Christmas, New Year's, Easter, July 4th and the Once Upon a Time of Fairy Tales – its due. *This book brings the Moon back into the calendar and humans back into haiku.* As this book has sold only a dozen or two copies since being published the *In Praise of Old Haiku* saijiki project has been temporarily suspended.

Re: **The Woman Without a Hole and other risky themes from old Japanese poems; also Octopussy, Dry Kidney & Blue Spots** (about 2000 dirty *senryû* essay 30 themes 2007, pp.500)

No reviews interesting enough to quote, but one sweet fan letter from Germany:

"I normally don't annoy authors, but I simply need to tell you how happy your "woman without a hole" book made me. It's so interesting, funny and well-presented, I loved it to bits, and I don't even speak Japanese. (perhaps I should add that I translated (and published, which was kind of not easy) Lord Rochester's poetry into German; which makes me, kind of, a colleague?)   Thank you very much!"
 – Christine Wunnicke (And, reader, if you read any German, buy her translation of John Wilmot, Earl of Rochester *Der beschädigte Wüstling** and you will thank *me*. It is *charming*.   *Like mine, not for readers under 18.)

Mad In Translation – a thousand years of kyôka, comic poetry in the classic waka mode. 2009, 740pp. *Kyôka,* usually translated as "mad poems" or "mad-cap verse," is usually identified with and exampled by late-18c Tenmei *kyôka* in Japan (in translation, all kyôka but those on surimono have been all but ignored) but, actually, the playful B-side of *waka* has existed as long as poetry has in Japan and is found by many names, and the *kyôka* of the 16-17c deserve as much attention as the later ones, as proven by example, 3000 poems, w/ original . . . annot. biblio, bio, poet & poem index, glossary. Much 'extreme translation' here!

Kyôka, Japan's Comic Verse: a *Mad in Translation* Reader 2009. A 300-page double distillation high-proof sample of the poetry and prose, with improved translations, re-considered opinions and additional snake-legs (explanation some scholars may not need). The scattershot of two-page chapters and notes have been compounded into a score of cannonball-sized thematic chapters with just enough weight to bowl over most specialists yet, hopefully, not bore the amateur and sink a potentially broad-beamed readership.

Topsy-Turvy 1585 – a translation & explication of Luis Frois S.J.'s Treatise listing 611 ways Europeans & Japanese are contrary (2004/5) in 14 thematic chapters, with essays of the history of topsy-turvy, cultural accomodation, China vs. Japan as *the* cultural antipode. As I was well-known in Japan for books challenging antithetical cultural stereotypes by showing deep similarity within superficial difference, it was both ironic and fitting that I read a book of differences. Frois wrote in Portuguese (included). In a 740pp. and 400 pp version. If you wonder why we sniff melons on top and Japanese sniff melons on the bottom, don't miss it! I often cite the book for it saves me the trouble of looking elsewhere.

Orientalism & Occidentalism – Is the mistranslation of culture inevitable? (2004 pp280). The odd "nihonjinron" world of antithetical cultural stereotype – the author's experience in Japan, discusssion of how and whether we can make sense of exotic tongues (to Japanese English and vice-versa), with especial attention to frequency of personal pronoun use vs the psychological impact and the problem of two conflicting ideas of faithful translation: maintaining word-order vs maintaining flow or connections.

Info re. *The Cat Who Thought Too Much;* summaries+reviews of my published books in Japanese at paraverse dot org.

www.ingramcontent.com/pod-product-compliance
Lightning Source LLC
Chambersburg PA
CBHW080536170426
43195CB00016B/2579